High on a Windy Hill
The Story of the
Prince of Wales Hotel

Ray Djuff

Chris Morrison, contributing editor

Rocky
Mountain Books

VANCOUVER • VICTORIA • CALGARY

Acknowledgements

High on a Windy Hill is the result of years of labour that began during my summers as an employee at the Prince of Wales Hotel. Anthony Flemming-Blake stoked my interest with his recollections of earlier times and characters. He rescued a disillusioned busboy from dining room drudgery and shared with him an appreciation for Waterton and its unique resort hotel. I will never forget his friendship and his tutelage, both in history and the art of mixology.

Betty Baker was a maid at the Prince of Wales Hotel the year it opened—1927. She was also the first person in Waterton I interviewed about the hotel's history. She willingly shared her memories and photographs, and was my entre into Waterton's close-knit community, introducing me to fellow longtime residents Ernie Haug, Delance Strate, Sophie Allison, George Annand and Bea Armstrong, among others. I could not have found a more gracious and generous hostess.

I owe a great debt to archivists and their staff at museums and libraries who spent countless hours trying to help me answer questions, fill in blanks and who pulled hundreds of linear feet of files from their storage boxes, sometimes on what seemed like little more than a whim. In particular, I'd like to single out Thomas White at the James Jerome Hill Reference Library in St. Paul, Minn., Dallas Lindgren at the Minnesota Historical Society in St. Paul, Minn., and Deirdre Shaw at the Glacier National Park archive, West Glacier, Mont.

Numerous other individuals have made important contributions to *High on a Windy Hill*, too many, unfortunately, to list all of them here. Mary O'Brien has been a steadfast friend and supporter, sharing memories about her father, Doug Oland, whose company built the hotel. Jeanne Stenerson at Toltz, King, Duvall, Anderson and Associates, Inc. in St. Paul, Minn., has been a wonderful resource for architectural information. And Frances Bellucci was exceedingly generous in helping me learn the background of Harley and Anna Boswell.

Contributing editor Chris Morrison has always been rock-steady in her convictions and a great sounding board in the writing process. Her advice and editing skills are unerringly accurate, and when on occasion I chose to ignore them, it was at my peril. It was her inquisitiveness about the Prince of Wales Hotel that resulted in my earlier history book, and I'll be forever grateful for that.

I'm also grateful to Tony Daffern and the staff at Rocky Mountain Books who worked with me under rigourous deadlines to make *High on a Windy Hill* possible.

Finally, and most importantly, there's been the unflagging love, support and understanding of my wife Gina, and, in time, our two children, Monika and Michael. I dedicate *High on a Windy Hill* to them.

Ray Djuff

High on a Windy Hill

The Story of the
Prince of Wales Hotel

Ray Djuff

Rocky Mountain Books
#108 – 17665 66A Avenue
Surrey, BC V3S 2A7
www.rmbooks.com

ISBN 978-0-921102-71-7

Library and Archives Canada Cataloguing in Publication

Djuff, Ray
  High on a windy hill

  Includes bibliographical references and index.
  ISBN 978-0-921102-71-7

  1. Prince of Wales Hotel (Waterton Lakes National Park, Alta.)—History.
I. Morrison, Chris, 1946- II. Title.
TX941.P75D58 1999   647.947123'401   C99-910355-5

Printed in Canada

Rocky Mountain Books acknowledges the financial support for its publishing program from the Government of Canada through the Book Publishing Industry Development Program (BPIDP), Canada Council for the Arts, and the province of British Columbia through the British Columbia Arts Council and the Book Publishing Tax Credit.

Table of Contents

*The Prince of Wales Hotel.
Author's collection.*

*Head bellman Victor Harrison and
front desk staff await the arrival
of the first customers at the
Prince of Wales Hotel on opening
day, July 25, 1927. T. J. Hileman
photo, author's collection.*

Introduction

There is little today to remind tourists of the origins of the Prince of Wales Hotel. Many visitors rightly guess "the Prince" was a railway hotel, assuming it to be a legacy of the Canadian Pacific Railway whose Banff Springs Hotel and Chateau Lake Louise to the north are synonymous with the Canadian Rocky Mountains. There's good reason for such an assumption: A CPR line runs just 35 miles (56 km) north of Waterton Lakes National Park, but Canadian Pacific did not construct the Prince of Wales Hotel. It was built by Great Northern Railway whose nearest line ran some 50 miles (80 km) to the south in Montana and the head office of which was in St. Paul, Minnesota.

That an American railway company would put up a single hotel in a Canadian national park is one of many unique facts about the Prince of Wales Hotel. Conceived and paid for by Americans, the hotel was constructed by Canadians who were barraged with design changes as building was in progress. Originally planned as several four-story structures with a low-sloping roof and 300 guestrooms, the plan was altered so dramatically during construction the hotel today bears little resemblance to the first set of blueprints. It ended up a solitary building with 90 guest rooms contained in seven stories under a steeply sloped roof capped by a 30-foot (9 m) tower. During the gruelling, yearlong process, the building was nearly lost twice—once to wind and once to fire. Constructed to show off Alberta's lake and mountain grandeur to wealthy American tourists, the hotel's lobby windows in fact mainly show Montana.

The story of the Prince of Wales Hotel is filled with such international novelties, peculiar circumstances and intrigue. It starts with the very reason the structure was built north of the 49th parallel. Great Northern executives saw it as a means to skirt Prohibition in the United States. The plan was to bolster travel on Great Northern's line by luring thirsty Americans to vacation at Great Northern's hotels and chalets in Glacier National Park, Montana, and then have them cross the border to Alberta where they could drink legally. Ironically, it was a purpose that was served for less than six years. Opened in 1927, the hotel became obsolete in late 1933 when Prohibition in the U.S. ended with the repeal of the Volstead Act.

While the Prince of Wales Hotel got off to a boozy start, its history since 1933 has been no less interesting. One of the largest all-wood buildings in the province, it has taken everything the elements could throw at it—flood-causing torrential rains, raging forest fires, hurricane-force winds and driving snow—and has survived intact. Fittingly, it was part of the setting that inspired the proposal to create the world's first international peace park. Economic depression and a world war forced its closure, yet the hotel was reopened after both occasions with renewed optimism for its future. It has had only three owners—always Americans—and suffered periods of neglect, but, in the caring hands of new staff, each summer season its lustre is restored with outstanding service, if not maintenance.

For all the optimism shown by Great Northern in building the hotel and the money poured into advertising it, the railway could not have picked a worse time to make such an investment. Construction of the Prince of Wales Hotel coincided with the zenith of rail passenger travel for tourism in North American. Rail arrivals to Glacier National Park peaked in 1929—a tally that would be exceeded only once in the next 40 years. Trains were losing way to the cost-effectiveness and personal freedom of the automobile. Faced with stagnation in passenger traffic to Glacier Park in the 1950s, Great Northern's directors decided there was no financial merit in holding on to the Glacier lodgings or the Prince of Wales Hotel and sought a buyer. An era ended when the hotels were sold in 1960 to Glacier Park Inc., a group of investors headed by Don Hummel of Tucson, Arizona. Hummel has since sold Glacier Park Inc., which is now part of Viad Corp.

As time passed, Great Northern's connection to the Prince of Wales Hotel faded. When the author worked at the hotel in the mid-1970s, the railway legacy was already but a distant memory and even the name Great Northern had disappeared, replaced by Burlington Northern following the merger of Northern Pacific, Chicago Burlington & Quincy, Spokane, Portland & Seattle and Great Northern in March 1970. Burlington Northern has since merged with Santa Fe, creating Burlington Northern Santa Fe.

A nod of recognition to the Prince of Wales Hotel's past was given in 1995 when it was declared a national historic site, commemorated for its architectural and historical significance. The hotel is the most prominent man-made structure in Waterton Lakes National Park and a regional landmark. It has no equal in Waterton, nor does the future hold a chance for it to be surpassed since the implementation of strict guidelines on new developments in the park. With its completion in 1927, the Prince of Wales Hotel not only opened its doors to tourists, but also created a gateway to the park. The hotel's prominence has brought it international attention and put it on the map as a must-visit site for anyone in southern Alberta.

Fascinated by what little he had been told of its origins when he worked there, the author started a quest to learn as much as he could about the Prince of Wales Hotel. *High on a Windy Hill* is the result of his 20-year search into this grand survivor of the golden age of railway resort development.

The Call of the Mountains

The Prince of Wales Hotel is an impressive sight, even from a distance. This one-of-a-kind structure, perched on a hill overlooking the Waterton Valley, fits into its setting in a remarkable way. The hotel appears dwarfed by the rugged mountains. Yet close at hand, the hotel is massive, with its many gables, steep roof and Swiss-style balconies. It beckons visitors and once inside casts its own spell of wonder.

The dark entry opens to a lobby where interior balconies of dark cedar and Douglas fir rise one after another to reveal open-beam construction, but the lobby's most striking feature is the way in which the view has been incorporated into the architecture. Two story-tall windows draw the visitor to an unequalled vista of a seven mile-long (11 km) lake straddling the Canada-U.S. border, framed by mountains and sky, with a tiny village below. The view is never the same as the light changes throughout the day, the wind whips the lake and the sometimes rapidly moving weather obliterates it altogether. Tantalizing to boaters, hikers and horseback riders, the setting has a hypnotic effect on all who visit, whether for the first time or for repeat trips. It's a

view that has not changed in a millennium and captivates the imagination.

It was the same view that Louis Warren Hill Sr., 41, then chairman of the board of Great Northern Railway, saw when he stood on the knoll one breezy September day in 1913. Hill let his imagination blossom before the dramatic geologic features. What he envisioned was a perfect site for a tourist resort—the Prince of Wales Hotel.

Louis Hill was the mastermind behind Great Northern's development of Glacier Park tourism. 'Every passenger that goes to the national parks, wherever he may be, represents practically a net earning,' Hill said. Courtesy M. J. Elrod, Glacier National Park, HPF-1950.

Waterton was a relative tourist backwater when Louis Hill visited the park September 1913. Jack Hazzard's hotel and rental cabins provided the only accommodations other than tenting for the 2,000 people who visited each year. For Hill, Waterton was an unspoiled paradise awaiting the transformation his mighty Great Northern Railway could bring. Courtesy Ernie Haug, author's collection.

'Empire Builder' James Jerome Hill. J. J. Hill Library.

It's a long, flat journey from St. Paul, Minn., where Great Northern had its headquarters, to Waterton Lakes National Park, and the contrast between the two places is stark. St. Paul is the capital of the state, an industrial centre and a major transportation hub between Chicago and the western plains, while Waterton is an unspoiled and isolated wilderness, where the prairies meet the mountains, in the southwest corner of Alberta. There was nothing to link the two places—until Hill arrived.

The journey that brought Louis Hill to Waterton in 1913 began more than half a century before, in 1856, when his father, James Jerome Hill, left his native Ontario looking to make his fortune and ended up in the twin cities of St. Paul-Minneapolis. The senior Hill found a niche in the burgeoning Mississippi riverboat industry and within 20 years had amassed a sizable fortune. Always on the lookout for ways to improve his financial status, the gruff but astute J. J. Hill began sizing up the money-strapped St. Paul & Pacific Railroad Company. While the railroad had twice been in default and its line, headed north from St. Paul to the Manitoba border, stopped far short of its desti-

nation, Hill saw potential, not to mention a lucrative land grant.[1] To assist with the purchase, he turned to Norman Kittson, his partner in the Red River Transportation Company, and acquaintance Donald Smith, chief commissioner of the Hudson's Bay Company. Aided by Smith's cousin, George Stephen, president of the Bank of Montreal, the foursome, known as "the associates," took control of the St. Paul & Pacific in 1878. With financing in place, Hill oversaw completion of the line to St. Vincent, on the Minnesota-Manitoba border, making it a primary supply route to Winnipeg and the Canadian West until completion of the Canadian Pacific Railway in 1885.[2] The St. Paul & Pacific and its associated land grant proved as profitable as predicted and, over the next decade, added even more cash to Hill's already bulging pockets.

Toward the end of the 1880s, Hill turned his sights to the Pacific coast, planning to capitalize on the second wave of westward migration in the United States. His railway would become the northernmost line in the U.S., running between the Northern Pacific's rails and the Canadian border, following settlement and mining exploration through North Dakota and into Montana.[3] The railway, now named Great Northern, punched a path through the Rockies at the recently "discovered" Marias Pass in northern Montana, reaching Seattle in 1893.[4] Along the way, J. J. Hill masterminded the railroad's expansion into mining, forestry, agriculture and related businesses and industries, earning the nickname "The Empire Builder" for his efforts and becoming one of the most powerful individuals in the northwestern United States.[5] Hill's economic dominance and political influence were recognized in 1915 at the Panama-Pacific Exposition in

San Francisco when he was named Minnesota's "greatest living citizen."

Following his father's lead, Louis joined the railway in 1893. Louis Hill was a willing pupil and, over the next five years, learned the basics of railroading, working his way up from section hand and office clerk to become his father's assistant. Although more reserved than his outspoken dad, who never hesitated in giving advice to his son or anyone else, Louis looked for all the world like a younger version of his stocky father, albeit with red hair, a more neatly groomed beard and prince-nez glasses.[6] The path of ascension was not unexpected. The hard-working Louis was appointed president of Great Northern in 1907 and, five years later, at the age of 40, was named chairman of the board.[7]

Louis Hill's entry into the corporate fold came at a turning point in railway operations and in society. America was on the move in the 1890s and 1900s. Industrialization was spreading wealth to an everwidening spectrum of society and with that came an increase in leisure time. Travel and vacations were no longer the domain of a moneyed elite. Driven by wanderlust, America's burgeoning middle class set out to see the sites that had been discovered by an earlier, fabled group of Victorian adventurers. Magazines like *Sunset*, *Wonderland* and *National Geographic*, which displayed the wonders of other civilizations and the beauty of the great outdoors, fuelled this lust. For railways, travel fever meant an increase in passenger traffic as the middle class sought access to destinations both near and far.

One of the first railways to exploit the tourism trend was Northern Pacific, which found the perfect opportunity in Yellowstone. Set aside in 1873 as the world's first national park, Yellowstone

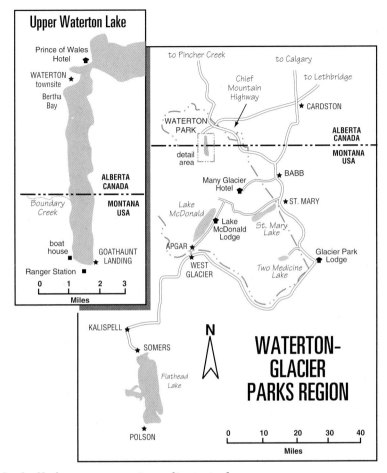

had all the necessary ingredients to lure inquisitive and thrill-seeking travellers: Vast expanses of remarkable scenery, plenty of wildlife, and the mystery surrounding the mineral waters, geysers and hot springs. It was also conveniently close to Northern Pacific's line. When the potential for increased rail-passenger traffic through tourism became evident, Northern Pacific positioned itself as the prime link to Yellowstone, using magazine and newspaper advertisements, brochures and posters to promote itself.[8]

Louis Hill had a natural interest in the affairs of Northern Pacific. Northern Pa-

A Blackfeet native gives Lucienne McGow and Fay Frederick a lesson in the use of the bow and arrow. Great Northern Railway used native imagery extensively in promoting tourism to Glacier Park, including paying natives to set up their teepees on the lawn of Glacier Park Hotel and to entertain nightly in the hotel lobby. Great Northern Railway publicity and advertising department, Minnesota Historical Society.

cific and Great Northern both had headquarters in St. Paul, Minn., and they had close historic ties that went back to the 1890s when J. J. Hill, along with J. P. Morgan, had a central role in reorganizing the line. By 1900, J. J. Hill was in control of Northern Pacific. As a leading executive of Great Northern, Louis Hill was keenly aware of any successes racked up by Northern Pacific, and he certainly noted the benefits that accrued from its association with Yellowstone.

Northern Pacific's venture into Yellowstone would have also appealed to Louis Hill on a personal level. Unlike his father, whose business was an all-consuming passion, the younger Hill took pleasure in other pursuits. He loved hunting and fishing and the adventure entailed in those sports. When time permitted, Hill enjoyed painting and photography. He also had a passion for the great West, studying it at close hand as Great Northern pushed its tracks ever farther from St. Paul toward the Pacific Ocean. The Blackfeet were particularly interesting to Hill, and he spent considerable time learning about their culture and collecting artifacts.* He appeared to have a genuine and respectful interest in the Blackfeet that transcended his railway's desire to exploit the natives for advertising and promotional purposes.[9]

Louis Hill eventually found his own Yellowstone in Glacier National Park, Montana. Legend has it he was instrumental in Glacier being designated a park.

---

* The tribes of the Blackfoot Confederacy are referred to by their preferred names. While the Siksika people were known as the Blackfoot in Canada, they are members of the Blackfeet tribe in Montana. Kainai are referred to as members of the Blood tribe and the Pikuni people as Peigan.

It was no mere coincidence Great Northern's line ran along what would become Glacier's southern boundary. Hill is credited with having persuaded Montana Congressman Charles Pray and Montana Senators Thomas Carter and Joseph Dixon to back the initial effort to create a park in the glacier-carved mountains, often called the backbone of the continent. It is hard to imagine today that anyone would oppose creating a reserve in an area as unspoiled and blessed with natural wonders as Glacier, but the proposal had its detractors in those who questioned the national park concept and didn't want the area's vast timber and mining resources lost from potential development.[10] It took three tries before Congress passed a bill setting aside 1,500 square miles (3,885 sq. km) for Glacier National Park. When it was feared the third bill had become stalled at the House committee level, Hill sent telegrams to two committee members urging them to help push the bill through.[11] As much as Hill played a role in the passing of the legislation, the work of Dr. Lyman Sperry and George Bird Grinnell, both of whom lobbied for and promoted the concept of a park in Glacier country for many years before Great Northern became involved, should not be overlooked or trivialized.[12] Hill, Sperry and Grinnell eventually got what they wanted when U.S. President William Howard Taft signed the bill into law on May 11, 1910.

Hill wasted no time in making his mark on the newly established Glacier National Park. He envisioned Glacier as "America's Switzerland," a theme Great Northern would use as the basis for all its buildings in the park and its advertising campaigns. Within a year, Great Northern had applied for and received concession leases for the undeveloped areas, mostly east of the Continental Divide. The railway constructed tourist cabins and tee-pee camps, followed later by Swiss-style chalets, at scenic points throughout the park. The locations were strategically chosen to be no more than a comfortable day's horseback ride apart. The building of Glacier Park Hotel, the first major establishment, was begun in early 1912. Many Glacier Hotel was started two years later. In 1914 these operations were consolidated as Glacier Park Hotel Company, a subsidiary of Great Northern.[13]

Besides chalets and hotels, the railway company also found itself building roads and trails at its own expense because congressional appropriations for Glacier Park were inadequate to cover the costs. Much of the Blackfeet Highway (Highway 89) on the east side of Glacier Park was originally built and paid for by the railway. It is estimated that for every $1 the U.S. government invested in Glacier Park during the first decade, Great Northern spent $10.[14]

Hill's involvement in Glacier Park developments was all encompassing. He devoted a great deal of time to their planning and expected the same commitment from his employees. "His enthusiasm was contagious," wrote H. R. Wiecking, a publicist for Great Northern. "There was hardly a department of his large railway organization that was not called upon to make its contribution to the work."[15] Contagious may not have been the word Great Northern's employees and contractors would have used in private, for they knew Hill was an uncompromising task master who took a keen inter-

Louis Warren Hill Sr.
J. J. Hill Library, LH 554.

Many Glacier Hotel. T. J. Hileman photo, Great Northern Railway publicity and advertising department, Minnesota Historical Society.

Dining hall at St. Mary Chalets. Postcard, author's collection.

Left: Sperry Chalets. T. J. Hileman photo, postcard, author's collection.

Belton Chalets. R. E. Marble photo, postcard, author's collection.

Luxury in the Wilderness

In Louis Hill's bid to develop tourism in Glacier, Great Northern Railway constructed hotels and chalets in nearly every corner of the Montana park. Reached by saddle horse, bus and tour boat, the facilities were oases of luxury in Glacier's vast Rocky Mountain wilderness. From these fully staffed Swiss-style hostelries, tourists could explore the "backbone of the continent" in total comfort.

Motor Vessel St. Mary and Going-to-the-Sun Chalets. T. J. Hileman photo, Great Northern Railway publicity and advertising department, Minnesota Historical Society.

15

The interior of Glacier Park Hotel was fashioned after the 'forest lobby' of the widely acclaimed Forestry Building at the 1905 Lewis and Clark Exposition. The hotel lobby features columns of tree trunks with the bark still intact. T. J. Hileman photo, postcard, author's collection.

est in every detail. For instance, when Hill learned a plumbing contract was to be let to a certain individual, he nixed it saying, "All the work he has done for us has been unsatisfactory."[16]

It was Hill who chose the Swiss-style architecture for the railway's Glacier Park developments. Glacier Park Hotel was his showpiece. The hotel was patterned on the Forestry Building at the 1905 Lewis and Clark Exposition in Portland, Oregon.[17] The 104 foot-wide by 206 foot-long (31.2 m by 61.8 m) Forestry Building was one of the outstanding features of the exposition. Its "forest lobby"—columns of tree trunks 54 to 70 feet (16 to 21 m) tall with the bark still intact—awed visitors. Hill wanted the same effect incorporated into the lobby of Glacier Park Hotel. In choosing this design, Hill was trying to capture the spirit of the West by romanticizing the cozy log cabin on a grand scale.[18] The use of tree trunks and logs captured the vernacular aspects of the cabin while Swiss themes provided interesting roofline treatments, balconies, fancy balustrades, decorative support brackets, and gingerbread scrollwork around window and door frames.

Hill was fortunate in that he had one of the pioneers in the use of vernacular/Swiss style in the northwestern U.S. readily at hand: Kirtland Cutter of Spokane, Washington.[19] Cutter had made a name for himself at the 1893 World's Columbian Exposition in Chicago with his design of the Idaho Building. Exposition judges awarded Cutter's firm the prize "for a type of architecture… which expresses the character of the state erecting it."[20] The building was derived from the chalets of the Bernese Oberland district of Switzerland, featuring deeply overhanging eaves, a low-pitched roof and balconies fronted by rustic balustrades. Great Northern hired Cutter to design several of its chalets in Glacier, and his work no doubt influenced Great Northern's architects, Samuel Bartlett and Thomas McMahon. Besides Sperry Chalet and his joint work with Bartlett on Many Glacier Hotel, Cutter also designed Lake McDonald Lodge.[21]

Hill was never far from the design process and monitored all the work carefully, particularly Glacier Park Hotel, the largest building commissioned and the first major structure most guests saw when arriving at the park. Hill repeatedly sent Bartlett books on Swiss designs from which the architect might draw inspiration. On one day, Hill exchanged five telegrams with Bartlett to ensure the blueprints for the hotel were satisfactory.[22]

Creating this tourist empire in Glacier set Great Northern apart from other railways. Most other lines were content to carve a niche for themselves in their chosen national park, constructing one or two hotels, like Canadian Pacific did with its Banff Springs Hotel and Chateau Lake Louise. Great Northern's widespread chalet system, with its Swiss architecture, gave a unity and sense of place to a region of

Louis Hill tries a Brewster brothers stagecoach which carried Glacier Park visitors between some of Great Northern's hotels and chalets. Stagecoaches were replaced by buses after two seasons. J. J. Hill Library.

The switch, in 1915, from stagecoaches to motor buses to carry visitors about Glacier Park did not always guarantee guests would make their destinations on time. J. J. Hill Library.

immense proportions that was unmatched anywhere else in North America.

Great Northern ensured the public knew its connection to the park through advertising. Pamphlets and brochures illustrating and describing the park and Great Northern's facilities were distributed throughout the United States. Advertisements in local newspapers encouraged readers to write to the railroad's passenger traffic department for these materials if they weren't readily available. Hill, a renowned booster who was once labelled "the best advertising man in the United States" next to Teddy Roosevelt, made numerous personal contributions to this promotional effort. It was he who coined the catchphrase "See America First" used in all railway advertising, and it was his idea to incorporate the park's indigenous Rocky Mountain goat into the railway's logo, beginning in 1921.[23] By 1914 the railway company was spending almost $330,000 a year to promote Glacier.[24] Great Northern was omnipresent and would eventually "own" Glacier, incorporating the park into itself rather than the other way around.

Throughout all the hectic building activity in Glacier Park, Hill never lost sight of the reason for the development: "The railroads are greatly interested in the passenger traffic to the parks. Every passenger that goes to the national parks, wherever he may be, represents practically a net earning," he said.[25] Hill was a reluctant developer, though. "We do not wish to go into the hotel business," he said at a national parks conference in 1911. "We wish to get out of it and to confine ourselves strictly to the business of getting people there just as soon as we can. But it is difficult to get capital interested in this kind of pioneer work."[26] In the end, he abandoned his misgivings: "The work is so important I am loath to entrust the development to anybody but myself."[27]

Hill's efforts came to fruition during the summer of 1913 when the doors of the Glacier Park Hotel opened to the first eastern guests. After stepping down from the Oriental Limited at Glacier Park Station, visitors were whisked by stagecoach or rickshaw a few hundred yards to the luxury hotel from which the splendour of Glacier Park was theirs to explore, on foot, by stage, horseback or excursion boat. The first season had inherent organizational problems: Stages were not always on time and when it rained the roads became impassable, stranding tourists for a day or two at one of the chalets. Despite these and numerous other minor inconveniences, the summer was a success.

Hill ended the season with a bang—a party to celebrate his father's 75th birthday. The younger Hill rounded up friends of his father from far and wide, as well as many of the early staff who had helped put the railroad on the map. Some 600 people attended the celebration, many brought to Glacier on specially chartered trains as much to see the new hotel and park as to mark the senior Hill's birthday. The banquet and subsequent party would go down in the railway's history as one of its most extravagant.

James Jerome Hill marked his seventy-fifth birthday at a gala put on by his son, Louis Hill, at Glacier Park Hotel in September 1913. About 600 people were invited to the party, many arriving on specially chartered trains. Here, J. J. Hill stands with his wife Mary in front of a bouquet of 75 American roses presented to them at the birthday celebration. J. J. Hill Library.

It was in the wake of the euphoria of this event that Hill travelled to Waterton, stood on the hill at the base of Mount Crandell and declared Great Northern would build what would become the Prince of Wales Hotel. Hill came to consider Waterton a future hotel site after a chance encounter with Reverend Samuel H. Middleton. Middleton was a newcomer to southern Alberta who emigrated from England in 1905 to take up cattle ranching. He discovered his abilities were in other areas and eventually joined the Anglican Church. In 1909, he was appointed headmaster of St. Paul's residential school on the Blood tribe reserve, northeast of Waterton.[28] Middleton literally fell in love with Waterton, where he vacationed each summer and ran a small camp for Blood children. He and Hill met on a hike in Glacier Park's Swiftcurrent Valley where Hill was choosing the future site of Many Glacier Hotel.[29] Middleton was keenly aware of Great Northern's activities in Glacier and believed similar developments would be beneficial to Waterton. Undoubtedly Middleton, in his quiet way, would have impressed upon Hill the desirability of Waterton as a possible site for a hotel.[30]

Hill took up the notion with his 1913 trip to Waterton and found an ideal location to build a Canadian link in his hotel chain. He said as much to the superintendent of Waterton Park, who dutifully recorded the event in his annual report: "Mr. Louis Hill stated that it was quite likely that his company would ... put up a 300-roomed hotel. If this is done it will bring a great many visitors to this park."[31] It was a bold statement by Hill and an accurate prediction by superintendent John George (Kootenai) Brown.

Kootenai Brown well knew the difference a resort could make to the future of

Kootenai Brown. Henson photo, Glenbow Archives, Calgary, Canada, NA 678-1.

Waterton was a popular spot for fishing and camping. Anglers could try their luck for rainbow and cutthroat trout below Cameron Falls, at left, or if the weather was calm, try some deep trolling in Upper Waterton Lake for lake trout and northern pike. T. J. Hileman photo, Great Northern Railway publicity and advertising department, Minnesota Historical Society.

the park. Brown had watched Waterton's evolution with interest since 1879, when he and his wife Olive became the first permanent residents of the area after building a cabin on the shore of Lower Waterton Lake.[32] Throughout the 1880s and into the 1890s, settlement encroached ever closer to the lakes and mountains. When an oil discovery on Cameron Creek precipitated Alberta's first oil boom in 1889-90, long-time residents realized the potential threat of development to the wilderness area, a prized spot for fishing and camping. F. W. Godsal, a Pincher Creek area rancher, urged the federal government to set aside the region for public use before tourists were crowded out and the district spoiled by settlement. It took two years for the government to act on Godsal's suggestion. On May 30, 1895, 54 square miles (140 sq. km) of land around the Waterton Lakes

Great Northern engine No. 2517 pulls the Empire Builder over the Stone Arch Bridge in Minneapolis, Minn. Great Northern Railway publicity and advertising department, Minnesota Historical Society.

A Pullman sleeping car ensured a good night's rest aboard the Empire Builder. Frank Willming photo, Great Northern Railway publicity and advertising department, Minnesota Historical Society.

All Aboard!

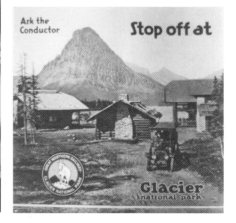

Ark the Conductor

Stop off at

Glacier national park

A westbound Empire Builder filled with eastern tourists eager to see the sights of Glacier National Park pulls into Glacier Park Station, the jumping-off point for summer vacations in the Montana Rockies. George Grant photo, courtesy National Park Service, GLAC-11489.

The Empire Builder lounge car offered a comfortable spot for passengers to relax and compare itineraries for their summer vacation in Glacier Park. Great Northern Railway publicity and advertising department, Minnesota Historical Society.

Returning home from a vacation in Glacier Park meant many happy memories of the holiday and time spent with new-found friends aboard the Empire Builder. Gilbert Seehausen photo, Great Northern Railway publicity and advertising department, Minnesota Historical Society.

Oil discoveries on Cameron Creek set off two mini-booms in the Waterton Lakes region in 1889 and again in 1901. The quantity of oil produced by the John Lineham well was insufficient to sustain a viable commercial operation and the well and nearby town, Oil City, were abandoned. Courtesy Ann Harrison, author's collection.

was set aside as Kootenay Lakes Forest Park, the fourth such reserve in Canada.[33]

Godsal, Brown and other advocates of preserving the Waterton Lakes district from development had but a short time to rest on their laurels. A second oil boom was sparked in September 1901 when a spot along Cameron Creek became the site for the first producing oil well in Western Canada. It created an instant town, Oil City, just outside the park and prompted the search that would eventually lead to the development of Alberta's now mainstay energy sector. The excitement in Waterton was short-lived, however, as the quantity of oil was insufficient to sustain a commercial well, and Oil City was soon abandoned. Again Godsal jumped to the fore, writing to the minister of the Interior urging expansion of the reserve to cover a much greater area. The results of lobbying by Godsal and John Herron, the local member of Parliament, eventually saw the region declared a national park in 1911.[34]

Despite the attention oil discoveries brought, Waterton remained a relative resort backwater with developers and tourists alike. Unlike Banff and Jasper parks farther north, Waterton did not have a railway to bring it fame through hotel development and promotion. The nearest main railway was 35 miles (56 km) away at Pincher Creek Station, and Canadian Pacific, owner of the line, considered it more important for coal, timber and freight than passengers or tourism. Besides, Canadian Pacific already had a substantial investment with its Banff Springs Hotel and Chateau Lake Louise and devoted its advertising to ensuring their continued success. The railway did not appear interested in taking on a resort in this far-flung corner of Alberta. So while Banff enjoyed international recognition, Waterton remained undeveloped and relatively unknown. It was a pleasant place to camp, picnic, hike and fish for the 2,000 residents from surrounding southern Alberta towns who stopped there annually, but with few tourist facilities. Ottawa didn't even deem it necessary to have anyone on site to oversee the park until March 1910 when Kootenai Brown was appointed game guardian and fisheries inspector.[35]

Hill would change the tempo of Waterton, but it was not in 1913 or immediately thereafter. The Prince of Wales Hotel would not be built for more than a decade and only after overcoming obstacles as diverse as climate, federal and provincial politics and Hill's own indecision on the final architectural design.

2 Haven for Thirsty Americans

It took 14 years for Louis Hill to fulfil his dream of opening a hotel in Waterton. Many circumstances played a part in realizing his proposal after all that time. Ultimately, it was a single event that made his wish become reality.

Within months of Hill uttering to Kootenai Brown his idea of building a hotel in the park, the world stood on the brink of war. Canadians were called to arms in the summer of 1914, from the outset of the First World War. While Hill ordered construction to start on Many Glacier Hotel that same summer, a similar development in Waterton was out of the question as manpower and resources in Canada were dedicated to the war effort for the next four years. The atmosphere for development dried up on the south side of the 49th parallel when the U.S. ended its neutrality in 1917 and declared war on Germany. To bolster its war effort, Washington nationalized the railways, including Great Northern. In one fell swoop the advertising department of Great Northern was essentially disbanded. Great Northern did not close its hotels and chalets in Glacier Park, but did not and could not go out of its way to promote them either since federal regula-

tors controlled the purse strings and operations of the railway. By 1920 the railways were back in private hands and Great Northern had reassembled its advertising department, kicking off an aggressive promotional campaign to entice war-weary Americans to take their first real vacation since the end of hostilities.

If Hill had any idea of reviving his plan for Waterton after the Great War, it was quickly squelched when the park became the centre of a disputed proposal that would have permanently ruined the location for a hotel. In 1919, Alberta govern-

Waterton's first ranger, Kootenai Brown, poses with his second wife, Isabella, in the back seat of a car that made the trip to Waterton. The missing headlight is testament to the rough road to the park, which had little or no signage, even less gravel and forced drivers to ford several rivers. Courtesy Ernie Haug, author's collection.

Louis Hill saw this knoll overlooking Upper Waterton Lake and realized it was the perfect site to build a summer resort hotel to complement those his Great Northern Railway was operating in Glacier Park. It would take 13 years from the time Hill visited this spot in 1913 until construction would begin on the Prince of Wales Hotel. One of the factors that prevented an earlier start was a proposal in 1919 to build a dam across the Bosporus, the narrows between the base of the knoll and Vimy Peak, at left, to raise the level of the lake to irrigate nearby farmland. Postcard, author's collection.

ment engineers recommended building a dam across the narrows between Upper and Middle Waterton lakes, including the promontory on which the Prince of Wales Hotel now sits.[1] Raising the lake level would have provided irrigation for farmland in southern Alberta that had suffered three years of drought.[2] It would also have flooded Waterton townsite, changing entirely the character of the area. Leasing of lots in Waterton was suspended while the dam issue was argued between the provincial and federal governments.[3]

At their headquarters in St. Paul, Great Northern officials followed the controversy through press reports. An internal memo suggests how the company viewed the issue: "I feel very sure there will always be too much opposition to (a dam) from all of that part of Canada for it to be carried out," Albert Hogeland, chief engineer for Great Northern, advised railway president Ralph Budd.[4] Hogeland's conclusion was correct.

A public outcry helped defeat the dam proposal and by 1921 leasing of lots resumed.[5] Several wet summers followed, ensuring the matter would not be revived.

Resolution of the dam question let loose a flood of pent-up demand for lots in Waterton. During the next five years dozens of buildings were constructed, from new businesses to private homes. By 1926, commercial and residential development in the park was taking on a life of its own, with each new addition acting as a further magnet for tourists. That spring a dance pavilion, commissioned by Ernie Haug and Dave MacLean, opened for business, offering live music each weekend during the summer tourist season. Down the street, Eddie Poulin of Calgary started upgrading his Waterton Lakes Hotel and Chalets.[6] T. L. Allred began glassing in the heated swimming pool, soon to be dubbed the Crystal Pool.[7] And requests for tours on Upper Waterton

Lake prompted the importation of more launches, from Gull Lake, bringing the total in the park to five.[8] Later that summer, C. A. Carnell and his brother expanded their dock on Steamboat Bay, now called Emerald Bay, added a boathouse, and made repairs to their boat, the *Allias*.[9]

Waterton's businessmen were not only working individually but also together to ensure the growth of tourism. They formed the Waterton Citizen's Committee to discuss ways to promote and improve the park. In the spring of 1926 the committee organized and raised funds to plant trees along Waterton Avenue as well as lay a wooden sidewalk along the dirt road. They also persuaded a bank to open a branch in the park for the summer season. Later, the committee ordered 100 road signs to mark the way to Waterton.[10]

The Parks Branch assisted the efforts of local businessmen by improving and expanding its facilities. Work had been going on for several years to build a proper road along the Akamina trail, west of the townsite. By 1926 the improved road had reached Oil City and was headed for Cameron Lake, with talk of pushing it over the Continental Divide, through British Columbia, and south to Glacier Park's Kintla Valley.[11] Waterton's hiking and horse trail system, which covered 150 miles (241 km), was also being expanded. Work was proceeding on a path to Hell Roaring Falls (which would become the basis for the renowned trail to Crypt Lake) and tree cutting to create Carthew trail was ongoing, while the trails to Bertha Lake and Goat Haunt were being improved.[12]

All of this development did not go unnoticed by Great Northern officials. What an improvement it was over the Waterton Park that Hill had visited just over a decade before: A one-street, one-hotel town

accessible only by fording several rivers. As encouraging as these improvements were, they were not motive enough for Hill to take the Prince of Wales Hotel plan from the shelf. Hill reacted to a much more powerful incentive: booze.

In October 1923, thirsty Alberta voters went to the polls and ended Prohibition in the province. After seven years under the thumb of the Drys, it was clear voters saw Prohibition as a noble experiment that had failed miserably. Crafty consumers had made a mockery of the law when it was discovered there was no ban on the interprovincial sale of liquor through mail order. While Albertans couldn't legally buy booze anywhere in the province, except for Prohibition near-beer or through a doctor's prescription, they could pay $11 for a gallon can of scotch from the Bronfman mail-order warehouse in Yorkton, Sask.[13] Moderationists used such failings in the law to convince voters it was wiser to have government control of the liquor trade rather than no control at all.

In accordance with the outcome of the Prohibition plebiscite, government liquor

As tourism to Waterton increased, the Carnell brothers expanded the services at their dock, adding rental canoes, a tour boat and building a boathouse. Author's collection.

The Victoria Day long weekend in May is the beginning of the summer tourist season in Waterton, here marked by a gathering outside Jack Hazzard's hotel in 1917. Courtesy Ernie Haug, author's collection.

stores began opening in May 1924 and several weeks later the first licensed hotels started serving the first full-strength, legal beer since the Great War. The availability of brand-name liquor versus the nameless and questionable bootleg varieties that were sold illicitly in the U.S., still in the throes of Prohibition, wasn't missed by Montanans. According to historian James Gray, when the Alberta government opened its store in Lethbridge, one of the first customers through the door was an American tourist.

"Gimme 10 cases of scotch," the tourist said, unrolling a wad of bills. The astounded clerk, who was still stocking his shelves, said that he did not yet have 10 cases of scotch on hand.

"Okay," said the American, "gimme 10 cases of whatever you've got." He loaded up with an assortment of booze and headed back to Montana.[14]

Not wanting to be party to rumrunning, the Alberta government eventually banned all liquor stores close to the border, forcing rumrunners to rely on liquor warehouses in British Columbia and Saskatchewan that had been set up to slake the thirst of mail order patrons.[15] The Crowsnest Pass, northwest of Waterton and the southernmost mountain pass between Alberta and British Columbia, became a hotbed for bootleggers.

South of the border, the dreary monotony of Prohibition was enlivened only by illicit sales of bathtub gin, costlier and better-tasting imported liquor smuggled from Canada, and, for those with money and the right connections, speakeasies. Unlike the plebiscite in Alberta, there would be no quick solution to Prohibition for Americans. In Canada it had been a provincial option, but Prohibition was part of the Constitution in the U.S., and mounting the support necessary for a constitutional amendment was no minor task. For those who had the inclination and the cash, it was easier to get a drink by circumventing the law than changing it.

Great Northern officials couldn't but be aware of the Alberta plebiscite and its outcome. Rumrunning was big business along the Alberta-Montana border, as there were few checkpoints. Trafficking in liquor became so widespread a group of special U.S. customs agents was dispatched to Montana to halt the flow. Based out of Great Falls, Charlie Sheridan's patrolmen had orders to shoot to kill.[16]

It was a strong order, but so was the lure of contraband alcohol and what people would do to get it. Hill understood the power of alcohol. Known to enjoy a tipple or two, he realized what a legal liquor licence could mean for a new hotel, especially one in Waterton. Great Northern had spent hundreds of thousands of dollars since the creation of Glacier Park in 1910 to promote the railway's hotels and chalets there and itself as the means to reach those scenic attractions. To make a hotel in an adjoining park in another country succeed, it would need more than just another dramatic expanse of scenery to lure Glacier visitors north. Legal alcohol provided the necessary incentive. Getting a liquor licence for a hotel in Waterton would put the hotel and the park on the map.

Great Northern was not the first to recognize the potential alcohol might have in luring tourists to Waterton. In May 1924, Lethbridge businessman Mark Rogers proposed building a new hotel in Waterton, but only if the province would grant him a liquor licence.[17] Rogers had purchased the Waterton Lakes Hotel and was ready to pull it down and replace it with a "first-class hotel," surrounded by 25 two-room bungalows. In case he didn't get the licence, Rogers said he would put the money into remodelling the existing hotel. Eager to have the bungalows ready for that tourist season, Rogers hired Thomas Stubbs as contractor to begin building them—even before a decision was made about the liquor licence application.[18]

Rogers didn't have to wait long for an answer to his request. "Emphatically no," announced Attorney General John Brownlee. "Mr. Rogers or no one else will get a beer licence at Waterton." Brownlee said the province saw no immediate need to sell liquor in the park, adding that Ottawa was also opposed to licensing a hotel in Waterton.[19] Rogers had Stubbs continue with construction of the bungalows, but his grand plan of luring tourists to the park with alcohol went nowhere quickly.

Great Northern did not make construction of the Prince of Wales Hotel contingent on getting a liquor licence. Railway officials had confidence they could muster the necessary support and, if need be, bring pressure to bear to put a beer parlour in the hotel. Great Northern quietly obtained the lease it needed to build in the park and got on with the preliminaries.[20]

The matter of announcing the new hotel project went to Budd, who carefully staged it as an offhand remark to journalists in New York. He didn't waste a moment letting the world know about the

Ralph Budd.
Author's collection.

Waterton's main street in the 1920s was the hub of a growing summer resort community. The growth was aided by the popularity of the automobile, which made it easier for people to reach this remote, southwest corner of Alberta. Courtesy Ernie Haug, author's collection.

Prince of Wales Hotel. In fact, he made the announcement in New York a day before the railway actually had the letter from Canadian parks officials in its hands saying it was okay to make public the proposal.[21] The choice of New York as the place to release the news was no accident; Budd wanted to make an impact in the eastern media. It was from the East that Great Northern drew most of its customers for its summer mountain vacation packages in Glacier Park. Any new development, especially one that offered legal consumption of liquor, was worth touting in this primary market. The publicity Budd got was more than he bargained for.

The *New York Times, New York Herald* and most other newspapers played the story straight, reporting Great Northern's "intention to build a 450-room hotel on ten acres in Canada to extend its hotel chain."[22] There was no hint in these reports of anything surreptitious in Great Northern's motive. The reporter for the *New York World*, however, dug deeper and his March 5, 1926, report told a different story. The hotel, the *New York World* declared, was to be a means for Americans to skirt Prohibition in the United States. "The Great Northern will build a haven for thirsty American travellers at Watertown [sic], Alberta, Ralph Budd, president of the road, intimated yesterday as he boarded the Broadway Limited. The dominion Department of the Interior, he said, has approved its project for a chalet type hotel with 450 rooms and a bar."[23]

While Great Northern was doing nothing illegal, the railway shunned such "negative" publicity even though the fact the new hotel would contain a bar was the underlying message it wanted conveyed. In the wake of the *New York World* story, Budd consulted friend and journalist Hoke Smith

about how to counter it. Smith advised: "If you do not emasculate this story too much, I am sure we can get it over (with), and thus correct the erroneous idea that has been given out concerning this new resort." To counter the publicity, Smith arranged to "slip out" his own, Great Northern-approved story over news wires to reveal the "true facts" of why the railway wanted to build a hotel in Waterton, emphasizing the beautiful scenery in the park as an adjunct to Glacier.[24] That the hotel would contain a beer parlour was to be viewed as little more than a happy circumstance. It would not be necessary to mention in publicity "that the situation in Waterton Lakes Park is any different in reference to Prohibition than in Glacier Park. Those who are interested will draw their own conclusions," a company memo noted.[25]

The eventual presence of a tavern in the Prince of Wales Hotel was no coincidence. Its existence was the result of a concerted effort by Great Northern officials, working in conjunction with the Alberta government. Great Northern waited until six months into the construction project— January 1927, long enough for suspicions to die down—before making an inquiry about a beer parlour licence.[26] An application was duly submitted and, as required by law, notices were taken out in local newspapers to permit the public to raise concerns or objections.[27] If railway company officials had had their way, that would have been the last anyone heard of the matter. Great Northern maintained a strict code of silence. Even guests invited by railway officials to tour Waterton were warned to steer clear of the subject. When confronted by the *Lethbridge Herald*'s correspondent, Nicholas Longworth, Speaker of the U.S. House of Representatives, said: "Ask me about anything but Prohibition."[28]

Great Northern, meanwhile, quietly marshalled its arguments and backing for the beer parlour application. With prompting, groups such as the Alberta Motor Association and the Moderation League of Alberta came out in support of the licence application for a tap room at the hotel.[29] In a petition to Brownlee, who was now premier of the province, the Moderation League pointed out that tourists to Waterton were being discriminated against since it was the only national park in Alberta where no liquor licences had been issued.[30] As for Waterton residents, there was no question where they stood. A vote of leaseholders showed 64 in favour and only 16 opposed.[31]

With such support it would have seemed an easy thing for Great Northern to obtain a beer parlour licence for the hotel. But there was a fundamental problem yet to be overcome: Waterton Park bordered the only part of the province that had voted to remain dry when Prohibition was repealed. The reason for the success of the Drys was Cardston was a town founded and predominantly populated by teetotalling Mormons. Dominated as the district around Cardston was by members of the Church of Jesus Christ of Latter-day Saints, it was no surprise when the vote turned out 1,521 for Prohibition while only 352 people voted to have the province control the sale of liquor and beer. As a result, no bars or liquor stores were permitted anywhere in the area.

Great Northern's plan for Waterton upset local Mormon leaders who readily voted to oppose the granting of any liquor licence at a location so close to their communities.[32] Knowing the religious dictates of the region, Great Northern officials decided to send a company representative to meet the Mormon bishop of Cardston to

explain the situation.[33] The tack taken in the meeting was to point out the benefits of having a bar in Waterton: The federal and provincial governments backed improvements in the park, of which the bar was a part; Waterton residents supported the application; and "a well regulated beer room" would help eliminate bootlegging.[34]

The latter point was no small consideration. For several years Waterton had been a prime spot for minor rumrunners. Just the previous summer Mounties had used an undercover officer to nab a bootlegger who had been selling liquor from his cottage in the park.[35] The opening of a dance pavilion that same year brought a new wave of public drunkenness. The *Lethbridge Herald* said the situation on Saturday nights had gotten to the point that it was "becoming a nuisance."[36] There had also been several automobile accidents related to drunk driving.

Fortunately for Great Northern's beer parlour application, it had the backing of no less than the liquor commissioner of the province, R. J. Dinning. While recognizing local opposition, Dinning took the stand Waterton "was no longer local in charac-

Cardston was a prosperous market community in southwestern Alberta founded by and predominantly populated by Mormons, many of whom vacationed in nearby Waterton. The teetotalling members of the Church of Jesus Christ of Latter-day Saints ensured this was the only corner of the province to remain Dry after Prohibition was repealed in Alberta in 1923. Church officials objected to Great Northern's proposal for a hotel in Waterton featuring a tavern. Glenbow Archives, Calgary, Canada, NC 7-656.

ter," that it had become an international playground and the wishes of the people in the province generally had to be respected. "We are satisfied the Great Northern will conduct a beer parlour along the very best lines. It will maintain a high standard," he said, adding that, for the first year, the operation would be monitored to ensure it was "operating in the best interests of the public."[37]

With Dinning squarely behind the application, the problem of Waterton being in a national park and next to a dry district was dealt with through a minor boundary adjustment. The move caught the attention of Reverend J. S. Knight of Edmonton who, along with a delegation of fellow Prohibitionists, accused the province of gerrymandering. Brownlee strongly denied the claim. Earl Cook, member of the legislative assembly for Pincher Creek, jumped to defend the action, noting requests to change the boundary had started four years ago, long before the hotel existed.[38] That last obstacle out of the way, the Prince of Wales Hotel was granted its tavern licence.

Publicly, Great Northern would never admit this reason for building the Prince of Wales Hotel. In official railway letters and memos, there is never a mention of it. The truth surfaces in private correspondence and then only between trusted individuals and after Prohibition in the U.S. was repealed, in December 1933. William Kenney, then president of Great Northern, admitted the role liquor played in the existence of the hotel in a 1935 letter to Howard Hays, president of Glacier Park Transport Company: "The reason for building this (Prince of Wales) hotel departed with the repeal of the liquor laws in this country."[39] In another letter to Hays lamenting the closure of the Prince of Wales Hotel during the Depression, Kenney said: "I can't see any value in the Prince of Wales Hotel, especially since Prohibition has been repealed."[40]

And so it was just as the *New York World* had claimed: The Prince of Wales Hotel would be built as a haven for thirsty Americans.

3 Road Wary

Louis Hill's vision of making a profit from Americans seeking a way to wet their whistle in Alberta was one thing, getting around to building a hotel that would be the attraction in Waterton Park was something else again. Little could he have anticipated the complications that lay ahead.

Hill was eager to get moving and as soon as he knew the railway was assured of the site it wanted in Waterton, he had the staff at Glacier Park Hotel Company and Great Northern's engineering department prepare preliminary cost estimates.[1] As had been done in Glacier Park with the two main lodges, Glacier Park Hotel and Many Glacier Hotel, the Waterton hotel was to be built in stages. The proposal brought to Hill in January 1926 showed a hotel comprised of a lobby, dining room, kitchen and one bedroom annex, for a total of 118 bedrooms. Each section would be connected to the lobby directly and by covered bridges or walkways.[2] Later, as need dictated, more bedroom annexes could be built, for a proposed total of 300-plus rooms. The cost of building the initial stage of the hotel was set at $642,500, including road construction, installation of a water and sewage system lines, and creation of an electrical supply.[3] Tentative plans were submitted for the approval of Canadian Parks Branch in Ottawa and in early March 1926 Great Northern received a letter from Ottawa stating "there would be no objection now" for the railway to publicly announce the project, which Budd did in New York.[4]

The announcement let loose a flood of mail to Great Northern offices in St. Paul, but none of it from thirsty Americans. Rather, dozens of contractors and suppliers wrote seeking a piece of the Waterton

This early sketch of the Waterton hotel was probably made by architect Thomas McMahon for Louis Hill in January or February 1926. It shows the north side of the building and closely matches the first set of Prince of Wales Hotel blueprints. Courtesy Toltz, King, Duvall, Anderson and Associates.

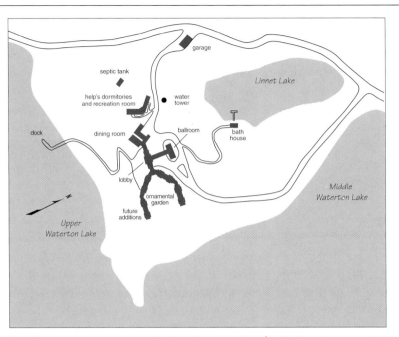

hotel project. Doing work for the prestigious Great Northern Railway was much sought after and the Grand Forks Builders and Traders Exchange in North Dakota said its members were "anxious to figure the work."[5] The president of the Lethbridge Board of Trade asked for an appointment with Budd regarding "matters of mutual interest to discuss."[6] J. McDiarmond Company of Winnipeg, Man., had the governor of Minnesota write a letter of recommendation so the company might offer a tender for the hotel project.[7] The landscaping firm of Morell and Nichols Inc. wanted to discuss the layout of the grounds, while Pittsburgh Glass Company was ready to fill any needs.[8] The Heintzman Piano Company's office in Calgary sent Great Northern a catalogue from which it might make a selection.[9] And a personnel company offered a manager "who has had a metropolitan experience in the largest of hotels."[10]

It didn't help the cause of some of the applicants that they had no real idea where the hotel was to be built. The Grand Forks Builders and Traders Exchange thought the hotel was "at Babb, Montana."[11] Great Northern politely pointed out Waterton was "near Babb."[12] The letter writers weren't aided by newspaper reports that sometimes had the location wrong (Babb) or referred to the Great Northern hotel project in "Watertown, Alberta."[13] Each letter received the response that it was premature for the railroad to be making any decisions, and then any appropriate inquiries were forwarded to Thomas D. McMahon, the architect who would design the hotel.

Before McMahon got too far with the blueprints, Hill wanted to clear up a concern about Waterton's strong winds. When Albert Hogeland had gone to Ottawa in December 1925 to work out the details of leasing land for the hotel, Canadian Parks Commissioner James Harkin had warned the chief engineer that Waterton was an extremely windy spot and the location chosen for the hotel put it directly in the path of the strongest prevailing gales. "I see no objections or obstacles, other than the suggestion regarding excessive prevailing winds at the point selected," Hill noted, heeding Harkin's advice.[14]

To answer the question of just how strong the winds were, assistant engineer Floyd Parker was sent to Alberta in March 1926 to set up a wind gauge. The readings over a 12-hour period showed an average wind velocity of 46 mph (74 km/h), with gusts from 60 to 75 mph (96 to 120 km/h).[15] Great Northern's engineering department told Hill the wind speeds were similar to those experienced at Glacier Park Hotel and the gusts shouldn't prove a difficulty—advice that Mother Nature herself would later contradict.

A more troubling issue for Hill than the wind was the length of the route to Waterton and the state of roads. To get tourists from Glacier Park would mean a 41-mile (66 km) bus trip from Many Glacier Hotel, through Babb to Cardston, and a further 35 miles (56 km) to Waterton townsite. It would be the longest single bus trip for tourists in the area, taking four hours. Chief Mountain International Highway, which now directly links Waterton and Glacier, would not be built until 10 years later. In Glacier, Great Northern had carefully planned the location of its chalets and hotels to avoid such long hauls; there was no such option on the road to Waterton.

Besides the length of the trip, the condition of the road between Cardston and Waterton worried Hill. He wanted a road that would stand up to the rigours of increased traffic from tourists lured to the park by the new hotel, as well as the regular runs of Glacier Park Transportation Company buses carrying Americans to and from Waterton.[16] The Cardston-Water-

ton road didn't meet those needs. It was based on a long-established wagon trail used by residents of Mountain View, Hill Spring, Leavitt and Beazer to reach Cardston, the major trading centre for that area of southwestern Alberta. Over the years, the trail had been graded, some gravel had been laid down and bridges constructed where travellers had previously forded the rivers. It compared favourably with other rural roads of the time, but could not fulfil the basic requirement Great Northern deemed necessary to build and maintain a resort hotel in Waterton—an all-weather highway.

The road between Waterton and Cardston was little more than a dirt trail in 1926 that quickly became a 'sea of mud' after a rain or wet snow. Great Northern officials wanted assurances from the Alberta government that the road would be made into an all-weather highway before the railway would construct a hotel in Waterton. Courtesy Ann Harrison, author's collection.

Without improvements to make the Waterton-Cardston road an all-weather highway, Great Northern feared a repeat of scenes like this from its early years in Glacier Park. J. J. Hill Library.

Great Northern's hotel in Waterton would not only be tied to its other hotels and chalets in Glacier by bus, but also by saddle horse tours arriving at Goathaunt Chalet at the head of Upper Waterton Lake. The railway planned to operate a boat on the lake to transport riders from Goat Haunt to the new hotel. T. J. Hileman photo, Great Northern Railway publicity and advertising department, Minnesota Historical Society.

Hill had learned the hard way in Glacier about the cost of jumping ahead without adequate roads. In his rush to open Glacier to tourism, Hill had authorized the spending of thousands of dollars of railway money to build some of the first roads in the area, expecting the state and federal governments to pick up where Great Northern had left off. That didn't happen quickly, at least not to Hill's satisfaction, and the results were disastrous. First stagecoaches and later buses regularly became bogged down on roads in and around Glacier. Guests were inconvenienced as they failed to get where they were headed, losing out on days of prepaid tour packages and missing train connections. Hill used his considerable influence to lobby Washington about boosting the appropriation for Glacier, but increases in the park's budget seldom hap-

pened fast enough to please him and remained a sore point for many years.[17]

Hill outlined his concerns about roads to Waterton in a May 1926 letter to George Noffsinger, head of the Park Saddle Horse Company. "We have about concluded not to start the Waterton Lakes Hotel," Hill wrote. "Without (road improvements) or any assurance of them ... we find it impracticable and inadvisable to build a large, expensive hotel without the various essential means of access to and from it."[18] Hill's letter to Noffsinger was more than a casual exchange between friends. The news was of vital importance to Noffsinger's Park Saddle Horse Company, which would need to know Great Northern's plans and make necessary adjustments to expand its concession operations in Glacier and link them to Waterton. Noffsinger would have to plan on whether to buy more horses, enlarge his corrals, what new backcountry trips to lay out, tent camps to set up and how many additional guides to hire.

Although not mentioned in the letter, there was growing alarm on the part of Hill and other Great Northern officials about finding a suitable contractor to undertake the hotel work. It was already May, the beginning of the prime building season in Waterton was at hand, and the railway still had no one signed to construct its hotel. The critical problem was finding a Canadian company to do the job. Railway officials had repeatedly turned down requests from American companies to submit a tender for the hotel contract saying, "We feel we should use Canadians."[19] Privately, Great Northern had considered using an American firm if a suitable Canadian one could not be found. The railway even went so far as to entertain a draft contract between its newly created Canadian Rockies Hotel Company subsidiary and the Walter Butler Company of St. Paul, Minn., "to have a hotel constructed at Waterton." The job was to be completed by July 1, 1927.[20] Great Northern officials also considered using Evensta and Company of Minneapolis, Minn., which had built Glacier Park Hotel and Many Glacier Hotel.[21] Hill was no doubt hesitant to let the contract to Evensta or Butler, though, knowing it would be a public relations headache to have a U.S. company build a hotel for an American railway in a Canadian national park.

Just when Great Northern should have been in the final phase of gearing up for construction to start, Hill ordered all expenditures on the hotel project stopped. Before any more work went ahead, Hill wanted to know if anything could be done about improving the condition of the Cardston-Waterton road.[22] He sent Hogeland to Alberta on a scouting mission to talk to Canadian officials about what options were available. Hogeland came back with disappointing news. He told Hill that neither level of government—federal nor provincial—would make road improvements until a hotel was built.[23] The most support Hogeland could muster came from the Lethbridge Board of Trade, which offered to look into the condition of the road on Great Northern's behalf.[24]

The Alberta government did offer a token show of good faith. Following Hogeland's trip, the Public Works Department announced it was tendering road repairs on a section of Highway 2, known as the Blue Trail, from Cardston to the U.S. border.[25] That would link it with the Blackfeet Highway in Montana, the final 11 miles (18 km) of which—from Babb to the border—was slated for $95,000 worth of upgrades that summer.[26] It would at least provide a dependable, all-weather road from the railway terminus at East Glacier Park to Cardston.

Adding urgency to the debate at Great Northern headquarters about what to do in Waterton was a perceived threat that Canadian Pacific Railway was also interested in the park. The *Lethbridge Herald*'s correspondent told readers there was a rumour CPR engineers were looking over possible hotel sites.[27] Hill wired Budd that he feared if they didn't act soon Great Northern might lose the hotel site to the CPR.[28] Hill needn't have worried that Canadian Pacific would snatch the lease; Great Northern had until the following summer, 1927, to build a hotel worth at least $100,000. Only if the railway didn't live up to that obligation could the Canadian government revoke the 42-year lease agreement.[29]

All of these considerations came at a particularly busy time for Hill. He was trying to wrap up a myriad of business and personal details before sailing to Europe in mid-June for an extended summer vacation with his family.

Glacier Park Transportation Company used 12-, 15- and 18-passenger White buses to ferry tourists between Great Northern's hotels and chalets in Glacier National Park. The same buses would be used to carry passengers across the border to Waterton. Author's collection.

*Douglas Oland.
Courtesy Rick Oland,
author's collection.*

The factor that turned the Waterton hotel plan around and saved Hill from having to cancel his own pet project was the discovery of contractors Oland and Scott of Cardston. "They have had considerable building experience, none however quite as large as this undertaking," Hogeland said in a memo describing Douglas Oland, 42, and James Scott, 38, to his superiors. "They are live, energetic men, familiar with the conditions there. They are not very strong financially, but the bank they do business with, together with a number of businessmen at Cardston, will stand back of them."[30]

Here, Hill figured, were men who knew the local road conditions well, would be capable of adapting to them and still meet the railway's construction deadline. He was right on the first two counts but, as he learned later, had only himself to blame on the third. That was still in the future, though. Great Northern had the Canadian contractors it needed and Hill didn't hesitate a minute in giving his approval to resume the Prince of Wales Hotel project once Oland and Scott had passed Hogeland's critical scrutiny.[31] It was a last-minute call; within hours Hill boarded the *S. S. Olympic* and set sail to Europe. Had Hogeland's review of Oland and Scott taken longer or some other factor cropped up to further delay the process, it is possible the hotel project would not have been approved.

The discovery of Oland and Scott was a matter of pure luck on the part of Great Northern, and the contractors nearly didn't make Hogeland's cut. Oland only learned by chance the railway had men in Waterton surveying the location for a hotel and looked them up on a whim. "I got acquainted with (assistant) engineer Floyd Parker and got the bright idea I would try and land the job of building the hotel," Oland says in his memoirs.[32] Oland and Scott fired off a letter to St. Paul. "I gave as references the mayor of Cardston, a friend of mine, and the Bank of Montreal Cardston manager, another friend. Although (we) had few assets and no money, we had always paid our commitments even though we had to go short ourselves."[33] This sense of fairness typified the pair and was one of the reasons they'd become such popular builders in and around Waterton.

Parker passed on Oland and Scott's names to Hogeland, who came from St. Paul to check the credentials of the contractors for himself.[34] Hogeland declared them "OK, better than Evensta or Butler."[35] Satisfied with Oland and Scott's skill, Hogeland asked them to make an offer.

"Then we really started figuring," Oland wrote in his memoirs.[36] They initially made an offer of cost plus five per cent commission, which was politely rejected. Hogeland suggested the builders might want to refigure the deal, taking into account the fact the contractors would have to furnish all construction equipment and run a camp to feed and house the crew, "at no loss to the railway." Oland and Scott countered with an offer of cost plus 6 1/2 per cent and sealed the deal, but not before one last, worrisome episode.[37]

Before signing the papers, Great Northern wanted an assurance Oland and Scott had the financial backing necessary to kickstart the project. Oland and Scott knew they'd need seed money and had arranged a bank loan for $12,000. When Oland took Hogeland to the bank to verify the loan was in place, "lo and behold the manager had gone on his holidays without telling the man he left in charge that he had gotten the loan approved by the Calgary superintendent. In those (days) bank managers did not have the authority to make a loan, even of this small sum."

Oland called Calgary only to discover, "as luck would have it, (the superintendent) was on his holidays." A trip to Lethbridge to consult the regional manager brought little good news. The regional manager put Oland off until the next morning when he would meet him at the Cardston bank branch. "Now I really began to sweat blood," he recalled. Oland turned to an old friend, Norris Stoltze, owner of the chain of Advance Lumberyard outlets in southern Alberta. Stoltze told Oland that if the bank wouldn't put up the money, he would. "Well, as you can imagine, I felt greatly encouraged."

The next day the regional manager said that "the bank, after careful thought, had decided to make the loan but, according to bank regulations, they would have to take an assignment of the contract." The statement made Hogeland livid, Oland recalled. "I will never forget the attitude of the Great Northern official. He told the bank manager that he had come to Cardston prepared to give Oland and Scott the contract mainly on the recommendation of the bank." If the bank was "too cold blooded" to trust Oland and Scott and the mighty Great Northern, Hogeland said, then they'd take their business elsewhere. Hogeland got up and left with Oland right behind.

Out on the street, Oland asked for Hogeland's indulgence and took him to a nearby lumberyard where Stoltze was waiting. It happened that Hogeland knew a wealthy relative of Stoltze's in St. Paul. Although Stoltze conceded he had no business dealings with his relative, he said he would loan Oland and Scott the necessary startup money and, if Hogeland would accompany him to the bank, he would provide proof that his

promise was good. Hogeland had had enough of the bank and its managers and took Stoltze at his word.[38] And so, with the signed contract in hand, Oland and Scott were ready to start work.

While Oland and Scott will be forever paired for their work on the Prince of Wales Hotel, they started their lives provinces apart and it was only after each moved to Cardston that they crossed paths.

Oland arrived in Cardston in 1905, having left his Nova Scotia birthplace to find employment and a climate more suited to his asthma.[39] It was in this small town of 700-plus people that Oland learned the basics of the construction business—on the job. "I started … at 20 cents a day. We worked nine hours a day, Saturday included," Oland said.[40] "During all this time I was picking up tools and must have been learning as I remember by the fall of 1906 I was put in charge of some … work for which I received 40 cents per hour."[41] Oland eventually struck out on his own and, in 1910, formed a partnership with Scott, a fellow Cardston carpenter.

Scott was born in Ontario in March 1888. He moved to Cardston about the same time as Oland and, also like Oland, learned the crafts of construction and carpentry on the job. Scott's skills were such that he was one of only a few non-Mormons hired to help build the temple in Cardston for the Church of Jesus Christ of Latter-day Saints, completed in 1923.[42] Oland and Scott worked together until the outbreak of the Great War in 1914, when Scott joined the army.[43] The partnership resumed after the war.

During their time together, the pair established a name for themselves constructing cottages and other buildings in Cardston and Waterton. Their motto was "A dollar's worth for a dollar." By the mid-

James Scott.
Courtesy Mary O'Brien,
author's collection.

The Waterton dance pavilion, opened in 1926, was Oland and Scott's biggest project prior to the Prince of Wales Hotel. Courtesy Rick Oland, author's collection.

Oland and Scott not only constructed the 112-foot square Waterton dance pavilion, they also designed it for owners Ernie Haug and Dave MacLean. The central pillar created a large, unobstructed dance floor, while overlooking balconies provided a place for dancers to catch their breath. Courtesy Rick Oland, author's collection.

1920s, they had dozens of buildings to their credit as word of their ability and craftsmanship spread.[44] In 1925 they got their biggest contract to date, from Ernie Haug and Dave MacLean, to build a dance pavilion in Waterton. Oland and Scott not only built the hall, they designed it. The dancehall, 112 feet (33.6 m) square, was one of the biggest in southern Alberta. With its second floor balcony, it had a capacity of 1,000 people.[45]

The opening of the dancehall on the night of May 15, 1926, was an impressive affair. The pavilion, illuminated by electrical generators against the dark sky, was like a beacon that enticed visitors to Waterton from near and far.[46] A *Lethbridge Herald* correspondent counted 165 cars outside the hall.[47] Also in attendance at the first dance were Floyd Parker and his crew, who were surveying the site for the hotel.[48] Although unconfirmed, it's likely Hogeland, McMahon and W. R. Mills, the general manager of Great Northern's advertising department, were there as well. They had been expected in Waterton the day before and would have wanted to see for themselves what Oland and Scott had done.[49]

Oland and Scott were more than worthy of the job Hill had in store for them.

Roads, Rain and Hill

The Prince of Wales Hotel that stands in Waterton today is not the building Oland and Scott set out to construct when they began work in the park in July 1926. Externally the hotel bears only slight resemblance to the original blueprints. The dramatic changes made to the profile of the hotel, as well as to its interior and exterior detail, were inspired by Louis Hill. Hill had been notorious for dipping his hand into every aspect of Glacier Park-related matters and it would be no different with the Waterton hotel project. Oland and Scott had to deal with more than just Hill, though. Other factors at work combined to influence the eventual design and construction of the hotel. In particular, there was wet weather and, as a result, the condition of the Cardston-Waterton road and other highways in the area. Those three elements—roads, rain and Hill—came together and coalesced in a remarkable way. One that resulted in a hotel unlike any other in the Rockies—then or now.

When talking to newspaper reporters, Great Northern officials indicated Many Glacier Hotel would provide the blueprint for its Waterton facility. That gave readers a ready reference, making it easy for them to visualize what the building in Waterton would eventually look like. It also made it very clear the railway intended to carry its Swiss design theme over from Glacier to Waterton. Although Great Northern was commissioning a building in Canada, there is no evidence to suggest the American railway executives ever considered following the chateau style used by Canadian Pacific Railway, exemplified by the different but related Banff Springs Hotel and Chateau Lake Louise. Hill was content to keep with tradition and have the Waterton hotel maintain the unity of design he'd established in Glacier.[1] The decision was a harbinger of the sentiment that would

Many Glacier Hotel was to be the model for Great Northern's new hotel in Waterton, maintaining the Swiss style the railway had developed for all its other facilities in Glacier Park. T. J. Hileman photo, copyright Glacier Natural History Association.

This blueprint shows the original design for the lobby section of the Prince of Wales Hotel. It clearly reflects the look of Many Glacier Hotel, from which it was adapted. Courtesy Toltz, King, Duvall, Anderson and Associates.

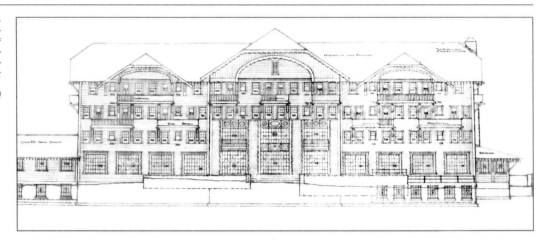

This blueprint shows the original design for the lobby section of the Prince of Wales Hotel. It clearly reflects the look of Many Glacier Hotel, from which it was adapted. Courtesy Toltz, King, Duvall, Anderson and Associates.

manifest itself less than a decade later, creating and reinforcing cultural ties binding two parks that already shared a natural connection, eventually joined as a peace park.

The selection of Many Glacier Hotel as the model for the Prince of Wales Hotel was no doubt also influenced by efficiencies of scale and the architect for the Waterton project, Thomas McMahon. When it came to architecture, Great Northern was no different than any other railway in having preset designs, such as bridges and stations that could be adapted to many situations. It saved the railway from having to re-invent the bridge or station each time its line crossed a river or entered a new town. That was the case with some of its architecture in Glacier: Cookie-cutter patterns for cabins and chalets that could be adapted to different sites were used throughout the park.[2] Just as with cabins, it would have made sense to adapt the design of a larger structure, like Many Glacier Hotel, to Waterton.

The selection of McMahon for the Waterton project was logical as he was one of the designers of Many Glacier Hotel, along with Kirtland Cutter of Spokane, Wash. An architect on staff at Great Northern's head-quarters in St. Paul, McMahon was well versed in Great Northern's Swiss style. With the overall look determined, it would be up to McMahon to resolve the layout and details, such as window and door-frame treatments, balconies and other such specifications.

For the exterior of the Waterton hotel, McMahon dutifully followed the look of the lobby section of Many Glacier Hotel, including the hipped-gable roofline and use of balconies with decorative balustrades. He broke with tradition elsewhere, though, in several key respects. The "forest lobby" dominates the main buildings of Many Glacier Hotel and Glacier Park Hotel. When entering each hotel, the focus is on the room, with the nearby mountains and lakes secondary to the interior of the building itself. In Waterton, McMahon put the setting first and designed the lobby to focus on it. So while the lobbies of the other hotels run parallel to the length of building and are meant to be the focus of attention, McMahon designed the lobby of the Waterton hotel perpendicular to its length and incorporated two-story "picture" windows that capitalized on the breathtaking view of seven mile-long (11 km) Upper Waterton Lake and surrounding mountains. The windows frame the scene to highlight it, much as an artist or photographer might do. Visitors entering the lobby would not have had the unimpeded view through the two-story windows that they have today, though. The blueprints show McMahon incorporated a second-floor mezzanine at the south end of the lobby as a sitting area, providing a view of the lake on one side while over-looking the rotunda on the other.

Abandoning the "forest lobby" also left McMahon room to be more creative with the details of the rotunda. Instead of mas-sive log columns, he drew slender, hand-carved posts and beams supported by matching braces and topped by queen posts. The carving was similar in detail to the ceiling rafters of the dining room and balcony supports at Many Glacier Hotel. Like the other hotels, McMahon retained the well four stories up the centre of the lobby to the roof. At the upper reaches of the well was the familiar open-beam, tim-ber framing, again featuring carved wood trusses rather than logs. Overall, the Wa-terton blueprints show a refinement and sophistication taken from the arts and crafts movement that is in sharp contrast to the more rustic, backcountry lodge at-mosphere of the other two main lodges.

After a reprieve of more than a decade, Hill was in his element again with this new hotel project, attending to the minu-tiae of another grand scheme. Hill tried to tone down his influence, but there is no mistaking his involvement with the design process or his position of author-ity. In a memo to Charles Jenks, vice-president of the Glacier Park Hotel Com-pany, Hill wrote: "I have asked Mr. McMahon, the architect, to furnish a set of rough drawings of the proposed Water-ton Lakes Hotel to Messrs. Noble, Blair,

Beck and Binder. If you feel interested enough to do so, I will be glad if you will ask Mr. Blair to bring the plans to your office, and … I will be glad to come down and hear his comments, criticisms and suggestions on any features of the plans."[3] There's no doubt who was boss or that Jenks would have dared not be in-terested in Hill's offer.

Almost as quickly as McMahon sat down at his drafting table to work, Hill began offering suggestions. "Have you con-sidered a Kodak darkroom in the new ho-tel?" Hill inquired.[4] Check the hotels in Yellowstone National Park for kitchen and dining room design ideas, he urged the ar-chitect.[5] Hill's penchant for getting in-volved in the design details knew no bounds. In one five-page letter to McMahon, Hill filled two pages with notes about the kitchen, walking the architect through the layout as the staff would use it. "While space is an important factor, what is more important is a proper arrange-ment of apparatus," Hill wrote. "The prin-ciple of a kitchen arrangement is with a view to having the traffic move through in regular order and avoid as much cross-walk as possible; also arranging apparatus to save cooks and workers as many steps as possible."[6]

Functionality was the essence of all Hill's suggestions, whether it concerned the needs of staff or was solely for the benefit of hotel patrons. In the same memo to McMahon about the kitchen, Hill recommended that "wall plugs should be provided (in bedrooms) for flat irons and curling irons. Nearly all women carry them with them now days." It was an astute observation.

Such detail was the last thing Oland and Scott had on their minds as they set about preparing to build the hotel. Time was wast-

Louis Hill.
J. J. Hill Library.

ing. They had lost nearly three weeks of good building weather from when they were approved by Hogeland in mid-June until there was a signed contract in their hands—the first week in July. As soon as the paperwork was completed, the contractors were quick off the mark to get on with the job. Their selection as the contractors to build the hotel was announced in the newspaper on Friday, July 9.[7] By Monday, Oland was in Waterton with a work crew.[8] He had no problem finding men. Local newspapers had been carrying regular reports about the proposed hotel for months. Lured by the prospect of a job, "a considerable number of men ... have been idle (and) have been hanging around here for five to six weeks anticipating the beginning of construction," the *Lethbridge Herald* noted.[9]

Despite the need to meet the June 1927 completion deadline, the first work undertaken by Oland's crew was not on the hotel. Instead, they started on a camp for construction employees between Linnet and Middle Waterton lakes.[10] This was necessary because there was insufficient rental accommodation in Waterton to handle the number of men who would be working on the hotel. To meet the initial housing need, Oland built a 72-foot by

24-foot (21.6 m by 7.2 m) dining room and cookhouse and four 22-foot by 32-foot (6.6 m by 9.6 m) bunkhouses.[11] Some of the workers chose not to stay at the camp. Many were married men who had brought wives and children with them when they realized they would be on the job for a year or more.[12] They had to find accommodation elsewhere.

The number of workers on the job grew quickly. The *Lethbridge Herald* reported on July 27, 1926, that Oland had 25 men building the workers' camp.[13] Four days later, the newspaper said the workforce had doubled to 50.[14] Oland's daughter, Mary O'Brien, recalled work was scarce at the time and her father received many letters from men wanting a job. "One letter came addressed 'Mr. Duck.' As Dad was so well known, the postman knew it must be for Dad."[15]

By the end of July, the camp was completed and work shifted to the top of the hill where excavation began for the hotel.[16] Already devoid of trees, owing primarily to strong winds and thin soil, the site was scraped of topsoil, gravel and rocks by horse-drawn equipment. There would be no bulldozers or engine-powered excavators used on the job as they were too costly and were not readily available.[17] The excavation proved troublesome because of the amount of coarse rock and number of large stones that had to be moved. Fortunately, Kenny and Jacobs of Mountain View, the excavation subcontractors, did not have to dig very far—only about 10 feet (3 m)—to place the deepest concrete footings.[18]

To aid Oland and Scott, Great Northern supplied all of the required lumber, most of it from its mill near Somers, south of Kalispell, Mont.[19] Advised of the hotel project, the mill started cutting wood even

Oland and Scott were required to build this camp by Linnet Lake for the Prince of Wales Hotel construction crew because there was insufficient accommodation in Waterton for the labourers.
Courtesy Toltz, King, Duvall, Anderson and Associates.

Doug Oland, standing second from right with arms crossed, enjoys a brief respite during the ground-breaking ceremony July 1926 for the Prince of Wales Hotel. At the plow is Waterton superintendent W. D. Cromarty. Courtesy Jack Oland, author's

before the contractors were in Waterton. The lumber was sent to Cardston by rail and then hauled to Waterton by trucks.[20] Great Northern also came to the aid of Oland and Scott by lending them power saws, planers and other equipment that had been used to build the hotels and chalets in Glacier Park.[21]

The start of work on the hotel proper attracted a host of officials curious to see the progress. Among the first to arrive, on August 10, 1926, were Budd, William Kenney, vice-president of Great Northern, Noffsinger and Hill's son, Louis Hill Jr. Budd waxed lyrical about the park for the benefit of the local press: "Many Glacier is always held as the gem of the mountains. Waterton Lake is equal to it."[22] Hill Jr. was equally effusive, saying: "I'll be here again, even if I have to walk."[23]

The visit to Alberta by two of Great Northern's top executives was more than just a courtesy call. Budd and Kenney were on a mission to make their case for improvements to the Cardston-Waterton road and would use whatever means necessary to achieve it. The lobbying took different

forms, ranging from the direct approach to using the power of the press to manipulate public opinion. In Waterton, Budd, Kenney and Noffsinger each made a point of speaking to the *Lethbridge Herald*'s local correspondent. Satisfied with progress on the hotel, Budd travelled on to Edmonton where he met Alex Ross, the provincial minister of Public Works, to lay out the railway's case "as vigorously as possible."[24] He also stopped in Lethbridge to talk to the board of trade about the railway's plans for Waterton.

Newspaper interviews with Budd, Kenney and Noffsinger provide a sketch of the tack taken in the presentations. Great Northern, Budd said, had more than just a hotel in its plans for Waterton. The railway was also considering the building of a chalet at Cameron Lake, it would be putting a launch like the *St. Mary* on Upper Waterton Lake and, if feasible, would mine coal from reserves Great Northern had near Pincher Creek.[25] Noffsinger said Waterton would gain the benefit of the railway's extensive U.S. advertising campaign, which would promote it and Glacier as "one great scenic unit."[26] That, Kenney added, could lay the groundwork for an economic boom in the region. "Let (eastern financiers) see the fertile country and its fame will spread," making it easy to float loans and bonds on the New York Stock Exchange.[27]

The only fly in the ointment was the state of the Cardston-Waterton road. Under the guise of friendly criticism, Budd noted the lack of an all-weather road had prevented Great Northern from authorizing the immediate construction of a 300-room hotel. Instead, the company was beginning cautiously, with just the 64-room lobby section. A bedroom annex would likely be added next summer, he said, presumably when the highway upgrade would be finished.[28]

Upon his return to St. Paul, Budd was flush with confidence about the success

The clearing of the hotel site was accomplished with a horse-pulled excavator. The amount of course rock and large stones at the site caused numerous headaches for contractor Kenny and Jacobs of Mountain View. The subcontractor had to dig 10 feet before the hotel foundation could be laid. *Courtesy Jack Oland, author's collection.*

of his Alberta trip and wrote to Hill that "enough sentiment in favour of doing this (road) work has been built up so that it will be done not later than the middle of next season."[29] While Budd may have felt public opinion was on his side, there was no letting up the pressure on the Brownlee government. Less than a week after his visit to Waterton, the need to upgrade the road was made again, this time by Roe Emery, head of Glacier Park Transportation Company, who was host to another group of dignitaries wanting to see the new hotel site. An all-weather road to Waterton was an "absolute necessity," Emery said.[30]

As luck would have it, the summer of 1926 was a fine one and the condition of the Cardston-Waterton road was not a concern. Oland and Scott made haste while the weather co-operated and by August 17, just a week after Budd's visit, the hotel's foundation was being poured. "At the present rate of construction, it is estimated that the whole building will be enclosed in a very few weeks," an August 19 report in the *Lethbridge Herald* stated.[31] Budd was equally optimistic in a note to Hill, saying "the contractors, Oland and Scott, seem to have taken hold in good shape."[32]

The speed at which Oland and Scott's crew was working soon began to outpace the rate at which McMahon could produce the necessary blueprints. When Hill had cut off money to the hotel project in May because of concerns about road conditions, he had also halted McMahon's work on the drawings. A month later, when the project was revived, McMahon had to scramble to make up lost time. Even as Oland and his crew framed their camp by Linnet Lake, they had little idea of what lay ahead. "Until the complete plans arrive, no detailed description (of the hotel) can be given," the *Lethbridge Herald* told its readers.[33] There

By August 1926, work was progressing quickly on the hotel, giving optimism to Great Northern officials that it would be ready to open by June 15 the following year. A fence was built to the south of the construction site to disperse Waterton's buffeting winds while the tower, centre right, housed an anemometer to record the force of the wind. George Anderegg photo, Great Northern Railway company records, Minnesota Historical Society.

is evidence Oland only received working blueprints as each stage of construction came up, and then not always on time. "Oland and Scott need detailed plans or there will be delays, especially detailed plans for framing," a memo from Hogeland warned in late August.[34]

There would soon be no need to rush. As Hogeland drafted his missive to Budd, rain showers hit southern Alberta. These sprinkles were followed by drizzle in early September that lasted nearly a week. A fortnight later, heavy, wet snow covered the ground. The effect of all this moisture was immediate and the road between Cardston and Waterton deteriorated quickly. The condition of the road was made worse by constant traffic—truckers hired to haul supplies to the park from Cardston, where Great Northern was sending freight cars loaded with lumber for the hotel. The vehicles churned the road up so badly it

Snow arrived early that fall of 1926, hitting Waterton in mid-September. George Anderegg photo, Great Northern Railway company records, Minnesota Historical Society.

became a "sea of mud," impassable for days at a time.[35] "I had to revert to horses (and wagons) and the more I hauled the worse the roads got," Oland said. A round trip that took a day in a truck took three days by horse and wagon. "I started paying $4 a thousand feet for hauling lumber and soon was up to $24 a thousand," Oland recalled.[36]

As the delivery of supplies from Cardston to Waterton slowed, construction on the hotel was likewise affected, the lack of material sometimes bringing work to a near halt. The holdups created a furore at

Exterior framing of the hotel had been completed for the first and second floors and was just beginning on the third when workers were forced to lay down tools while revisions to the design ordered by Louis Hill were being incorporated into the blueprints. Doug Oland laid off 25 men in October as they waited a month for the new plans to arrive. As yet no work had been done on the central portion of the hotel. George Anderegg photos, Great Northern Railway company records, Minnesota Historical Society.

Great Northern's headquarters. An ominous note was sounded in a September 27, 1926, article in the *Lethbridge Herald*. The news story said "people in contact with Great Northern officials" were about to curtail expenditures on the Waterton hotel to $500,000—half what had been planned—"on account of the abominable roads." It went on to say there were rumours that, if the Cardston-Waterton route was not made into an all-weather highway, railroad officials would propose a straight road from Glacier to Waterton via Beazer and bypass Cardston.[37]

The rumour, obviously planted by the railway, did not go unnoticed. The Cardston Board of Trade started a membership drive that same afternoon to make area businessmen aware of what was at stake if Great Northern opted for a direct route and bypassed the community. Within days, the board of trade had signed up 100 members and a meeting to discuss the issue was planned for the following week.[38] It was exactly the response railway officials were hoping for.

Budd applied more pressure three weeks later in a letter to Oland, verifying the rumour about scaling back the hotel. "From my personal experiences with the road from Cardston to Waterton Park on two occasions during August last, I am satisfied that the hotel company is not justified in spending any more money there at this time than now contemplated," Budd wrote. "If, however, the road from Cardston to Waterton Park could be gravelled and put in first-class shape early next season, I feel sure that the hotel company would be justified in going ahead with additional units in order to properly take care of the heavy tourist travel that will surely want to visit that very attractive point."[39]

Little could Oland and Scott have imagined what was actually happening in St. Paul. Great Northern officials were reconsidering the Waterton hotel project, but not in the way that was being let on publicly. Yes, the state of the Cardston-Waterton road was a concern and, yes, plans for the hotel were being redrafted, but the two were only somewhat connected. At the centre of the hubbub was Louis Hill, refreshed from his summer-long vacation in Europe. Hill was back in his office in St. Paul in September 1926 and he quickly immersed himself in the details of the Waterton project to catch up on its progress.

He turned his attention first to reviewing the hotel blueprints, and he didn't like what he saw. "They were not satisfactory as to the size of rooms and arrangements thereof, or as to the exterior, and as to the general arrangements of the main building," Hill told Hogeland.[40] Before McMahon had a chance to explain the reasons for what he had drawn, Hill began coming up with his own ideas about how the layout of the project should be done. Hill thought the lobby section of the hotel, with its 64 rooms, was too small. "I think we should consider preparing plans to build the 'Help's Dormitory.' ... This could be used for hotel guests as an overflow," he wrote.[41] Hill also proposed "a few—say six or more—small cottages," similar to the Doll House group in Carmel, Calif. "These cottages, with rooms which are small—not much larger than a Pullman stateroom—seem to please tourists and are very inexpensive to build from odds and ends of lumber. ... Such cottages would be the cheapest way of accommodating an overflow of people and no doubt would be popular."[42]

The prospect of expanding the Waterton project alarmed Hogeland, who knew too well the transportation problems to the park. "I think we should go slowly there and not do more than already planned, until we see some definite move towards gravelling the road from Cardston to the park boundary," Hogeland wrote.[43] Hill was not to be deterred. He ordered a set of blueprints of the Doll Houses, a set of rental cabins he had noticed, for McMahon to review.[44] At Budd's suggestion, Hill authorized the hiring of Beaver Wade Day of Toltz, King and Day in St. Paul as consulting architect to assist McMahon in revising the hotel design.[45]

Next on Hill's agenda was the matter of an excursion boat for Upper Waterton Lake to complement the hotel. Hill's initial thought had been to relocate the launch *St. Mary* from St. Mary Lake in Glacier to Waterton and build a replacement.[46] Great Northern officials turned for advice to Capt. J. W. (Bill) Swanson, a tour boat operator and boat builder of considerable experience in Glacier.[47] Swanson nixed Hill's idea. Although a large vessel at 65 feet long (19.5 m), the *St. Mary*, Swanson said, was not substantial enough to take the wind and waves, which can be generated, on Upper Waterton Lake.[48] A new vessel would have to be designed specifically for use in Waterton—the *Motor Vessel International*—and Swanson was hired to undertake the job.

Last on Hill's list of concerns was arranging to have local natives produce "picture writing" canvases for the lobby walls

Great Northern Railway approached Canon Samuel Middleton about enlisting his assistance to have elders of the Blood tribe create pictographs to decorate the lobby of the Prince of Wales Hotel. Glenbow Archives, Calgary, Canada, NA 2345-59.

of the new hotel. Native imagery had played an important role in Great Northern advertising and promotion from the outset of its Glacier developments. The nearby Blackfeet Indians were renowned in the "buffalo days" as a warrior tribe and they had a longstanding connection with the Glacier area, which was part of their reservation before being ceded to Washington in 1896. Great Northern capitalized on the history and fame of the Blackfeet tribe, featuring photos and drawings of tribe members in its brochures and posters as well as including descriptions of native customs and legends. Easterners were urged to visit Glacier to see these legendary figures of the West. To ensure they did, the railway paid members of the tribe to set up teepees on the lawn of Glacier Park Hotel each summer and perform each evening in the lobby.[49]

Hill, who was a great admirer of the Blackfeet culture and a master promoter, ensured native themes were incorporated into the buildings, such as the use of plaster-cast buffalo skull lamps in the lobby of Glacier Park Hotel. Great Northern officials

Shinny hockey games, dances and basket socials kept workers in the construction camp entertained throughout the winter. Courtesy of Jack Oland, author's collection.

also arranged for respected Blackfeet leaders to make pictographs for the lobby walls of the Glacier Park and Many Glacier hotels. Hill wanted the same feature used in Waterton so, on his instruction, Canon Middleton was approached about enlisting elders in the nearby Blood tribe to paint the pictographs.[50] As principal of the Anglican residential school on the Indian reserve, Middleton was respected by the natives and could be counted on to gain their support for the project.[51] The pictographs would tie in well with Great Northern's established advertising campaigns.

While Hill was resolving these matters, the flow of blueprints from Great Northern's offices to Oland slowed to a dribble and then dried up completely as McMahon and Day revised the drawings in an attempt to fulfil the railway chairman's new ideas. Without blueprints from which to work, Oland and Scott laid off 25 men.[52] They were able to use the idle time, however, to clear a lumber logjam in Cardston. Shipments had become so backed up by the rain and snow in September that Scott had to build storage sheds in Cardston to handle the continuous arrival of material by rail.[53] The road to Waterton was improved markedly by cold weather in October that froze the ground and Oland and Scott made haste while they could. In the last two weeks of the month, 340,000 board feet (802 cu. m) of lumber and over 200,000 pounds (90,700 kg) of freight were unloaded in Waterton in preparation for the resumption of work.[54]

To keep up the spirits of his employees, Oland arranged a number of social functions. Dances were held at the camp kitchen for the workers, their families and Waterton residents. "We had a very good orchestra from the men at camp," Mary O'Brien recalled. "If the (members of the band) took a weekend off and went to Cardston or Pincher Creek, Dad would have his Victrola carried over to the cookhouse." For square dances, Oland would ask Cpl. Andy Ford, Waterton's sole RCMP officer, to be the caller.[55] Basket socials were also organized, with some of the funds raised used to buy hockey equipment.[56] The construction crew formed one of three teams in the Waterton Lake Hockey Club, playing on a 70-foot by 170-foot (21 m by 51 m) hockey rink on Linnet Lake. A generating plant loaned to Oland by Great Northern supplied power to light the rink so his men could play at night.[57]

The slowdown in work on the hotel, combined with Great Northern's threats of scaling back the project, were all the proof needed to spur members of the Cardston Board of Trade into action yet again. They dispatched a copy of Budd's latest letter to the provincial capital, hoping it would prompt early action on gravelling the Cardston-Waterton road.[58] Government officials were immune to Great Northern's veiled blackmail, saying they had no intention of making any immediate improvements. The road "will not be gravelled this year," was highways commissioner C. A. Davidson's response.[59]

Determined to get the province to move more quickly on the issue, the Cardston Board of Trade organized a "good roads" conference for November 24, inviting delegates from all over southern Alberta to attend. Publicity about the road had caught the attention of many local politicians, who made a point of attending the meeting. Among them were George Stringham, member of the legislative assembly for Cardston, and L. H. Jelliff, the member of Parliament for Lethbridge. Great Northern's hotel project should not be "left stuck in the mud," delegates to the conference

said, noting Waterton was the only national park in Canada at that time without a rail connection. They overwhelmingly voted in favour of a one-cent increase to the existing two-cent gasoline tax, with the money to be earmarked for road improvements, which Floyd Parker said would cost $200,000. Jelliff said he would urge Ottawa to put up 40 per cent of the cost.[60]

It was predictable that Great Northern's push to improve the Cardston-Waterton road would find local support. It represented the plea of nearly every car driver in the province. Albertans had been quick to take to automobiles: From nearly 10,000 cars in 1916, the number of vehicles on provincial roads hit 40,000 in 1921 and would top 100,000 by the end of the decade.[61] Rural families were among the most enthusiastic car owners, gaining newfound freedom and mobility. The pace at which car ownership and use grew outstripped the ability of the province to act. Alberta only set up its Highways Branch in 1923, the first provincial road map was published in 1924, and it wasn't until 1926 that the provincial government took over responsibility for highway signage, previously a task left to local clubs and towns.

In response to the province's inaction, the Alberta Motor Association and Good Roads Association sprung up to act as lobby groups for drivers, giving a more powerful voice to complaints about poor road conditions and the lack of services.[62] All the talk about roads sparked by Great Northern's Waterton hotel project prompted the Alberta Motor Association to open a divisional office in Lethbridge— the third in the province after Calgary and Edmonton.[63] Lethbridge area residents were so eager to support the motor association they lined up to pay the $6.50 annual fee even before the applications were

Mary O'Brien.
Courtesy Mary O'Brien.

As soon as the new blueprints arrived, in late October, Oland had his men back to work and within two weeks framing was completed on the third floor and progressing quickly on the fourth floor and the new, steeper roof. The sense of urgency to get the project done on time is evident in the fact workers are on the job (right) despite it being a holiday, Remembrance Day. George Anderegg photos, Great Northern Railway company records, Minnesota Historical Society.

ready.[64] People were desperate for any improvement in the current situation.

Great Northern officials could never have evoked the public sympathy they sought for gravelling the Cardston-Waterton road without the indirect backing of Senator W. A. Buchanan. Buchanan resided in Lethbridge but also owned a rambling cottage in Waterton, where he spent summers with his wife and family. Buchanan had a soft spot for the national park and was referred to as the "senator from Waterton."[65] He made a point of meeting Great Northern officials as they came to inspect the site of their new hotel.[66] Budd and Hill welcomed the senator's interest, for Buchanan also owned the *Lethbridge Herald*, the biggest and most influential daily newspaper in the region. The *Herald* made sure readers knew every detail about the state of the Cardston-Waterton road.

As lobbying efforts continued, Oland and Scott waited to see what Hill would spring on them once McMahon and Day had finished the revisions to the hotel's design. Like the public, the contractors must have also wondered whether Great Northern would make good on its threat to cut the size of the proposed development. What Oland and Scott saw when the new blueprints finally arrived was both shocking, given the extent of the architectural changes, and pleasantly surprising. Instead of cutting back on the main hotel building, the number of rooms was increased, from 64 to 78, and the whole structure enlarged. The hotel had gone from four to seven stories high by increasing the pitch and height of the lobby roof. The eave-line for the roof of the wings was dropped from the fourth to the third floor, the pitch was increased, and 12 dormers replaced the original four gables on the wings. More balconies were added to the exterior, and a 30-foot (9 m) tower now topped the building.[67]

The apparent discrepancy between what Great Northern was rumoured to be considering and what actually happened had been a ruse. It was a convenient cover for the design changes sought by Hill, who figured the size of the lobby building was too small. Despite what Budd had said, Hill's vision of a 300-room hotel in Waterton was still very much intact. Hill was only making revisions to the first stage, the lobby section currently under construction by Oland and Scott.[68] Budd simply exploited the situation with cagily worded letters to make it seem like the revisions were a form of scaling the project back to heighten pressure on the government.

So successful was Budd's media blitz that members of Brownlee's own party, the United Farmers of Alberta (UFA), began siding with the railway even after it was revealed the revisions would mean a bigger first stage than initially planned. At a UFA constituency meeting in Lethbridge, delegates easily passed a resolution urging the province to make the Cardston-Waterton road a main trunk highway, which would force the government to begin the needed upgrades.[69] And support was spreading. The *Calgary Daily Herald*, which generally focused its reporting about parks exclusively on nearby Banff, came out with an editorial in favour of gravelling the Cardston-Waterton road to enhance tourism in the province.[70] The need for improvement is not in dispute, the paper said, the question is affordability.

The public backing Great Northern had garnered was cold comfort to Oland and Scott. The jolt of seeing revisions ordered by Hill and realizing the extent of the work that would be required took their toll on Oland, who worried that he and Scott might not be able to complete the job on time. "He was normally a very easy-going man," said his daughter, Mary O'Brien. "He became very fretful."[71] Just how much of a setback the revised plans had on construction is evident in weekly records kept by George Anderegg, Great Northern's field accountant in Waterton. In Anderegg's October 25, 1926, report to his superiors in St. Paul, he stated that construction on the hotel was 40 per cent complete. The next week, when the revised blueprints arrived, he lowered his estimate to 30 per cent.[72]

To the credit of McMahon and Day, the new design was created with an eye to saving as much of the existing construction as possible. Few drastic changes were made to the first three floors of the wings of the hotel, which was as far as Oland and Scott's crew had gotten before the plan changes started and work was halted. The architects reserved the majority of their revisions for the central section and areas of the wings that had yet to be built.

Nonetheless, the revisions were a drastic change from the blueprints Oland and Scott had started out with. The cozy original plan, that would have sat low—almost hunkered down—on the hill overlooking Upper Waterton Lake, was replaced with a towering, scene-stealing monument, reaching for the sky as if to challenge the mountains around it. It wouldn't look anything like Many Glacier Hotel, upon which it was supposed to be based, or Glacier Park Hotel. Instead, Oland said, Hill "wanted (the hotel) to look like the French

George Anderegg, courtesy Mary O'Brien, author's collection.

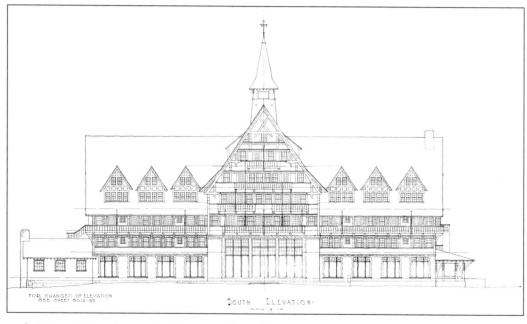

and Swiss chalets he saw in Europe" during his vacation.[73] Much as he had done with the design of Glacier Park Hotel, Hill inundated McMahon and Day with suggestions and ideas about how he wanted the Waterton hotel to look. Instead of books on Swiss architecture that Hill collected earlier, this time he had a collection of photographs and postcards.[74]

The look McMahon and Day created for the Prince of Wales Hotel was a unique interpretation of Swiss style. The rooflines were distinct, with no real Swiss equivalent, while the exterior walls and balconies mimicked alpine style. Layers of ornate fretwork or gingerbread mouldings were used to enhance decorative balcony supports and door and window openings. They are more the products of fanciful designs in pattern books than a faithful reproduction of anything seen in the Alps.[75]

For the interior, McMahon and Day kept the same refined look with which

McMahon had started. Raising the roofline to seven stories meant the trusses were now hidden from view, so they created a new, decorative, open-timber framework below that would be visible from the rotunda. And the mezzanine overlooking the rotunda was eliminated, providing an unobstructed view from anywhere in the lobby through the two-story windows on the south wall.

With the new blueprints in hand, Oland and Scott's crew got back to work. It was now early December, five months since they had broken ground for the hotel foundation. Nearly 30 days' work had been lost owing to bad roads and the slowdown caused by Hill's revisions to the design. It took the construction labour force a month and a half to make up the time that had been lost because of the plan changes.[76] There was no telling whether Oland and Scott would have the hotel ready in time for its scheduled opening date of June 15, 1927, seven months away.

5 Windswept Designs

As much as Oland and Scott may have wished it, there would be no immediate reprieve from southern Alberta's notoriously fickle weather or Louis Hill's ever-changing idea about what the Prince of Wales Hotel should look like. In the final seven months of construction, the resolve of the contractors to complete the hotel project would be tested over and over as they raced to meet their June 15, 1927, deadline. They were eventually able to contain Hill's enthusiasm, but there is no controlling the elements and they twice came close to undoing Oland and Scott's handiwork.

Oland and Scott pulled out all the stops to try and get back on schedule following the major redesign of the hotel dropped on them in late October. Oland went so far as to get permission from the federal government to let his crew work on Sundays, weather permitting.[1] But the weather worked against them. Recurring snowfalls throughout the winter of 1926-27 cut off transportation to the park for days at a time, yet again holding up shipments of vital supplies and stopping construction in the process. One storm dropped 46.5 inches (118 cm) of snow on Waterton in three days.[2] Another prevented postmaster Arthur (Pop) Harwood from making his twice-weekly mail run—only the second time in eight years he'd been unable to bring in the mail.[3] "The total fall of snow (that winter) was about 14 feet (4.2 m)," Oland said. "Each time it snowed I had to lay the carpenters off and put on a crew of labourers to clear the building. Before the winter was over, I had spent $5,000 on shovelling snow."[4] One particularly violent snowstorm, on December 10, 1926, would stand out from the others.

A tractor plows through a Waterton snow drift. About 14 feet (4.2 metres) of snow fell in Waterton during the winter of 1926-27, and each time it did, work on the Prince of Wales Hotel had to be halted until the scaffolding could be cleared. Courtesy of Betty Baker, author's collection.

Oland and Scott's crew made quick work on the hotel once the new plans arrived, but by December they had still not seen blueprints for the centre section. Plenty of wood and some of the 28 pillars that would be used for the lobby have been carefully piled ready for use. A boom with block-and-tackle rigging, centre left, was constructed for each wing to cut down on the manual hauling of lumber. George Anderegg photo, J. J. Hill Library, LH2500.

The hotel's construction crew knew it was not going to be a routine Friday when what started as a mild breeze from the south developed into a howling gale. The average wind speed was 66 mph (106 km/h).[5] Buffeting blasts made it unsafe to be on scaffolding around the hotel, so workers were instead ordered to gather loose lumber and secure it with large rocks.[6] It was no easy task. The wind played havoc with pedestrians, making walking anywhere on the hill or in the townsite below a dangerous activity. Men were knocked off their feet and rolled along the ground, "one man being blown clear over on his head and nearly turned completely over," the *Lethbridge Herald* reported. Another was "blown flat and his nose used as a plow in the gravel."[7]

The already strong gales increased in fury, to hurricane strength, during the late afternoon, whipping Upper Waterton Lake "into a mass of foam and spray" and creating waves 12 feet-high (3.6 m). The mist was carried clear over the hotel site,

150 feet (45 m) above, soaking it and the camp at Linnet Lake.[8] Workers at the hotel site abandoned their posts and ran for their lives when the wind began picking up the lumber they had stacked and supposedly secured. "Planks and boards were seen flying over men's heads, who not even looking back to see if any more were coming, only put on a little more speed," the *Herald* said, adding: "Records for running were broken by old and young alike."[9] A group of men unloading supplies that had just arrived from Cardston had a miraculous escape when scaffolding on the west wing of the hotel worked loose and came crashing down about them.[10]

There were many other close calls. "One man with a truck load of timber was just getting out of the cab on one side when a plank was driven through the window on the opposite side. He lost no time in crawling under his truck until the flying timbers had landed on the ground."[11] A story was later told of a plank that ripped through the wall of a building and "cut the legs clean off a chair in which a man was sitting, but without injury to the man other than to his dignity."[12] Some weren't so lucky, as several men were hit glancing blows and knocked down by flying lumber.

Throughout the night the hotel's construction crew huddled in fear as lumber picked up by the wind slapped onto their bunkhouses. Several attempts were made to get readings at the wind gauge on the hill, "but it was impossible to read the meter and on some of the attempts impossible to even get to it," assistant engineer Floyd Parker wrote.[13] The following morning, Saturday, workers ventured out into 15 inches (38 cm) of new snow to assess what damage had been done. What they saw was dumbfounding. Small boards and shingles were strewn all over the knoll and far along the north shore of Middle Waterton Lake. The four foot-high (1.2 m) boards of the skating rink on Linnet Lake were blown down.[14] At the hotel site, the gasoline storage hut was turned over and the front of the lumber shed to the west of the hotel had been torn off.[15] When Oland went into his office, he found the floor littered with small stones. Looking up, he saw what appeared to be bullet holes in the window panes. The wind had been so strong that it had "shot" the rocks through the glass.[16] "I would judge that the maximum velocity was over 90 mph (145 km/h)," Parker wrote.[17]

Incredibly, the hotel had survived the storm intact. "The east wing received the brunt of the strain, as the wind was slightly from the west and blew into the open end of this wing," Parker wrote in a report to his superiors in St. Paul. "(I) figure the temporary six-inch by six-inch (15 cm by 15 cm) diagonal braces we placed at the west end of the east wing was all that saved this

wing."[18] After careful inspection, the only fault Parker could find with the hotel was that the wind had knocked each of the wings about three inches out of plumb. Horse-powered winches mounted in front of the hotel were used to pull sections back into alignment.[19]

"The wind was a very severe test on the hotel building and, taking into account its present weak condition of same, it stood up better than I would generally expect," Parker said.[20] Surprisingly, Great Northern had to pay out of pocket for damage incurred at the construction site—about $180. "Our (insurance) policy … covers fire only as (we) did not think it necessary to carry wind and tornado insurance," Parker noted.[21]

The damage was small compared to how much the railway might lose if the Cardston-Waterton road was not improved in time for opening. Members of the Cardston Board of Trade were well aware of that and the potential for lost benefits to themselves if Great Northern balked at plans to expand the hotel project or decided to push for a more direct route between Waterton and Glacier parks. The efforts of the board of trade to get the province to improve the Cardston-Waterton road were motivated by

The delay in enclosing the lobby allowed snow to drift into this fourth floor corridor. The diagonal bracing is what held the hotel together during the December 11, 1926, hurricane gale. The stairway leads to the boom used to haul lumber and supplies to upper floors. George Anderegg photo, J. J. Hill Library, LH 2492.

Mortises were cut into the lobby pillars where the tenons of the timbers at the upper reaches of the lobby will be fitted into place. George Anderegg photo, J. J. Hill Library, LH 2488.

more than greed. Oland and Scott were longtime members of the Cardston business community and, as in any small town, business people relied on each other for referrals and as customers. As well, Oland and Scott were their friends.

In January 1927 the Cardston Board of Trade formed a strategic alliance with its Lethbridge counterpart, hoping the added numbers might help sway the province to cough up money for road repairs. Joseph Card of Cardston headed a joint delegation that travelled to Edmonton to meet Premier Brownlee. Card's plea was not much different than earlier appeals: Great Northern was ready to double the capacity of the Prince of Wales Hotel if the Cardston-Waterton road was improved. Card also noted federal funds would be available to offset the cost of upgrading the road, should the province decide to give the go-ahead. Brownlee was sympathetic but unmoved. The premier said the problem with roads in Alberta was tremendous and would have to be dealt with in its entirety, adding a plan was just being drawn up.[22]

It was a cautious statement by a politician ever-thoughtful of the consequences of his words. At the time there was also pressure on the premier to improve the roads to Banff and Jasper parks. If Brownlee could find $100,000 plus for the 30-mile (48 km) Cardston-Waterton road, advocates of Banff and Jasper would soon be on his doorstep asking for money for their considerably longer routes. It was a can of worms the premier would just as soon not open.

Members of the Cardston Board of Trade had reason to think they had possibly made an impact with the premier when the province announced it was raising the gasoline tax a penny to three cents a gallon.[23] The board had recommended just such a hike. The additional revenue, Brownlee said, would go to improve roads throughout Alberta.[24] The question on everyone's lips was: When?

The condition of the Cardston-Waterton road and what to do about it was far from the mind of Louis Hill at that particular time. It was typical of Hill to resolve situations when he deemed necessary, which was not necessarily the best time for others. The matter of the Cardston-Waterton road had not yet risen to the top of his priority list. In part that may have been because there was no immediate road problem; the mud was frozen solid and Oland and Scott were making relatively satisfactory progress on the hotel.[25] In the meantime, Hill busied himself with other issues.

For months, the railway's advertising department had been urging Hill to make a decision about a name for the Waterton hotel so work on next season's promotional literature could begin. Budd had proposed three names: Canadian Rockies Hotel, Boundary Hotel and Moraine Hotel, but Hill wasn't impressed with any of them and put the matter off.[26] The question finally came to a head when Edward Ward, a retired newspaper reporter living in Wa-

terton, wrote Great Northern saying he had met a company official who said the hotel was to be named for the Prince of Wales.[27] Ward asked if it was true and if it were, suggested that Edward, the Prince of Wales, be invited to the hotel.

Ward's inquiry prompted a flurry of memos at Great Northern's headquarters to determine if indeed the hotel would be named for the prince. Although it was believed Hill himself had indicated the Prince of Wales Hotel name might be used, it was unclear just how firm the decision was.[28] The railway, attempting to cover all bases, asked the Canadian government if it had any restrictions on what the hotel could be called. Great Northern was free to choose any name it pleased, Ottawa replied.[29] Finally, Budd asked Hill: "Do we use Prince of Wales Hotel as the name?" "O.K. with me," Hill scrawled at the bottom of the memo.[30] Three days later, Budd was able to tell Ward: "It has definitely been decided to call the hotel Prince of Wales."[31]

Hill may be credited for making the choice, but the suggestion had come from Canon Middleton.[32] As Middleton recalled later, the company representatives "expressed (a) desire to 'Indianize' the name, but for lack of euphony the idea was dropped."[33] It was British-born Middleton, a firm believer in the monarchy, who gave them the idea of naming the hotel after Edward, Prince of Wales.[34] Like many Canadians, Middleton was a great admirer of the prince. In October 1919 when the Prince of Wales visited Fort Macleod, it was the cadet corps that Middleton had founded on the Blood tribe reserve that provided the prince's honour guard.[35]

Also on Hill's plate was the question of who would build the excursion boat that would ply Upper Waterton Lake. Although Capt. Swanson drew the plans for the *International*, it was not intended that he necessarily build the $24,000 vessel. The first offer went to Oland.[36] Oland's boat-building experience was limited, however.

Edward, Prince of Wales. Glenbow Museum, Calgary, Canada, NA-4388-1.

According to his memoirs, he had helped with the construction of the *Gertrude*, a steamer constructed in Waterton in 1907 to haul logs from the shores of Upper Waterton Lake to John Hanson's mill on Maskinonge Lake.[37] Mary O'Brien also remembers her father building small pleasure boats in his spare time during the winter.[38] Regardless of Oland's qualifications, he was in no position to take on the job of building the *International*. He was focusing his attention on finishing the Prince of Wales Hotel and Kenney felt he could not be spared.[39] Hill instead turned to Swanson to construct the vessel.

All the while Hill was handling these and other issues, he continued fiddling with the design of the Prince of Wales Hotel. Dozens of detail changes were made between December and April, many at his urging. They ranged from relocating the elevator and revising and adding fire escapes to adding decorative metal brackets to lobby pillars and trusses, and changing the dimensions of the gift shop windows and doors. It was nit-picking attention McMahon—and Oland and Scott—could have done without.

The most extensive revision to the hotel's blueprints was the creation of a fifth floor in the east and west wings. This entailed tearing apart each of the 12 flat dor-

This artist's illustration shows how Great Northern officials originally planned to dock the excursion boat for Waterton at the base of the knoll. The rendering shows a boat that resembles the St. Mary, which the railroad had initially considered moving from Glacier to Waterton. The idea was abandoned because it was thought the St. Mary would not be able to withstand the rugged conditions on Upper Waterton Lake. Courtesy Toltz, King, Duvall, Anderson and Associates.

mers on the roof and rebuilding them into a peaked or gable design. While Hill was able to increase the number of rooms in the hotel to 90 by making the change, it meant even more time lost for Oland and Scott. It was not an unusual situation. Hill's tinkering with the plan "meant that a lot of the structure as it now is had been built four times (over)," Oland said.[40] Each change in the blueprints arrived by mail from Great Northern's headquarters. It got to the point that Oland dreaded opening any letters postmarked St. Paul.

Not only was Hill seemingly conspiring against Oland and Scott to keep them from completing the hotel on time, the weather continued to play havoc with their construction schedule. In March, Waterton took a lashing when wind speeds reached 80 mph (129 km/h).[41] Work was halted to check the integrity of the hotel. While not quite as strong as the December 1926 storm, the buffeting winds had once more knocked the building out of plumb. Framing was so far along that Oland feared structural damage if the building were winched into alignment, so he left the hotel out of rack.[42]

Bad roads returned to haunt Oland and Scott when spring came early to southern Alberta, thawing the ground and melting snow. Familiar with how easily the Cardston-Waterton road could be churned up by heavy traffic, Oland and Scott took to rerouting some shipments of lumber, wallboard, pipes and fixtures through Hill Spring. Unfortunately, it didn't take long for the detour to deteriorate, as progress reports to St. Paul revealed. "Roads bad, nearly impassable," the April 12 update stated. The roads "are impassable for trucks," the April 18 report said.[43] Once again, work on the hotel slowed as delivery of supplies was delayed.

The news of these recurring road woes was never far from the ears of Cardston's Board of Trade members and they took up the cause of highway improvements with renewed vigour. In a telegram to their representative in the legislature, the board of trade said it had an "absolute guarantee" Great Northern would spend $1 million in Waterton by June 1, 1928, if the road was improved. The board warned against waiting for Ottawa to act because that could mean a delay of several years. If tourists were forced to travel mud roads to reach Waterton, it would a very long time before the area recovered from the "bad advertising."[44] The plea was to no avail. The Brownlee government was not about to spend anything in the near future on major road projects, a stand reinforced when the budget estimates for 1927-28 cut $576,000 from highway improvements compared to the previous fiscal year, despite collecting substantially more from the increased tax on gasoline.[45]

At Great Northern's headquarters, concern over the road issue was growing every day as the summer tourist season approached and no breakthrough seemed imminent. Taking matters into his own hands, Budd again sent Hogeland to Alberta. Unlike the previous foray, this time Hogeland did not go empty-handed; he carried with him an offer that Budd hoped would prove irresistible. The railway was prepared to buy thousands of dollars worth of government bonds if the province would order the necessary improvements to the Cardston-Waterton road.[46] Brownlee said he would have to talk the offer over with his cabinet colleagues.

A couple of weeks later, the government made a counter offer. It would upgrade the road if the railway agreed to buy up to $125,000 in provincial bonds—and waive

A lone workman stands beside the hotel tower. The worker has an excellent view of the reconstruction on the dormers, which were converted to gables so a fifth floor could be added to each wing, increasing the number of rooms in the hotel. *George Anderegg photo, Great Northern Railway company records, Minnesota Historical Society.*

the interest payments for the first four or five years.[47] "To simply take their bonds bearing 4 per cent interest does not mean much to them, as they can market such bonds quite readily," Hogeland wrote in his explanation of the Alberta government's stance to his superiors in St. Paul. "I feel satisfied the government will not go ahead with the improvement of the Cardston-Waterton Park road unless we agree to bear all, or a substantial part, of the cost, or take their bonds and waive interest for a few years," Hogeland added.[48] Hill rejected the proposal out of hand.[49] Kenney suggested an end run around Brownlee, saying the railway would be better served lobbying for a new highway

At nine tons each, the two boilers for the Prince of Wales Hotel were too big for any nearby trucks to haul from Hill Spring. They were accompanied by two equally big fuel storage tanks. Even if a truck could have been found, the road conditions were so bad it would have never gotten to Waterton. The problem of transporting them was solved when a late spring snowstorm inspired creation of makeshift sleds pulled by teams of horses. The snow was followed by a chinook, but the teamsters reported the sled ran as well on mud as snow. Author's collection.

Nine ton boilers

that would directly connect Waterton and Glacier, eliminating the need to use the Cardston-Waterton road.[50] Hill agreed.

A few floors from Hill's offices at Great Northern's headquarters building in St. Paul, Howard Noble and his Glacier Park Hotel Company staff had their own set of concerns about what was going on with the Prince of Wales Hotel project. Noble's staff was taking bookings based on Oland's calculation he would have the hotel ready for opening June 23.[51] But Anderegg's building update reports indicated otherwise. Despite adding manpower weekly, work on the hotel was progressing at a snail's pace because of the weather and road conditions.[52] From March 15 to April 12, the reports indicated the contractors were only able to complete as much work as they would have normally done in a week.

As word of construction delays and slowdowns poured in, Noble began to wonder whether Oland and Scott could make the deadline or even come close. Floyd Parker, Great Northern's on-site engineer, didn't think so. He wasn't even sure Oland's construction crew could have the

Workers make adjustments to the tank that will hold the oil for the boilers. In the empty bay beside it will go the diesel fuel tank to supply the hotel generators. George Anderegg photo, Great Northern Railway company records, Minnesota Historical Society.

This 100,000-gallon tower (454,000 litre) sits upon a 100-foot (30-metre) pedestal, supplying the hotel, laundry and boilers with fresh water. George Anderegg photo, Great Northern Railway company records, Minnesota Historical Society.

The 'powerhouse' contained the hotel's boilers, laundry and electrical generating plant. George Anderegg photo, Great Northern Railway company records, Minnesota Historical Society.

The hotel generators.

The transformer switchboard.

The pump for the hotel's fire hydrants and roof sprinkler. George Anderegg photos, Great Northern Railway company records, Minnesota Historical Society.

be cancelled. I wrote them at once that I now had the roof on and that if they would guarantee me delivery of materials as I needed them and would quit changing the plans, I would give them the hotel. They told me to try it."[54]

At last Oland and Scott were able to rein in Louis Hill; the flood of plan changes emanating from his meddling in the design process would stop. As for guaranteeing delivery of supplies to Cardston, that wouldn't be a problem for a railway like Great Northern and the resources it could command.

The factor that neither Great Northern nor Oland had addressed was the weather. May 1927 would go down in memory as one of the wettest on record, even if the statistics don't back it up. Repeated periods of rain and snow saturated the ground. Both the Cardston-Waterton road and the Hill Spring detour deteriorated rapidly into a mess the consistency of thick porridge that held tenaciously to vehicle tires and wagon wheels. "Impossible for trucks to haul now and (we) had two loads of lumber come in today by team that had to unload part of their loads in order to come through, the full loads sinking in up to the hubs in places," Parker reported, adding, "(We) had a load of lumber on the way from Hill Spring the past week that mired so deep it was impossible to pull out and was left standing."[55] Six railway carloads of material for the Prince of Wales Hotel were sitting on the tracks in Cardston waiting to be unloaded.[56] Oland and Scott resorted to digging culverts at their own expense to divert groundwater away from roads.[57]

The hotel site faired no better. "No outside work done account snow and rain," Parker wired Hogeland. "Two feet snow outside park and one foot here. ... Telephone lines down." Hogeland laid bare

hotel ready before July 1.[53] Fearing the complications and bad publicity that would come from cancelling and rescheduling reservations if the opening had to be changed—possibly more than once—Great Northern officials tried to pin Oland down on a completion date.

"Finally, in early April, they wrote me from St. Paul that they were afraid they would have to delay the opening of the hotel one year on account of the terrible weather and the plan changes," Oland recalled. "They had already accepted a lot of (guest) reservations that would have to the facts for Hill, Budd, Kenney and Noble to see, ending his letter: "This situation is interfering seriously with the completion of the job."[58]

In Great Northern's boardrooms, executives argued about the best solution to the road problem. Budd favoured taking the Alberta government's offer, even though the province would pay the railway no interest on the bonds for a period. Kenney and Hogeland were opposed. "I am not in favour of contributing anything to the improvement of this road," Hogeland stated.[59] Hill sided with Hogeland and Kenney.[60]

Budd turned to Senator Buchanan for advice. After contacting Brownlee's office, Buchanan wired Budd: "Am still strongly of the opinion (it is) worthwhile having personal interview with premier as you might be able to influence him to undertake the highway this year. I know he is in a sympathetic mood."[61] Noble agreed, saying he had the "impression (the) provincial government (is) now desirous (of) cooperating and inclined (to) consider in substance original proposal made by us."[62] Over the objections of Kenney and Hogeland, Budd told Buchanan to contact Brownlee to arrange a meeting. It was set for June 9 in Calgary at the Palliser Hotel with Brownlee and his public works minister. Great Northern's delegation included L. C. Gilman, executive vice-president of Great Northern, Noble, Hogeland and Howard Hays.

Each of the parties had powerful incentives to work out a deal. On Brownlee's part, he was eager to address the continuing and building bad publicity his United Farmers government was taking in the press and from its own members over the on-going dilemma about improving the Cardston-Waterton road. "The papers have been carrying stories about this bad road

This is one of only a handful of views showing the interior of the hotel during construction. George Anderegg photo, J. J. Hill Library, LH 2515.

that reflects no credit on the government," Noble noted, adding Brownlee was becoming "sensitive to this criticism."[63] Months of lobbying had taken their toll on the premier. "Local organizations and citizens who recognize value to province and to community of tourist traffic are clamoring for (a) remedy," wrote Andrew Hogg, the Lethbridge lawyer who handled legal affairs for Great Northern in Alberta. "Provincial government which lately decided against improving road this year now seems repentant and might yield readily

This view of the hotel construction site from the water tower was taken less than a month before the hotel opened. The trench running from the foreground to the hotel is for the hotel's water and steam supply. The two buildings in the foreground are the lumber storage shed and wood-working shop, where all the fancy scroll work and other decorative detail pieces were fabricated. *George Anderegg photo, courtesy of the J. J. Hill Library, LH 2523.*

to demands direct from heads of your company presented so as to impress general public with emergency and give government good political excuse for reversing decision even without valuable consideration."[64] Brownlee could ill afford further attention being focused on a road that was becoming a microcosm of problems across the province, especially the Edmonton-Jasper Park route. The difficulty, as had been previously pointed out to Great Northern officials, was the province "cannot undertake one road without the other, unless there is a particularly strong reason."[65] Just buying government bonds was not enough; but an offer to waive interest on the purchase of bonds would supply the necessary reason.[66]

Great Northern came to the table because it was desperate for a solution. The immediate problem was to get the hotel completed in time for the summer season. Even if the hotel was opened, without road improvements "there will be periods of from a day to a week when people will be marooned at our hotel," Budd noted. Then there was the question of expanding the hotel. Tentative plans for a three-story, 39-bedroom annex to the Prince of Wales Hotel had recently been issued. Work on the 40- by 86-foot (12 m by 25.8 m) building, which would contain the beer parlour, was to start in June.[67] Unless the railway was ready to do what it had done in Glacier, and build or repair the road itself, it didn't have any options.

Several days prior to the meeting in Calgary with Brownlee, Noble and Hays made a stop in Waterton to see how construction on the Prince of Wales Hotel was far-ing. What they got was firsthand experience of the desperation of the situation. There was no way to reach Waterton directly from Cardston. Instead, Hays and Noble had to make a 110-mile (177 km) detour through Fort Macleod and Pincher Creek to get to the park.[68] Even then their car became stuck several times, with Canon Middleton coming to the rescue on one occasion, summoning a farmer with a tractor to pull the vehicle free.[69] When Noble recounted their difficulties at a Lethbridge Rotary club luncheon meeting, Reverend Cecil Swanson, himself a Waterton cottage owner, attempted to humour him with a ditty. Sung to the tune of *Old Folks of Home* (*Way Down Upon the Suwannee River*), it evoked gales of laughter.

Way out beyond the Belly River, far, far away;
There's where I'll have to stay forever, me and my Chevrolet.
All up and down the unpaved highway, sadly I roam;
Still waitin' for a team to haul me back to my dry, warm home.
Oh, the road is deep and soggy, everywhere I roam;
Please come and fetch me in a buggy, back to my dry, warm home.[70]

When the Great Northern officials finally headed home following their meeting with Brownlee, it was with a considerable dent in the corporation's pocketbook. They had agreed to buy up to $150,000 worth of Alberta government bonds at 4 1/2 per cent interest over 15 years to get the Cardston-Waterton road repaired. The two sides argued over the length of time during which interest would be waived; Great Northern was able to reduce it from four years to a year and a half.[71] With cash in hand, the province began work almost immediately. Unfortunately for Oland and Scott, it would be of little help. It was initially believed the road could stay open during upgrading, with traffic detoured as necessary. It quickly became clear the road's condition was so bad it had to be closed for the summer, and all traffic was rerouted through Hill Spring.[72] "While we will be handicapped this year, it looks as though we will open next year with a good dependable road," Noble wrote Kenney.[73] A longstanding hurdle had been cleared. The question that remained was how soon Oland and Scott could have the hotel ready.

With the deadline now extended to July 15, the contractors threw themselves at their task. The extent to which they went to get the job done became the basis for one of the most enduring tales about the construction of the Prince of Wales Hotel: The arrival of the boilers.

The hotel was to have two boilers to supply hot water for patrons, the laundry and the heating system.[74] At six feet (1.8 m) in diameter and 12 feet (3.6 m) long, the boilers were an imposing sight when they arrived in Cardston by rail in May 1927. Accompanying the boilers were two equally large fuel storage tanks. These huge vessels created a problem. There was no truck big enough to haul any of them and even if one could have been found, all the roads to Waterton Park were in such bad condition no truck could have gotten through.[75]

A partial solution came when Canadian Pacific Railway opened its spur line to Hill Spring.[76] The boilers were moved there to cut the hauling distance to Waterton, but the problem of how to get them to the hotel site remained. A heavy snowfall provided the answer.[77] It allowed the equipment to be loaded onto skids and towed to the hotel site. With no time to spare, horses were taken to Hill Spring and hitched to the jerry-rigged sled. Using 24 sturdy steeds pulling, eight or more pushing and four teamsters on the reins, the boilers and tanks were hauled to the park.[78] The first arrived May 30, 1927.[79] The snow that had made the sledding so easy didn't last. By Wednesday, June 1, one of southern Alberta's famous chinooks blew in.[80] That didn't stop the hauling. "This was one time where the mud and water helped considerably, the skids sliding over the mud and wet grass quite easily," the *Lethbridge Herald*'s Waterton correspondent noted. One of the teamsters said the sleds actually ran better through mud than on snow.[81]

The scene on the hotel hill those last weeks was one of controlled chaos. Despite everyone's best intentions, the opening of the hotel had to be delayed a further 10 days, to July 25.[82] Oland and Scott were not to blame for the deadline extension. The holdup was caused by delays in getting the electrical and plumbing hookups completed, the job of subcontractors, some of whom were sent by Great Northern directly and not hired by Oland and Scott.[83]

Until the subcontractors' jobs were done, Oland and Scott were unable to complete finishing work throughout the site.

One of the last jobs to wrap up construction of the Prince of Wales Hotel was the painting, and it almost proved to be the undoing of a year's hard labour. Knowing the potential for fire at the all-wood hotel, Oland ordered the painters not to leave their cleaning rags around the building overnight. He provided an iron barrel away from the hotel for their disposal. One day, "when the weather was unusually hot, this barrel exploded, blowing burning rags into the air."[84]

The night watchman "thought he smelled smoke," Oland said. He at once investigated and traced the smoke to a closet where the door was tightly stuck. When he opened this door, he saw that a fire had started from rags and had burned through the floor and started burning the joists. The watchman, having pails and water close at hand, soon had the fire out.

"This gave us all a terrible scare." Had another hour passed before the fire was discovered, "nothing could have saved the building," Oland said.[85]

The week the Prince of Wales Hotel opened, Oland and Scott took out an advertisement in the *Lethbridge Herald* trumpeting their creation. The hotel, the ad read, is "a tribute to our efficiency—built to last, and a product of speedy construction." The contractors were obviously proud of their handiwork and had every right to be. During the 12 months it had taken to complete the hotel, they had overcome obstacles that would have overwhelmed lesser men. The hotel was, as the ad said, "a monument of beauty, dignity and character"—its beauty was Hill's inspiration, dignity the architect's design, and character the result of Oland and Scott's craftsmanship.

The Lodestone

In the spring and early summer of 1927, the focus in Waterton was preparing for the opening of the Prince of Wales Hotel. Great Northern was one of the mightiest railways in the United States and the fact it had decided to build a hotel in Waterton was the biggest thing to happen to the park since the discovery of oil on Cameron Creek at the turn of the century. Great Northern's promotional campaign had achieved wonders in boosting tourism to Glacier Park in Montana and optimism was running high about what would happen in Waterton. Howard Noble predicted the opening of the hotel would see tourism double within a few years.[1] In fact it would nearly triple, but little did anyone know that then. The Prince of Wales Hotel was viewed as a lodestone that would alter the future of Waterton and the fortunes of those who lived there. Directly and indirectly, it would be responsible for many changes and improvements to the park.

Among local entrepreneurs, construction of the hotel prompted a wave of ideas about what new services Waterton would need. William Peacock figured the park should have a movie theatre.[2] Win Chow, who was operating the Beach Cafe, talked about leasing two lots in town and putting up his own hotel.[3] And the Atkinson brothers of Hillcrest proposed erecting a garage near the Strate butcher shop that would offer gasoline and vehicle repairs.[4] In time, some of these developments would take place.

W. J. Baker of Twin Butte and his son George were among the first business people to take action. During the spring of 1927, they were hard at work building their 50-foot by 75-foot (15 m by 22.5 m) Park Transport Garage and filling station on Mount View Road. The Bakers were not alone in readying to meet the needs of the motoring public. Dell Ellison was also building a garage, across from his store.[5]

W. J. Baker of Twin Butte and his son George planned the opening of the Park Transport Garage and service station so it would be ready for an influx of tourists expected with the opening of the Prince of Wales Hotel. Ray Djuff photo, author's collection.

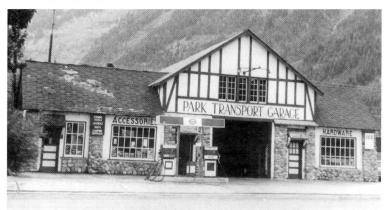

The opening of the Prince of Wales Hotel was the biggest thing to happen in Waterton since the discovery of oil more than 20 years earlier, prompting local businessmen to make improvements or expand their operations. It also attracted new entrepreneurs to town, expanding existing services. T. J. Hileman photo, Great Northern Railway publicity and advertising department, Minnesota Historical Society.

Besides the Prince of Wales Hotel, Great Northern Railway considered building a chalet at nearby Cameron Lake. The railway asked about a lease for a chalet, but the proposal never went any further. T. J. Hileman photo, Great Northern Railway publicity and advertising department, Minnesota Historical Society.

Still in the planning stage, but soon to become a reality, was Nahor (Dil) Dilatush's idea for a new hotel in Waterton. Dilatush, owner of the Tourist Cafe, had been working all winter for Oland and Scott, operating the kitchen at the camp for the crew building the Prince of Wales Hotel. Oland had gone through a series of cooks, but couldn't seem to find the right man who could turn out good meals and not end up cheating him in the process. Desperate to find a happy medium, Oland even tried a stint at doing the job himself but quickly gave up when he realized running a kitchen wasn't his forte. That's when

Oland turned to Dilatush for help.[6] The deal worked out well for both men: Oland had a reliable and honest cook and happy employees. Dilatush, with his winter's earnings, decided to build his own small hotel, with space for two, main-floor shops, beside his Tourist Cafe on Waterton Avenue. Dilatush's Stanley Hotel was completed in 1928.

In building the Stanley Hotel, Dilatush was counting on the fact not every new visitor to Waterton would want to or could afford to stay at the Prince of Wales Hotel. There would be an obvious need for more moderately priced accommodations. No one knew that better than Eddie Poulin, who owned the Waterton Lakes Hotel and Chalets. Poulin realized he could not compete with the Prince of Wales Hotel for opulence, but he was not about to be completely overshadowed in the market. For the 1927 season, Poulin paid for a series of upgrades to the chalets, a group of cottages beside his hotel.[7] It was the second year in a row Poulin had poured money into his summer resort.

Poulin's improvements to the chalets and his decision to open the hotel earlier than usual that season caused a problem for Waterton's school teacher, who was forced to find a new location for her class. The school's population had jumped from about a dozen in June 1926 to 36 that September, boosted by the children of Prince of Wales Hotel workers who had brought their families to the park for the yearlong construction project.[8] Miss G. MacDonald was used to teaching lessons in her home, but come September she was forced to find larger premises to accommodate the increased enrolment. The teacher and students ended up in what would eventually become the tavern of Poulin's hotel, a fact her pupils would later boast about.[9] Forced to move again in the spring of 1927, the students and their new teacher, Sylvia Ward, who had taken over the one-room class from MacDonald in December 1926, found a temporary home in R. W. Bradshaw's cottage.[10] Acknowledging the inevitable, the Waterton school board issued a tender in the spring of 1927 to build a proper facility.[11]

Poulin, Dilatush and the Bakers were not just playing a hunch that tourism was about to take a dramatic turn in Waterton. There were other signs. In March 1927, Brewster Transport Company Limited of Banff announced it would be starting the first regularly scheduled bus service to Waterton.[12] The prediction by Great Northern officials that the opening of the Prince of Wales Hotel would make Waterton a stepping stone for tourists going between Banff and Glacier Park was coming true. Getting to Waterton from Banff was no joyride. The journey was a 1 1/2-day ordeal, including an overnight stop in Calgary. The last leg of the trip was a gruelling nine hours, with a one-hour stop for a meal in Fort Macleod.[13]

When the first Brewster bus pulled into Waterton at 6 p.m. on July 21, 1927, it held only three passengers from Philadelphia.[14] But there were more people to come— many more. The Morris brothers, who had been contracted by Great Northern to supply horse-outfitting services to the Prince of Wales Hotel, had been warned to expect a lot of visitors. They added 100 head to their string of stock in the park, anticipating increased business from guests at the Prince of Wales Hotel.[15]

To control the anticipated onslaught of motoring tourists, two additional RCMP officers were brought in to assist Cpl. Andy Ford at the local detachment.[16]

A new floating platform was added to Linnet Lake for the summer of 1927 and a log boom was put in place to mark the swimming area. The shallow Linnet Lake is considerably warmer than Upper Waterton Lake, which is fed by snow and streams high in the surrounding mountains. T. J. Hileman photo, Great Northern Railway publicity and advertising department, Minnesota Historical Society.

Later that summer, Oland and Scott would build a police barracks, including a lockup, office, residence and stable at the corner of Cameron Falls Drive and Waterton Avenue.[17]

There was little question that North America would soon know about the hotel and the park. Besides newspaper stories in the *Lethbridge Herald* and elsewhere describing progress on the hotel's construction, the silver screen was about to reflect Waterton's wonders. In June, a representative of Associated Screen News of Montreal arrived to film scenes around the park. These clips would be used for newsreels, shown before the main attraction at cinemas throughout Canada and the U.S. As it was still early in the season, the photographer recruited the talent of "five pretty girls," who volunteered to act as tourists and sit under the spray of Cameron Falls.[18] He also filmed scenes at the Prince of Wales Hotel.

A Glacier Park Transport Company bus on Akamina Highway, heading toward Cameron Lake. Photographer Tomer Hileman used Prince of Wales Hotel employees and their relatives to play 'tourists' in the bus, including hotel manager Capt. R. Stanley Harrison (white moustache), and five year-old Margaret, the daughter of hotel chef Len Moores. T. J. Hileman photo, Great Northern Railway publicity and advertising department, Minnesota Historical Society.

Like private enterprise, the Parks Branch was investing in Waterton's future, updating and improving facilities. In the spring of 1927, it bought an electric generator to light Waterton's main street, the entrance to the campground, the registration office and other government facilities.[19] The superintendent made sure his house was also supplied with electricity, one of the first private residences in the park to have power.[20] Other improvements included continuing with an experiment in oiling roads to keep down the dust, gravelling others, grading the tennis courts and installing high netting around them.[21] At Linnet Lake, a log boom was put in place to mark the swimming area and a new floating platform was constructed.[22] A bonus came from Ottawa when Senator Buchanan announced that two years of lobbying had finally garnered approval to build a trout hatchery at Spring Creek, near the park entrance.[23]

Parks Branch activity was not restricted to the townsite. On the arch announcing the entrance to the park, which had been put up the year before, the words "Water-

ton Lakes National Park" were added to ensure tourists knew exactly where they were visiting.[24] And just above the town, work resumed on widening Akamina Highway and completing the road as far as Cameron Lake. There was no missing the construction: Dynamite explosions rocked houses and showered debris over parts of the town. Pop Harwood, Waterton's postmaster, was almost hit when he didn't hear the clearout notice and a rock came through the roof of his home.[25] With construction of the Prince of Wales Hotel, Akamina Highway was taking on more importance. Many people were talking about pushing the road beyond its current terminus, at Cameron Lake, west over the Continental Divide and south into the U.S. to make Waterton a stop on a loop road linked to Glacier Park in Montana rather than the last point on a dead-end highway.

That summer, Waterton was also linked to the outside world by air. Where the highway into the park crosses Pass Creek, the Parks Branch had tendered a project to construct a 30-acre (12 ha) landing field for forestry planes.[26] Jock Palmer, a founder of the CJOC radio station in Lethbridge, made good use of the airfield to promote his Lethbridge Commercial Airlines. He and Charlie Elliott flew from Lethbridge to Waterton, covering the 80-mile (129 km) distance in 70 minutes. They stayed in the park for several days, making special promotional passenger flights.[27] Palmer and Elliott were jumping on a bandwagon of interest in civil aviation created by Charles Lindbergh, who in May 1927 had made his historic solo crossing of the Atlantic in the *Spirit of St. Louis*.[28]

For all the high-flying high jinks, Waterton's residents remained relatively grounded. They did permit themselves a few luxuries with cash earned from work associated with the Prince of Wales Hotel. That was particularly evident in the number of newer model vehicles roaming local streets. The new vehicle owners included George Allison, who purchased a Ford light delivery truck, George Baker who picked up a Chevrolet truck, Jack Lea a Paige sedan, and Jack Jensen a Star tourer. Even Oland treated himself to a new Paige sedan.[29] The man responsible for many of these vehicle sales was Art Baalim, a Lethbridge car dealer who had a summer home in Waterton.

The flush of public interest Great Northern had created in Waterton with its new hotel was also evident in the number of people talking about building residences in the park. The *Lethbridge Herald*'s correspondent estimated 20 new cottages would be constructed that year.[30] Certainly the deal the railway had worked out to improve the road to the park helped make up the minds of some would-be cottagers.

Waterton residents didn't have to go as far as the highway to see the difference the Prince of Wales Hotel had made to their lives. It was as close as the telephone on the wall. As the hotel would have a phone in every room, Alberta Government Telephones was forced to install new phone and trunk service to Waterton to handle the increased requirements.[31] Installation of a new line and switchboard, operated by Harwood, provided for more private lines in town and, for the first time, 24-hour long-distance service. Harwood's switchboard, however, would only be open 12 hours a day, from 8 a.m. to 8 p.m.[32] The hotel also came to the aid of one of the men who was hurt putting up the new telephone lines. Jim West of Calgary, foreman of the telephone construction crew, was injured when a pole his men were raising slipped and fell on his leg. West was im-

mediately rushed to the infirmary at the hotel, which had opened two days before, where he was treated by the resident nurse before being taken to hospital in Pincher Creek.[33]

The advent of the hotel improved life in the park in other, more mundane ways. Mail volume, boosted by the hotel's construction crew, had increased to such a point Harwood was forced to find bigger facilities. He relocated from a building near the park registration office, by Linnet Lake, to an extension built onto his home on Fountain Avenue.[34] And delivery was increased from twice to three times weekly to prevent too many letters from piling up.[35] The new post office also featured lock boxes so local residents could pick up their mail when they pleased rather than having to use the general delivery wicket during business hours.[36]

All the improvements and effort spruced up Waterton for visitors in general, but there was one person in particular Great Northern officials hoped would show up—Edward, the Prince of Wales. Their hopes lay in the fact Prince

The hotel nurse. Courtesy Ann Harrison, author's collection.

The increase in tourism to Waterton created by the opening of the Prince of Wales Hotel warranted the construction of a new RCMP barracks, including lockup, office, residence and stables. It was built by Oland and Scott. Author's collection.

Edward, Prince of Wales, centre, chats with Guy Weadick, left, one of the founders of the Calgary Stampede, at the prince's E.P. Ranch southwest of Calgary. At the right is W. L. Carlyle, who managed the ranch for the prince. Glenbow Archives, Calgary, Canada, NA 2800-13.

Edward, later to become King Edward VIII and still later the Duke of Windsor after his abdication in 1936, had planned a tour of Canada that summer to mark the 50th anniversary of Confederation. While his itinerary was vague, it was known he would be spending about a week in August at the E.P. Ranch, 110 miles (177 km) north of Waterton.

The E.P. Ranch held special symbolism for the prince and southern Albertans. The prince had bought the ranch on a whim after visiting the adjoining Bar U Ranch during a 1919 trip to Canada. "What I saw in North America stirred me deeply—most of all the beauty and grandeur of the Canadian Rockies," Edward wrote in his biography many years later.[37] "My impulse in making this investment—the only piece of property that I have ever owned—was far removed from Imperial politics. In the midst of that majestic countryside I had suddenly been overwhelmed by an irresist-ible longing to immerse myself, if only momentarily, in the simple life of the western prairies. There, I was sure I would find occasional escape from the sometimes too-confining, too-well ordered, island life of Great Britain."[38] And escape he did on two subsequent visits to E.P. Ranch; the first in September 1923 and the second in the fall of 1924.

The fact the prince had bought the property and returned relatively frequently, for a royal, earned great respect from southern Albertans. Edward was more than just another of the prosperous Englishmen who had bought ranches in southern Alberta as an investment, to be run by local administrators who sent periodic updates to their bosses "across the pond." The prince's keen interest in his ranch and personal involvement set him apart and made him a less-distant figure.

For Great Northern, having the Prince of Wales appear in Waterton or anywhere in close proximity to the namesake hotel would be a public relations coup sure to attract worldwide attention. Railroad officials, however, were loath to make the invitation themselves. They preferred that a private individual or group suggest a "quiet trip" to the hotel as an outing while the prince rested at his ranch.[39] The Lethbridge Board of Trade, with Great Northern's encouragement, sent the invitation. Since the prince had already toured both Banff and Jasper, the expectation was he'd make an effort to visit Waterton.[40] Time would tell whether the Prince would be among the throngs heading for the park that summer to see its latest attraction.

The Call of the Mountains
Vacations in
Glacier National Park
Waterton Lakes National Park

The colour of the roof of the Prince of Wales Hotel was a hotly contested topic between Great Northern Railway and the Canadian Parks Branch. Government officials wanted the roof painted green to conform to the recommended park colour scheme. Louis Hill's wish was that the cedar shingles be allowed to weather and turn grey, as shown in this rare 1941 colour photo. The Parks Branch eventually got its way and in 1950 the roof was painted green, much to the chagrin of later hotel owners who would have preferred the lower maintenance of a natural finish. Herman Rusch photo, courtesy Herman Rusch.

A Glacier Park Transport Company gearjammer, looking smart in his driver's uniform, stands beside one of the touring cars used to ferry private parties and dignitaries between hotels and chalets in Waterton and Glacier parks. Drivers were held personally responsible for the washing, waxing and cleanliness of their vehicles, as well as ensuring they received necessary maintenance. The care heaped on these vehicles is evident in the fact the White buses bought in the mid 1930s still operate, carrying tourists throughout the parks. Herman Rusch photo, courtesy Herman Rusch.

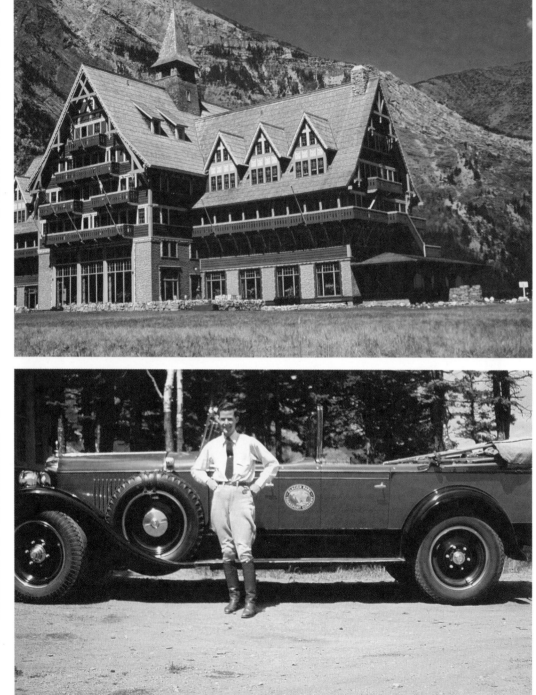

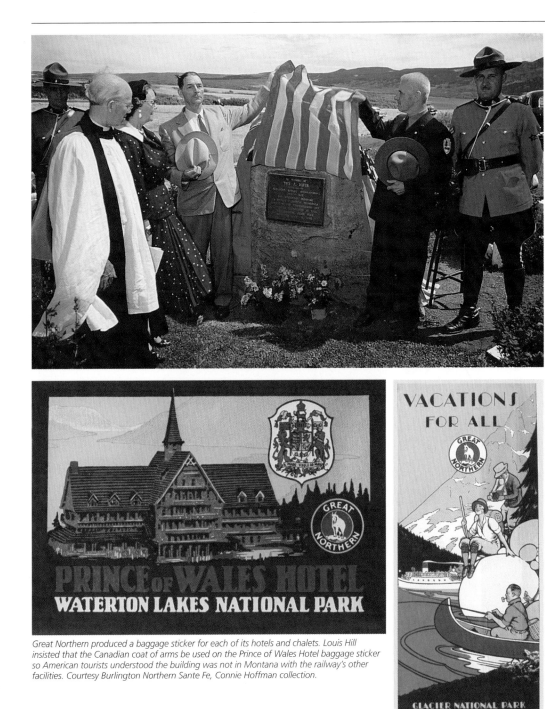

Waterton superintendent J. H. Atkinson, left, and Glacier superintendent J. W. Emmert raise the flags of the United States and Canada to unveil a plaque outside the Prince of Wales Hotel honouring the late Tom J. Davis, a president of Rotary International. Davis was active in the establishment of Waterton-Glacier International Peace Park, the first of its kind in the world. Also participating in the mid-1950s ceremony are Canon Samuel Middleton, chairman of the peace park committee and one of the originators of the concept, and Mrs. Tom Davis. Kathleen Revis photo, copyright National Geographic Society.

Great Northern produced a baggage sticker for each of its hotels and chalets. Louis Hill insisted that the Canadian coat of arms be used on the Prince of Wales Hotel baggage sticker so American tourists understood the building was not in Montana with the railway's other facilities. Courtesy Burlington Northern Sante Fe, Connie Hoffman collection.

With the opening of the Prince of Wales Hotel, Great Northern began marketing Glacier and Waterton parks as one big scenic unit, evident in this Vacations for All pamphlet. Despite their best efforts, Rotarians were unable to cajole the railway into referring to Waterton and Glacier as an international peace park. Railway officials considered the name too long and awkward. Courtesy Burlington Northern Santa Fe, author's collection.

This portrait of Plume was one of many Blackfoot confederacy natives painted by German-born artist Winold Reiss for Great Northern. The portrait was one of a series produced as prints. Plume is described on the print as "a modern representative of the Kainahs —proud owner of many lodges, horses, and a large herd of cattle." Print of Winold Reiss portrait, courtesy Burlington Northern Santa Fe, author's collection.

Long Time Pipe Woman was the wife of renowned Blood Chief Shot-Both-Sides. Winold Reiss's portrait of Shot-Both-Sides appeared in a Great Northern calendar issued in 1928. The calendar was so popular Louis Hill commissioned Reiss to produce more portraits of members of the Blackfoot confederacy, which appeared in railway calendars and other promotional literature for the next 30 years. Print of Winold Reiss portrait, courtesy Burlington Northern Santa Fe, author's collection.

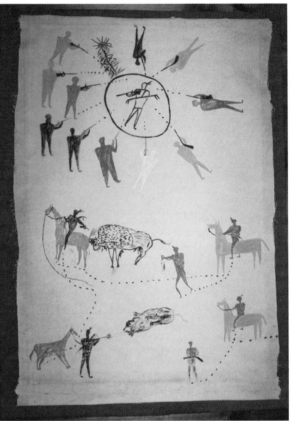

Many Mules was one of the Blood artists who created pictographs that were displayed in the lobby of the Prince of Wales Hotel. Many Mules, an elder in the Blood tribe, was 82-years old at the time this portrait was painted and rode 32 miles on horseback to have it done. Print of Winold Reiss portrait, courtesy Burlington Northern Santa Fe, author's collection.

This pictograph, or picture writing canvas, was painted by Many Mules for display at the Prince of Wales Hotel. Each artist produced his own pigments for the pictograph. Ray Djuff photo, author's collection.

A portrait of each artist and a framed text, shown here, describing the artist and the meaning of his pictographs were hung in the lobby of the Prince of Wales Hotel. Ray Djuff photo, author's collection.

The lobby of the Prince of Wales Hotel has been redecorated several times over the years, usually in an attempt to "modernize" it. This popular postcard image shows how the lobby looked through much of the 1960s to 1980s. Mike Roberts photo, copyright Glacier Park, Inc.

The teak and walnut used to construct the wheel house of the Motor Vessel International gleam in this rare colour photograph showing the vessel prior to a major overhaul in 1953. During refitting, the canopy was removed, diesel engines were installed and a smokestack was added. Walt Dyke photo, courtesy Burlington Northern Santa Fe, author's collection.

This advertisement promoting travel to the Pacific northwest and Glacier National Park on Great Northern's Empire Builder and Western Star trains appeared in the April 1953 edition of National Geographic. The railway was proud of its modern streamliners and featured them prominently in advertising its Chicago-Seattle route. Courtesy Burlington Northern Santa Fe, author's collection.

For a great vacation

Pacific Northwest
by way of Glacier National Park

Vacation *all the way*...Go Streamlined
EMPIRE BUILDER or *WESTERN STAR*

New vistas await you in the majestic Pacific Northwest! ... the Cascades and the Columbia ... Puget Sound and Mt. Rainier. On your way, stop in Glacier Park, in the Montana Rockies. See it all on one great trip. Go carefree, be carfree. Go Great-Northern!

Write P. G. Holmes, Great Northern Ry., Dept. N-43, St. Paul 1, Minn., for details on a Western "Vacation-of-a-Lifetime."

● Glacier Park served only by Western Star, June 15 thru September 10.

SEE AMERICA FIRST

GREAT NORTHERN PASSENGER AND FREIGHT OFFICES IN PRINCIPAL CITIES OF UNITED STATES AND CANADA

7 The First Season

When the doors to the Prince of Wales Hotel were opened to the public for the first time, at noon on Monday, July 25, 1927, it heralded the beginning of a new era in tourism for Waterton Lakes National Park. The hotel brought a level of luxury and service to the park that was previously unknown. Uniformed staff, hot and cold running water and a bathtub in each room, in-room telephones, and Waterton's only electric elevator were just some of the features that set it apart. The hotel also marked the park's entry onto the national scene as a major tourist destination and the beginning of international prominence for Waterton, linked as the Prince of Wales Hotel was to American-based Great Northern Railway. And the hotel was a unique design unparalleled anywhere in the Canadian Rockies, making the building as much an attraction as the astounding scenery it was meant to show off.

There was no official ceremony to mark the opening of the hotel. Instead, Great Northern opted for a low-key dinner for invited guests, including a who's who list from southern Alberta, Waterton and Glacier.[1] A few lucky tourists who arrived shortly after noon on the first red buses from Glacier Park were included in the celebration.[2] They got to partake in a lavish eight-course meal, which included hors d'oeuvres, soup, salad, fish, entrees and desserts, and, later, an impromptu dance amid upturned carpets in the east-wing lounge.

Conspicuous by his absence was Louis Hill. Aside from the fact his presence would have overshadowed the true heroes of the day—Oland and Scott—Hill had toured the hotel little more than a month

The first Glacier Park Transport Company tour car and buses carrying owner Howard Hays Sr., other dignitaries and tourists from Glacier Park arrived at the hotel shortly after noon on opening day, July 25, 1927. T. J. Hileman photo, Great Northern Railway publicity and advertising department, Minnesota Historical Society.

This decorative bracket support for a third floor balcony is a composite of several pieces of wood. Contrasting paint colours were used to highlight these architectural details. Ray Djuff photo, author's collection.

before.[3] He learned of the opening in a telegram sent by William Kenney, who stood in for him. "Prince of Wales Hotel opened for business yesterday 25th," Kenney wrote. "172 for dinner. 80 house count. Everything went fine."[4]

Throughout the day and during the dinner, the attention of guests was equally divided between ogling the new surroundings and heaping praise on its builders, Doug Oland and Jim Scott. The pair deserved the attention. On what had been a barren, wind-blown hill just a year before was now an impressive, modern edifice. They had built a 90-room, $370,000 hotel in a wilderness area and overcome incredible obstacles to do so. At 212 feet (63.6 m) wide and 122 feet (36.6 m) tall, it was the biggest man-made object in the park. The task had taken 12 months and used 100 railway carloads of lumber.[5]

The two-story windows at the south of the lobby offer an unparalleled view of spectacular Upper Waterton Lake. Plush chairs and sofas, selected by Louis Hill at the Eaton's store in Winnipeg, were an invitation to guests to pause to enjoy the scenery. Commenting on the flagstone terrace, one tourist said, 'Do you get your stone masons drunk before starting on stone work?' T. J. Hileman photo, courtesy of the National Archives of Canada.

The staircase allowed guests to descend either into the lobby, far side, or the east wing lounge. T. J. Hileman photo, J. J. Hill Library, LH 2825.

The finished building stood as a monument to Oland and Scott's determination and craftsmanship. Oddly, despite the involvement of both an architect and an engineer in this hotel, none of the drawn plans, either original or revised, indicate specifications, a practice that is now unheard of given today's strict engineering standards. Oland and Scott were to use their common sense, their know-how and their experience to get the job done.[6] And while it was a major job, no heavy machinery had been used to excavate the foundation and no crane had been used to erect any of the timbers. Each of the 28 Douglas fir pillars in the lobby and the 14-by 20-inch (35.5 by 50.8 cm) trusses that lock into them were moved into place by block and tackle and the sheer force of human muscles. Oland was particularly pleased with how the post and beam construction in the lobby had turned out.

The dining room featured fine cuisine in an elegant atmosphere. The table settings included Blue Willow china, silverware featuring the Glacier Park Hotel Company monogram and linen napkins. For those without a view out the windows, on the wall were murals of scenes of Glacier and Waterton parks painted by Chicago artist John Fery. T. J. Hileman photo, copyright Glacier Natural History Association.

"There are no nails in it anywhere," said Mary O'Brien, Oland's daughter. Huge mortise and tenons were cut and each of the pieces was fitted into the other, secured with pegs and then and set off with iron braces. "Dad was very proud of that." [7]

Everywhere visitors looked, the builders' attention to detail could be seen, for example, in the grain of the wood on the posts and the balustrades in the lobby. The grain was raised and off-set by what appeared to be a two-tone stain. The effect had been achieved by taking a blowtorch and lightly scorching the wood, then removing the charred portions with a wire brush. The wood was then polished with wax to bring out the colour. It was a small but representative example of the thought that had gone into the design and the work necessary to execute it.

Long before guests found time to admire the details, they couldn't help but be overcome by how the lobby capitalized on Waterton's scenery. The lobby was—as it still is today—dominated by three 12 foot-wide (3.6 m) and 18 foot-high (5.4 m) windows along its south wall, providing a commanding view of Upper Waterton Lake, 150 feet (45 m) below, and the mountains of green and red argillite and white and grey quartzite that rise 4,000 to 6,000 feet (1,200 to 1,800 m) around it. For many local people, it was possibly the first time they'd been able to take in the view from this spot in comfort—no wind to buffet them or, in extreme cases, knock them over.

For all the praise Oland and Scott received about their handiwork, the job was by no means done. "There still remains considerable construction work to be completed," Anderegg reported to St. Paul the week after opening. One hundred and forty men were working on the hotel and related facilities, he said.[8] A fortnight later, there were still 50 workers on site, cleaning the grounds, finishing the powerhouse, adding a soda fountain room—a last-minute plan change—and doing detail work.[9] As a result of ongoing construction, the hotel operated the first two weeks without laundry facilities, forcing the hotel to send all of its sheets, towels and linen to Lethbridge to be cleaned.[10]

As Oland's crew and the subcontractors finished the last details of the hotel project, inside the building staff hustled about in their stiff, new uniforms, getting accustomed to the togs while learning new jobs and acting as if they were old hands at their work. It was the presence of these uniformed staff and their numbers, as much as anything, that set the Prince of Wales Hotel apart from it counterparts in town. The employees promised services that no other hotel in the park could offer. The nearest comparable hotel was the Palliser in Calgary, which had been opened 13 years earlier by the Canadian Pacific Railway.

From the moment guests arrived, they were in the presence of 75 staff wearing uniforms: A page boy in red suit and cap, bellmen in brown jackets with contrasting piping, and waitresses in Swiss-style costumes. The uniforms continued behind the scenes, with chambermaids in crisp, white smocks and kitchen staff outfitted with aprons and hats or caps.

Planning trips to see other hotels in the chain was as easy as checking with the transportation agent, who could provide the schedule and fares of Glacier Park Transport Company's buses to any destination in Glacier, as well as the arrival and departure times of Great Northern trains and Brewster bus line connections to Calgary and Banff.

Besides the regular staff, the hotel also featured the contract services of a beautician and barber, both of whom had offices in the basement of the east wing. Next to them was the dispensary run by a resident nurse, Miss MacDougall, who could call on Dr. J. K. Mulloy of Cardston if the situation required.[11] And for the latest news, a souvenir of the park or postcard to send home, there was a well-stocked gift shop and newsstand along the northeast wall of the lobby run by James Ridler.

Adding to the sense of cosmopolitan opulence was the variety of activities that guests could enjoy while staying at the hotel. Not far from the hotel the Morris brothers had a string of saddle horses tethered, ready to offer individual rentals or guided group trail rides. If hiking was more appealing, it was a short stroll to a variety of trailheads. On the shore of Steamboat Bay, there were several gasoline excursion launches operating from C. A. Carnell's dock, providing lake tours and fishing trips. Just north of the hotel at Linnet Lake was a sandy beach and bathhouse for swimmers. For those with more refined tastes, there was the steam-

It's six days since the Prince of Wales Hotel opened and workers were still on site completing details to the main building and related facilities. The piles of lumber at the lower right were in preparation for construction later that summer of a proposed bedroom annex to the east of the hotel. George Anderegg photo, Great Northern Railway company records, Minnesota Historical Society.

Manager Capt. R. Stanley Harrison doted all summer on Margaret, the five year-old daughter of hotel chef Len Moores. Courtesy Irene LaFlamme, author's collection.

Len Moores, seated, and fellow hotel employees. Courtesy Irene LaFlamme, author's collection.

heated, indoor Crystal Pool in town.[12] Elsewhere in town were tennis courts, curio shops, three restaurants and a dance hall that featured live music by an eight-piece band every Saturday night.[13] A short drive from the hotel was a nine-hole public golf course with a resident pro, E. H. Wagstaff.[14]

All this luxury came at a price: $8-12 per person per day—up to four times the rate charged for accommodation elsewhere in the park.

Keeping watch over the entire operation at the Prince of Wales Hotel was the manager, Capt. R. Stanley Harrison. A short, stocky man, about 50 years old, he looked and played the part of the proper English gentleman—a stern but fatherly figure for the staff.[15] Harrison came with an impressive set of credentials. He had worked his way up the ladder in the hotel industry. At one point he had owned his own hotel in Boston, later moving to Canada where he worked in managerial positions at the Windsor Hotel in Montreal and the Marlborough Hotel in Winnipeg, Man. The fact that he could call on the mayor of St. Paul, Minn., to write a character reference for him speaks highly of Harrison's contacts and renown. "(He) is a thoroughly experienced hotel man, both back and front of the house, and I really believe just the type of man that would be most suitable for your hotel," Mayor R. H. Webb said in his letter of recommendation to Great Northern.[16] It was Harrison, as much as anyone, who set the tone for the hotel and ensured the service was as good as any in its class.

Harrison proved himself even before the hotel opened its doors. Early in July, Kenney and a party had arrived to discuss last-minute details with Oland and to get an update on construction progress. Harrison was able to provide his unexpected guests with meals and fourth floor rooms for an overnight stay.[17] A few days later, Kenney's wife, son Charles and some friends arrived for a sneak peek at the hotel. Again, Harrison was able to accommodate them. Nicholas Longworth, Theodore Roosevelt's son-in-law, and Henry Spencer of the Fruit Growers' Express Company, a major Great Northern client, followed them.[18]

Kenney was impressed with how Harrison had handled these situations, given he'd had little time to organize the staff and the trying circumstances under which they were operating—with carpenters, plumbers and electricians still scurrying around the building, only some of the furniture, bedding and tableware available, and the kitchen not fully operational. "I think Harrison is a very good man in charge of the hotel, and he apparently has some good help," Kenney wrote Hill.[19]

Harrison went to great lengths to ensure he got the best people he could for senior posts at the hotel. Harrison scoured Western Canada for suitable candidates. Finding a chef was particularly problematic and showed just how much Harrison was willing to dicker to ensure he got whom he wanted.

Len Moores was living in Winnipeg, Manitoba, when he read a newspaper advertisement for a chef at the hotel. Moores was both qualified and experienced, and Harrison offered him the job, but Moores initially turned it down. The wage was not up to standard, said Moores' daughter, Irene LaFlamme. Harrison, however, would not budge on the salary. A deal was finally reached when Harrison agreed to give Moores' wife a token job in the housekeeping department and provide her with free room and board.[20]

During the negotiations, Moores had failed to mention he had two daughters, Irene and Margaret. Given the compromise that had been struck, LaFlamme said her father decided he couldn't just show up with two more in the party. So Irene was shipped off to spend the summer with grandparents in Saskatchewan while Margaret would accompany her parents to Waterton. As luck would have it, Harrison took a shine to five year-old Margaret and doted on her throughout the summer.[21]

The dining room hostess and waitresses kick up their heels during a bit of fun between meal shifts. Courtesy Ann Harrison, author's collection.

The girls who worked in the hotel laundry were referred to by other staff as 'bubble queens.' The hotel operated without a laundry for several weeks, until all the water and steam lines and electrical fittings could be completed. Courtesy Ann Harrison, author's collection.

Try as he might, Harrison was unable to fill some positions. Repeated newspaper advertisements failed to turn up anyone to run the hotel laundry.[22] With only days remaining until the hotel's opening and the position still vacant, Harrison turned to Harold Templeton, manager of the Lethbridge Steam Laundry, for help. Harrison persuaded Templeton to train the Prince of Wales Hotel's staff and return from time to time to check on the operation, which he did.[23]

Maids pose with empty beer bottles outside the hotel tavern. Delays in constructing the tavern meant it was not ready until two weeks after the hotel opened, causing some of the hotel's first American guests to miss having a drink of legal alcohol, as the U.S. was still in the throes of Prohibition. Courtesy Betty Baker, author's collection.

Harrison's attempts to run a picture-perfect operation were sometimes fouled by things beyond his control, none more so than the problem with the hotel's water system. The water reeked of creosote—a toxic, tar-like wood preservative used to coat wooden water pipes. Added trouble came from globs of the substance dislodging from the pipes and clogging taps in the hotel.[24] The smell and taste were initially so bad, hotel staff took buckets and drew water directly from the lake for use in the dining room and kitchen.[25]

When Hill learned of the problem, he became livid and demanded to know how creosote had gotten inside the pipes. Hogeland was ordered to investigate. The reason for the creosote problem, Hogeland learned, was because the manufacturer of the pipes had recommended they be coated on the inside as well as outside. Regrettably, there had been insufficient time between the installation of the pipes and opening of the hotel to thoroughly flush the pipes of "surplus oil," as the manufacturer recommended.[26] Fortunately, the odor and globs were out of the system by the next year, assuring guests fresh mountain water.

A familiar problem—bad roads—haunted Harrison, as it had Oland before him. Since the Cardston-Waterton road was being upgraded, traffic was rerouted through the Blood tribe reserve and Hill Spring. When it rained heavily, however, the detour turned out to be little better than the old route.[27] On a couple of occasions, food orders being trucked to the hotel from Lethbridge got stuck on the rain-soaked road. By the time the merchandise arrived it was spoiled, causing the chef headaches as he rushed to prepare alternate meal plans.[28]

Glacier Park Transport Company buses also had trouble traversing the detour when it was wet. On one occasion, a bus from Many Glacier Hotel "became mired in a mud hole this side of Hill Spring, and another bus going out from here to help it was also stuck for a while. Both buses finally were pulled out, however, and arrived safely at the Prince of Wales Hotel about midnight."[29] What had started out as a four-hour excursion ended up being an all-day nightmare for the passengers.

Liquid of another kind—beer—posed yet another set of challenges, this time for Harrison's bosses at Great Northern's headquarters. The whole point of building the Prince of Wales Hotel was to provide a way for Americans to skirt Prohibition in the United States. But because of a technicality in the law there was no bar when the hotel opened its doors on July 25. A beer parlour licence had been approved for the hotel, but the Alberta government wouldn't hand it over until a room was actually constructed.[30] This caught the railway off guard, since no one knew exactly where the bar would be located. The plan was to put it on the east side of the hotel, either in a bedroom annex or just off a corridor to a bedroom annex.[31] But the annex, which was to have been started in June, was held up by the delay in completing the hotel. To expedite the matter, Hill had the plan for the existing hotel revamped to include a beer parlour at the east end of the main floor. The blueprints were finished too late for the tavern to open the same day as the hotel. Customers had to wait until Monday, August 9, to belly up to the bar.[32]

In the absence of the beer parlour, head bellman Victor Harrison quickly found a niche for himself. Harrison, no relation to the manager, had a permit that allowed him to procure alcohol for hotel guests. He became popular with patrons and townsfolk alike by ensuring orders were filled when the hotel's supply truck went on its regular forays to Lethbridge.[33] Harrison's sideline continued even after the bar opened. Alberta law did not permit hard liquor or wine to be served in bars, only beer. Harrison was the only ready source for stronger stimulants.

Such minor faults as smelly tap water and muddy roads did nothing to deter tourists from visiting the Prince of Wales Hotel or Waterton Park. Once word of the hotel's opening spread, the park was overwhelmed with tourists, notable and otherwise. Among the more prominent to show up were liquor commissioner R. J. Dinning, R. B. Baxter, deputy minister for Alberta Government Telephones, Capt. J. T. Shaw, leader of the provincial Liberals, Congressman Fritz Lantane from Fort Worth, Tex., and noted poet Arthur Guiterman, who made the trek on foot from Many Glacier Hotel.[34] The flow of people set a park attendance record.[35] Traffic was heavy enough to warrant the full-time use of a motorcycle policeman.[36] He nailed half a dozen speeders in short order, levelling fines of $1 each for not keeping to the posted 15 mph limit in the townsite.[37]

Adding to the traffic were people sent to Waterton by Great Northern as part of its advertising and promotional campaigns. Both Winold Reiss and James Willard Schultz came to the park to follow up on work they'd been doing related to native people. Schultz was a renowned western writer who had gained fame for more than two dozen books he penned about his life with the Blackfeet prior to the turn of the century. Great Northern, which featured the Blackfeet in its advertising for Glacier, picked up on Schultz's writing and promoted titles like *My Life as an Indian* and *Blackfeet Tales of Glacier National Park* in conjunction with its advertising campaigns. Reiss was a painter who was so enthralled by Indian legends that he left his native Germany to come to America. Reiss's brother, Hans, who worked as a mountain guide in Glacier, introduced Winold to Hill, which resulted in a commission to paint Blackfeet people.[38] Hill liked what he saw and a deal was struck to have Reiss return.

Both Reiss and Schultz were in Waterton to focus attention on elders of the Blood tribe who had painted pictographs dis-

Head bellman Victor Harrison, second from left, was strict with his staff and demanded a percentage of all tips they earned. He also held a permit that allowed him to fill liquor orders whenever the hotel's transport truck went to Lethbridge, which made him popular with guests wanting stronger spirits than the beer served at the hotel tavern. Courtesy Betty Baker, author's collection.

American author James Willard Schultz was invited to Waterton to interview members of the Blood tribe for stories for a new book. Schultz, who married a Peigan woman in the 1880s, wrote dozens of novels about the life of the Blackfeet. He is seen here in Waterton with Bloods, from left, Bobtail Chief and his wife, Mrs. Weasel Tail, Many Mules and Weasel Tail. T. J. Hileman photo, courtesy Hugh Dempsey collection.

played on the lobby walls of the Prince of Wales Hotel. Schultz hoped to interview some of the Blood tribe elders and use their stories for a new book.[39] He readily persuaded Weasel Tail and Eagle Plume to set up a teepee camp with their families on the lakeshore below the Prince of Wales Hotel. Schultz paid regular visits to the camp during August 1927 to learn the native people's stories.[40] When Reiss arrived, he dropped by to meet Weasel Tail and Eagle Plume and arrange some of his first portrait sittings.[41]

Reiss and Schultz were not alone in their interest in the Blood tribe. Great Northern's publicity about native involvement in the Prince of Wales Hotel had aroused curiosity far and wide. Henry Balnick, a Dutch portrait painter living in Santa Fe, New Mexico, came to Waterton that summer to paint portraits of members of the Blood tribe.[42] Peggy Nichol, a young Ottawa artist, also visited the Blood reserve, to paint portraits for the Canadian Indian Affairs Department.[43] F. C. Campbell, superintendent of the Blackfeet Indian reservation in Montana, showed up for a stay at the Prince of Wales Hotel and to visit the Bloods, as did Dr. Duncan Campbell Scott, deputy superintendent for the Canadian Indian Affairs Department.[44] With all this activity, there was some suggestion Waterton might become an artist's colony. It was even rumoured Charlie Beil, a student of renowned western artist Charlie Russell, was looking for a suitable location for a studio.[45] He would eventually find it in Banff.

Since the opening date for the Prince of Wales Hotel had been delayed several times and finally occurred halfway through the summer tourist season, Great Northern was forced to cancel reservations and shuffle others. In the first 38 days after the hotel opened, Glacier Park Transport Company buses carried only 407 passengers north, less than 15 a day—far short of filling the building.[46] Great Northern's advertising and passenger traffic departments made use of the spare rooms by having their people tour the hotel to become familiar with Waterton and spread the word about it over the winter.[47] To prepare next year's brochures, photographer Tomer J. Hileman of Kalispell, Mont., was hired to take publicity stills of the hotel and the park and portraits of the Bloods who painted the pictographs.[48] W. R. Mills, the railroad's top publicist, arrived in the park with a motion picture crew.[49]

Surely the great disappointment of the summer for Great Northern officials had to be the failure of the Prince of Wales to visit his namesake hotel in Waterton. While Prince Edward and his brother Prince George spent most of the week of August 10-17 in Alberta, including four days at his E.P. Ranch, they did not find time to see Waterton. The scheduling for the princes appeared somewhat chaotic, and southern Albertans learned only days before their arrival that they'd be unable to visit Waterton.[50] On their departure, however, the princes made a 15-minute whistle stop in Lethbridge where they met their loyal subjects. Great Northern had made a gamble with the invitation to Prince Edward, one that would have paid off in spades had it succeeded. Unfortunately, it didn't.

On the walls behind the front desk and suspended from the lobby ceiling are examples of the pictographs painted by members of the nearby Blood tribe. Later, photographs of the artist would be placed with each pictograph on the lobby walls, along with a plaque translating the picture writing. T. J. Hileman photo, copyright Glacier Natural History Association.

This is a pictograph illustrated by Eagle Arrow. The Bloods who painted the pictographs obtained the colours from various natural sources, like vegetable colourings and minerals, mixing the pigments with grease. The colours were applied with a sharp or pointed stick about the size of a pencil. Author's collection.

Blood tribe members greet New York artist Winold Reiss and his son Tjark in Waterton. Some of the Reiss's portraits of these natives would be used in Great Northern's advertising promoting tourism to Waterton and Glacier parks. From the left are: Owns Different Horses, Riding Black Horses, Falling Over a Bank, unknown man and child, Tjark, Winold Reiss, unknown, Takes a Good Run (Mrs. Riding Black Horses), Shot-Both-Sides, head chief of the Bloods, unknown, Plume, Jack Low Horn and Gros Ventre Boy. T. J. Hileman photo, courtesy Hugh Dempsey collection.

Sixty-five year-old Mike Oka was one of the Blood elders who painted pictographs for the Prince of Wales Hotel. T. J. Hileman photo, author's collection.

As it was, Louis Hill had much to be pleased about when the first season ended with the closing of the hotel's doors on September 15. In seven weeks, it had racked up 2,616 guest days, and staff had served 7,558 meals.[51] But more than that, the Prince of Wales Hotel had been established as the premier attraction in Waterton and southern Alberta, acclaimed far and wide. The august *Wall Street Journal* deemed the hotel "striking and unique."[52] Proof of the hotel's attraction was in the statistics. Visitors had come in record numbers from the U.S. and Canada despite bad roads and periods of rain.[53] Great Northern had spent $371,465.50 to build the hotel and another $300,000 on the complementary facilities, including the water tower and related plumbing, temporary construction buildings, engineering costs and furnishings.[54] It now had a top-notch draw and a prosperous future apparently lay ahead.

8 Unfinished Business

When the doors of the Prince of Wales Hotel closed in September 1927, work on the hotel project was nowhere near completed. There were a number of matters that still needed attention before the season could be considered wrapped up.

Topping the list of items was progress on the *Motor Vessel International*.[1] From the time building an excursion boat to ply Upper Waterton Lake had been proposed, the *International* project had been fraught with complications. The original idea had been to have the 56-ton (51 tonnes), 250-passenger boat on the lake by June 15, in time for the anticipated opening of the Prince of Wales Hotel. Like the hotel, the *International* was not completed anywhere near the expected deadline.

The building of the boat had been arranged as a multi-stage process. First, Capt. Swanson fabricated major sections of the 73 foot-long (21.9 m) hull at his Kalispell shop. When these parts were completed, in the spring of 1927, they were transported by train to Cardston. The initial plan was to build the *International* on the Canadian side of the border and Great Northern's accounting department made

out the authority for expenditure to the railway's Canadian subsidiary, Canadian Rockies Hotel Company.[2] This was later changed when Great Northern officials realized the major cost-saving of having all the work done at Goat Haunt, on the U.S. end of Upper Waterton Lake.[3] It is estimated the railway was spared paying $7,000 for Canadian duty and taxes, which would have been on top of the proposed $24,000 cost for the vessel.[4]

To achieve the saving took a fair bit of organizing on the part of Great Northern,

Goathaunt Chalet, nestled in the trees, was a stop on the North Circle Tour, a five-day trek offered by the Park Saddle Horse Company that started and ended at Many Glacier Hotel. T. J. Hileman photo, Great Northern Railway publicity and advertising department, Minnesota Historical Society.

Capt. Bill Swanson and his construction crew pose for photographer Tomer Hileman in September 1927 prior to a test inspection of the Motor Vessel International at Goat Haunt, at the south end of Upper Waterton Lake.
T. J. Hileman photo, J. J. Hill Library, LH 2812.

including arranging the necessary permissions from the U.S. National Park Service to lease land at Goat Haunt, build a boathouse and then construct the *International* there.

The project hit several snags once the parts Swanson had fabricated in Kalispell arrived by rail in Cardston. Swanson had hoped to get an early start on building the shed at Goat Haunt in which the *International* would be fabri-

cated, but a late breakup of ice on Upper Waterton Lake held him up.[5] Getting supplies to Waterton also proved to be as difficult for the boat as it had been for the hotel. The contractor hired to move the boat pieces from Cardston to Waterton, where it would be taken by barge to Goat Haunt, was stalled for days at a time until the road became passable.[6]

Actual construction of the *International* was a slow and tedious process. The conditions at the worksite were primitive, even by the standards of the day. There was no electricity at Goat Haunt to power saws or planers; all cutting and fitting was done with painstaking accuracy by hand. Living conditions were equally rustic. The work crew spent the summer in relative isolation, except for visitors who sailed down the lake or arrived at Goathaunt Chalet, across the lake, on saddle horse trips from Many Glacier Hotel. The crew made occasional excursions to Waterton to take in dances at the pavilion.

Like the construction of the Prince of Wales Hotel, the *International* required a myriad of related details to be sorted out. Some, like the choice of wood and design, were left to the knowledgeable Capt. Swanson. Others, like matters that arose because the boat would be plying international waters, were not as simply handled. Since the *International* would cross the border daily, picking up passengers, such as trail riders at Goat Haunt, Waterton would become a port of entry and Canadian customs officials insisted an agent be stationed in the park to monitor arrivals.[7] Railway officials were taken aback that Ottawa expected Great Northern to cover the $110 a month salary to fill this seasonal position, as well as provide room and board for the customs agent and pay any overtime costs. Rather than start a fight with the federal government, Great Northern officials went along with the request to expedite matters, but planned to launch an appeal of the arrangement at a later time.[8] It was agreed that Glacier Park Transport Company buses could cross the border unobstructed at Carway and Bill Young, the appointed customs inspector at the hotel, would clear passengers when they arrived, as well as check boat passengers.[9]

A further challenge arose in August 1927 as workers were preparing a site below the hotel, on Steamboat Bay, for the *International*'s dock. The plan was to construct a 100 foot-long (30 m) wharf at the base of the hill, close to the hotel and the customs inspector. Lumber was gathered and digging began for piles. It didn't take long to discover the location would not work. The lake bottom was too deep and uneven for the piles to be easily driven. Instead, the dock was moved across the bay to the townsite, where an additional benefit of shelter from prevailing winds made moorage more practical.[10]

The *International* was completed in September—three months later than anticipated. A test inspection by U.S. officials found it shipshape.[11] "All of the inspecting officials were very decided in their praise of the workmanship, the stout construction of the boat, its design and arrangement and its power plant," Howard Noble reported. The inspection process was eased by the fact Canadian naval authorities agreed to a reciprocal arrangement with the U.S. so that once the vessel passed inspection there, it was deemed to meet all pertinent Canadian regulations.[12]

Another leftover matter from the first season was what to do with the portraits of Blood, Peigan and Blackfeet people Winold Reiss had been commissioned to

A Winold Reiss painting of Shot-Both-Sides, head chief of the Bloods, was featured on a 1928 calendar issued by Great Northern Railway. It was so popular, Great Northern would continue issuing calendars with Reiss's paintings for the next 30 years. Author's collection.

paint. Reiss had completed 51 portraits, including many of prominent Bloods like Weasel Tail and Chief Shot-Both-Sides, who had painted pictographs for the lobby walls of the Prince of Wales Hotel. While Hill was only committed to purchase a few paintings, he was so pleased with Reiss's work he bought all of them.[13] Hill and the

These sketches for cottages proposed for the Prince of Wales Hotel were based on the design of the Doll Houses of Carmel, Calif. J. J. Hill Library.

Roy Childs Jones was an architect at Toltz, King and Day in St. Paul, Minn., and also a professor at the school of architecture at the University of Minnesota. Courtesy Toltz, King, Duvall, Anderson and Associates.

railway's advertising department recognized their promotional value and part of the collection was sent on a tour of every major city in the United States. Besides reaping accolades, the travelling show prompted thousands who viewed it to make travel arrangements to visit Waterton and Glacier parks.[14]

The portraits also became the basis for a calendar Great Northern issued for 1928. Chief Shot-Both-Sides was one of the natives featured in that calendar. The paintings garnered such acclaim, Great Northern commissioned Reiss to return in 1928 to do more portraits. It was the beginning of a lasting business relationship. For more than 25 years, the railway distributed calendars featuring Reiss's paintings.[15]

Overshadowing all other issues was whether additional guestrooms would be built for the Prince of Wales Hotel. Improving the state of the Cardston-Waterton road was Great Northern's condition for expanding the hotel and that had been addressed. In the minds of many Waterton residents, the only questions to be answered were how large an addition would be constructed and when would work begin.

Great Northern officials had hinted all summer during interviews with newspaper reporters about what might be expected, but details were sketchy and var-

ied greatly. William Kenney indicated that at least two options were being contemplated. One was to build detached cottages around the hotel, similar to those at Jasper Park Lodge.[16] The second option, which Kenney considered most likely, was to construct a 90-room annex, which Oland and Scott would start soon after the hotel closed for the season.[17]

Budd had other ideas. "He gave the impression that he was more in favour of help's quarters being immediately erected than the 90-room hotel annex planned," the *Lethbridge Herald* reported.[18] Budd had good reason for his suggestion. During that first summer, staff had occupied most of the rooms on the fifth and sixth floors of the hotel as no residences had yet been built for them.[19] Capt. Harrison had purposely selected local people so he could minimize the number of employees needing on-site accommodation.[20]

Whatever Budd thought, he still had to contend with Hill who was keen on expansion. To that end, architect Roy Childs Jones was sent to Waterton to sketch possible expansion scenarios.[21] Jones was an associate with Toltz, King and Day, the firm Hill had asked to assist McMahon with design revisions during construction.[22] Leon Arnal, a fellow professor of architectural design at the University of Minnesota, accompanied Jones. They spent a week in the park, with Jones making pencil sketches of his ideas for expanding the hotel.[23] Jones created at least seven different scenarios that would have added anywhere from one to four annexes to the building.[24]

All Jones' sketches show additional buildings being constructed to the east of the hotel; only two have annexes to the west. In most cases, the annexes to the east are attached to the lobby section via a walk-

This retouched photograph of the Prince of Wales Hotel was probably sketched by architect Roy Childs Jones to show how his proposed plans for expansion would affect the profile of the hotel on the hill. All sketches on this page courtesy Toltz, King, Duvall, Anderson and Associates.

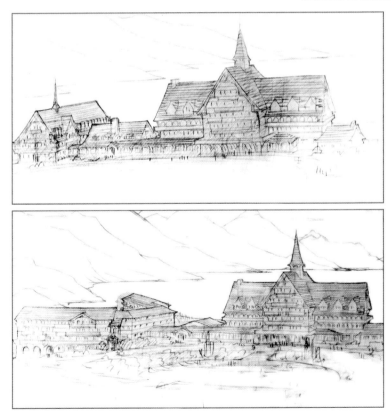

Thoughts of expansion

These three sketches show different treatments proposed by architect Roy Childs Jones for expansion of the Prince of Wales Hotel. A tavern or ballroom was to be located between the hotel and bedroom annexes.

Snow lays thick on the recreation hall, top, and three hotel staff dormitories built by Oland and Scott over the winter of 1927-28. George Anderegg photo, J. J. Hill Library, LH 2552.

The dorms were ready for the 1928 season, freeing rooms in the hotel that had been occupied by staff the previous summer. George Anderegg photo, J. J. Hill Library, LH 2564.

was in an expansive mood. He urged federal officials to rush completion of Akamina Highway to Cameron Lake, envisioning it as a vital link in what could eventually be a loop road between Waterton and Glacier parks.[27] It was a pipe dream that Hill was neither the first nor the last to propose.[28]

Upon his return to St. Paul, Hill began discussions with Budd and Noble about hotel expansion. As he had previously, Budd worried about spending any large sum on the hotel until completion of repairs to the Cardston-Waterton road were assured. "The way government work is carried out ... I do not believe that the road will be gravelled before August 1928, and probably not much before September. During all that time detours will have to be made, which become practically impassable every time it rains."[29] The practical thing to do, Budd said, would be to build staff dormitories. "This would in effect enlarge the hotel greatly by taking the help out of the rooms which they now occupy in the hotel proper," he wrote.[30]

In the meantime, Budd said, a thorough study and plans could be made for an annex and, if approved, work could start in 1928. "It would make it possible to have the material ordered and ready to move in the beginning early in September, 1928, thus taking advantage of the early fall for hauling and with the new road, the expense would be greatly reduced from what it would be to undertake to get material in this coming winter."[31] In the end, Budd's view prevailed. New construction at the hotel was limited to expanding the kitchen, adding a private dining room, to the south of the existing dining room, and building three staff dormitories and a recreation hall to the west of the hotel.[32]

way along the northeast wall of the wing (where the gift shop is presently located). Jones used a variety of treatments for the annex buildings. They range in style from those that mimic sections of Many Glacier Hotel, featuring three or four stories and a low-sloped roof, to designs that more closely reflected the roofline of the Prince of Wales Hotel. In the latter instances, Jones added gables and capped the annex roof with a tower. A bar figures prominently in many sketches; those that lack a tap room feature a large dance hall.[25]

Hill made a personal inspection of the hotel, his first since it was opened, just before Labour Day 1927. Also on hand to offer their perspective and opinions were Noble, Noffsinger and Howard Hays.[26] Hill

As Hill, Budd and other Great Northern officials argued the merits of expanding the Prince of Wales Hotel, Oland sat waiting in Waterton for a decision. "I got the plans for the kitchen and dining room but by October had received no plans for the dorms," Oland recalled. "I got very anxious to get started before winter hit me in the neck, so I decided to go to St. Paul and see what was holding up the plans."[33]

Oland's arrival coincided with a meeting of the railroad's directors. The builder "was invited to meet the whole bunch." He learned plans existed for the dormitories, but the cost estimate was more than the railroad was willing to pay. "Budd asked me if I could figure any way to cut the cost," Oland said. Furnished with a copy of the blueprints, he stayed up all night reworking them. When he met Budd the next morning, Oland had made changes that would save $30,000. Budd immediately replied: "Go home, Oland, and go to work." Oland did, and completed the dorms and recreation hall in early 1928, "just under my own estimate."[34]

While Oland was wrapping up work on the dorms and recreation hall, a Toronto company raised the prospect of Great Northern expanding its Waterton operations in an unexpected way. J. R. Mills of Stanley Thompson and Co. Ltd. wrote to Budd saying he had heard the golf course in Waterton was being turned over to Canadian Rockies Hotel Company. Mills, whose company had designed the links for the Banff Springs Hotel, offered to send an engineer to Waterton to make a preliminary report on its nine-hole golf course.[35] There had been rumours in Waterton that Great Northern had been eyeing the golf course, but they were just that—rumours. "Have you any thought of putting in a golf course up there?" Budd asked Hill.[36] The answer came back an emphatic No![37] Hill was still haunted by what had happened the previous summer when he tried to have a golf course constructed at Glacier Park Hotel. The work went over budget and deadline, with Hill eventually firing the contractor.[38]

Hill was not averse, though, to throwing a little money Canon Middleton's way. Middleton had been raising funds for some time to build an Anglican church in Waterton. Hill came through with a substantial donation—a way of thanking Middleton for his help overseeing the creation of the pictographs featured on the lobby walls of the Prince of Wales Hotel. When it came time to dedicate the tiny All Saints Anglican Church in Waterton in July 1928, Hill was an invited guest. As he was leaving the service, Hill turned to Middleton, pointed to the Prince of Wales Hotel and said: "There on the hill is the big show; here is the jewel."[39]

By the time the Prince of Wales Hotel opened for the summer of 1928, little remained to remind tourists that this had been the scene of a major construction project just the year before. Gone were the

Louis Hill.
J. J. Hill Library.

The dining room annex, to the west of the entrance, and extensions to the kitchen and staff cafeteria were the only modifications authorized by Great Northern for the Prince of Wales Hotel after its 1927 opening. Despite originally indicating the hotel would encompass as many as 300 rooms and plans being drawn for a bedroom annex, no further expansion of the hotel was ever approved.
T. J. Hileman photo, Great Northern Railway publicity and advertising department, Minnesota Historical Society.

Louis Hill made a substantial donation to Canon Samuel Middleton so he could construct All Saints Anglican Church in Waterton in 1928. The contribution to the church building fund was Hill's way of thanking Middleton for co-ordinating the pictographs painted by members of the Blood tribe for the Prince of Wales Hotel. Atterton's Studio, Glenbow Archives, Calgary, Canada, NC 7-656.

lumber storage shed and woodworking shop to the west of the hotel. Oland's office, the timekeeper's shack, the out buildings and all the other temporary structures had also been removed. Grass and wildflowers had grown over the slashes made by trenches dug into the hill for water pipes, and the road and parking lot were freshly gravelled. Only the house that Oland had built for himself at the workers' camp near Linnet Lake remained, the bunkhouses and cookhouse having been torn down.

At the dock in Waterton, several dozen people hailed the *International* on its maiden voyage. It arrived June 10, with flags flying, walnut woodwork polished and brass gleaming, ready to serve hotel patrons and others alike. Hill's vision for Waterton was complete.

Although Great Northern had no more immediate work for Oland, Hill was not yet finished with his services. In June 1928, Hill contacted Oland about building a home in Waterton. Exactly what possessed Hill to want a house in the park is not known. From Oland's account, Hill simply showed up, they had a short discussion about what Hill wanted and agreed on a site for the house, south of Cameron Falls on Evergreen Avenue, and the cost, $3,500.[40] Hill instructed Oland "to build the house just as quick as you can" and produced a roll of bills "the size of a grapefruit" from which he pulled five $100 bills as a down payment to seal the deal.[41]

Mary O'Brien, Oland's daughter, recalls the scene somewhat differently: "(Hill) had a large car with a black man who was chauffeur and carried rolls of money for him. Hill, I understand, disliked carrying money so his chauffeur paid the bills," O'Brien recalled. "Well, when it was decided Dad would do the job, (they finalized the deal) by handshake only. Louis Hill drew a plan on brown paper sack and (the) chauffeur pulled off many $100 bills as a down payment."[42] Oland acknowledged receipt of $500 cash and the deal in a letter dated June 2. The one-story house was to be completed by the end of the month.[43]

Hill must have had sober second thoughts about the size of the house, realizing it would be too small for his family, let alone any guests. At the bottom of his copy of the letter to Oland, Hill wrote a note indicating he wanted to add a second story, if it wasn't too late to make the change.[44] Two days later, Hill asked Noble to contact Oland about getting a set of rough sketches of the house so Hill's architect could modify them. Hill also wanted Noble to tell Oland: "I may wish to change the plans so as to add second story under four gable roof with balcony porch (under) each gable. … Hope he can delay the work till I can promptly send him revised plans for all of which, of course, I will pay extra."[45]

For Oland, the letter from Noble must have brought back vivid memories of his experiences constructing the Prince of

Wales Hotel. Yet again, Hill was tinkering with the design. Somewhat wiser, Oland submitted the necessary drawings, asking: "If it is unnecessary to change the foundation plans, I would like to receive a wire from you to this effect so that we can go ahead and place the foundation and cellar walls."[46] Oland wanted to ensure there'd be enough work to keep going without losing time or manpower.

Despite Oland's request for a quick reply, it wasn't until a week later, on June 15, he got word work could go ahead on the foundation.[47] The two-page, single-spaced letter also outlined in detail the second-story addition and other changes Hill desired. As with the Prince of Wales Hotel, the redesign Hill sought was extensive. "I have made a rough sketch of the second floor, which provides for four bedrooms, one sleeping porch, three balconies, and one bath and toilet room; also providing for three or for more wash basins in the bedrooms," Hill wrote. He had even thought to add a toilet and slop sink "for the help" in the basement. "This should make a fair size house; practically six bedrooms and two sleeping porches."[48]

With all these changes and a week of heavy rain, there was no way Oland could keep his deadline of August 1. He rescheduled completion for August 20 but in fact did not finish Carthew Lodge, as the house was named, until August 29.[49] The invoice for the work came to $9,600, including insurance and lot rental until the lease was issued in Hill's name.[50] "In as much as there was no agreement entered into prior to the execution of this work," Oland left the matter of the commission "to Mr. Hill's discretion." Just as with the Prince of Wales Hotel contract, Hill paid Oland a commission of 6.5 per cent.[51]

Carthew Lodge was built in 1928 in Waterton by Doug Oland as a private home for Louis Hill. A few hundred yards from Cameron Falls, it has a view of Waterton townsite and Vimy Peak. Curiously, neither Hill nor his family ever occupied the home. Courtesy of Fred Udell, author's collection.

Curiously, Hill would never occupy the house. And according to Oland, Hill never stepped inside the completed Carthew Lodge, named for one of the mountains in Waterton.[52] Oland said Hill's excuse was he didn't like the location, despite Hill having said he "was greatly pleased with what he saw" during a visit to the site during construction.[53] Incredibly, Hill told Oland the fact he didn't want to use Carthew Lodge didn't matter because he was going to have the contractor build a new cottage by the hotel.[54] He didn't. A more likely reason Hill never used Carthew Lodge is because he had three other rural homes: One in California, North Oaks Farm outside St. Paul, Minn., and a cabin on St. Mary Lake across from Sun Point in Glacier Park. It is doubtful Hill had much time to make frequent retreats to such a distant spot as Waterton when his other residences were more readily accessible. Hill was also a year from retiring as chairman of the board of Great Northern. Possibly he had second thoughts about where he wanted to spend his retirement years.

Not inconceivable is the idea that Hill had the house built in part to keep Oland

available in case Great Northern decided to go ahead with last-minute expansion of the Prince of Wales Hotel. After the disappointment of seeing only minor additions to the hotel over the winter of 1927-28, there would have been little to keep Oland on standby throughout the summer of 1928. Construction of Hill's house made a convenient bridge should the railway have changed its mind about building an annex.

Oland played out his option, waiting until the fall of 1928 to see what Great Northern would do. In October, Oland wired Albert Hogeland to ask if any more work was contemplated.[55] When Hogeland replied none was planned, Oland moved his family from the temporary house in Waterton to their home in Cardston.[56] Sixteen months after the Prince of Wales Hotel had opened its doors, Oland and Scott's work for Great Northern was finally done.

Profits and Losses

For three seasons, the Prince of Wales Hotel was the focus of unprecedented attention. Thousands of people from across Canada and the United States came to luxuriate in its many services as well as take in its unique design and remarkable setting. Visitation to Waterton Lakes National Park nearly doubled in 1928 from the previous season—26,002 versus 14,134 in 1927—and again in 1929, when it hit 48,592.[1] The hotel was the crown jewel in Great Northern's chain of Rocky Mountain hotels and chalets—a must-visit—and was featured prominently in the railway's advertising. The hotel's unique design, its location in a Canadian park and singular purpose for existence—to foil Prohibition laws in the United States—reflected the optimism and daring of the 1920s. It was a brief but shining moment. The following decade would be one of hardship and the Prince of Wales Hotel would face numerous threats to its existence, from humans and nature alike.

The bravado that caused the decade to be labelled the Roaring Twenties gave out with the stock market crash of October 1929. The economic collapse brought a gradual end to the Prince of Wales Hotel's time in the spotlight. Tourism dwindled as the Great Depression and coinciding drought took their toll on personal fortunes and disposable income. The number of tourists arriving by rail at Glacier Park sank from 10,182 in 1929 to 2,988 in 1932.[2] Fewer and fewer people could afford the luxury of a summer vacation to the mountains. An all-expense, overnight stopover

Guided tours by the Park Saddle Horse Company steadily lost business during the 1930s as the cost became prohibitive for many park visitors. T. J. Hileman photo, Great Northern Railway publicity and advertising department, Minnesota Historical Society.

A U.S. army captain and guest review the menu in a Great Northern dining car. The menu cover features a photograph of the lobby of the Prince of Wales Hotel. The china is the railway's Glacier pattern, introduced on the newly equipped Oriental Limited in June 1924. A later, 1940 china pattern, Glory of the West, would feature scenes inspired by Glacier Park.

The lounge car of the Empire Builder provided a relaxing place to enjoy passing scenery and the company of fellow travellers. Frank Willming photo.

Arrivals at Glacier Park Station declined during the early 1930s as the Depression put the cost of taking a summer vacation in the Rockies beyond the means of many people. The numbers would pick up later in the decade, but not match or exceed the pre-Depression tallies. T. J. Hileman photo.

All photos Great Northern Railway publicity and advertising department, Minnesota Historical Society.

in Glacier National Park went for $16 US, exclusive of rail fare—the same as a month's rent for a modest apartment. A three-day stay was $42.50 while five- and seven-day sight-seeing excursions, which had been a staple prior to the Depression, were usually not listed as they were beyond the means of most travellers and seldom called for. The resulting drop-off in business was felt at every hotel and chalet Great Northern owned in Glacier and, in turn, the privately owned Park Saddle Horse Company, Glacier Park Transport Company and Glacier Park Boat Company.

The Prince of Wales Hotel was shielded for a while from the drop in rail traffic to Glacier. While Great Northern passengers on sight-seeing visits made up a portion of its clientele, the hotel always relied less on rail passengers than the other lodges in the chain, attracting guests from nearby large cities in southern Alberta, like Lethbridge and Calgary. Tourism to Waterton dropped only slightly in 1930, decreasing 7.8 per cent to 44,827 visitors, and fell even less in 1931.[3]

As the Depression deepened, thousands of people throughout Alberta found themselves unemployed, some homeless. Farmers were hit by the double whammy of low wheat prices and varying degrees of "dust bowl" conditions. In 1932 visitation to Waterton fell to 35,334, down nearly 20 per cent from the previous year. It hit its lowest ebb the following year, with only 32,844 people visiting the park.[4] "The travel in that region is getting less and we are naturally suffering considerably at our Prince of Wales Hotel as a result," lamented William Kenney, who had succeeded Ralph Budd as president of Great Northern in 1931.[5]

As economic despair in Alberta was headed for rock bottom, the Prince of Wales

Hotel was the site for an inspiring idea—one that would have lasting and historic significance. It began July 4, 1931, with a goodwill meeting of 100 representatives of Rotary clubs from Alberta, Saskatchewan and Montana. During the gathering, Canon Middleton and Harry Mitchell of Great Falls, Mont., sponsored an unprecedented resolution. They proposed the Rotary clubs petition their respective national governments to join Waterton and Glacier as an international peace park. Fellow Rotarians heartily approved the resolution, which passed unanimously. Lobbying of the governments soon began in earnest.[6]

In later years, Middleton would give credit to Kootenai Brown for inspiring the original idea of linking, or "internationalizing," the two parks.[7] An avid outdoorsman, Brown realized the border means nothing to the wildlife that populate the area and that animals treat the contiguous regions as a continuous entity. "It might be well to have a preserve and breeding ground in conjunction with the United States Glacier Park," Brown wrote in an annual report to Ottawa.[8] Middleton took the idea and expanded it from linking just natural resources to fostering cultural ties. Great Northern had played a role in developing that sort of thinking. With construction of the Prince of Wales Hotel, the railway began including Waterton in its promotion of Glacier as "one great scenic unit." The peace element of the proposal was a reflection of the lasting horror of the Great War, which had ended only 13 years before. Situated as the parks are, across from each other on the longest, undefended border in the world, there was much the rest of the world might admire in the peaceful relations between Canada and the United States. It was apropos the Prince of Wales Hotel should be the setting for

Upon buying an all-expenses paid Great Northern vacation, visitors would be issued a ticket book from the Glacier Park Hotel Company with coupons for bus trips, boat cruises, hotel rooms and meals.

Two thousand people gathered at Glacier Park Hotel on June 18, 1932, for the dedication ceremony that created Waterton-Glacier International Peace Park, the world's first peace park. Courtesy of Glacier National Park.

making the peace park resolution, overlooking, as it does, Upper Waterton Lake, which spans both sides of the border.

In Canada the bill to create the peace park was sponsored by Alberta MP Brig.-Gen. J. S. Stewart while its backer in the United States Congress was Scott Leavitt of Montana. "The main purpose of this bill," said Leavitt, "grows out of the fact that Glacier National Park in Montana and Waterton Lakes National Park in Canada join to form one great scenic area. They are really one great park, and it is perhaps the supreme place along the border that can be dedicated to commemorate the long existing friendship and spirit of good will between the two nations."[9]

Following passage of similar bills in both Canada and the United States, 2,000 Rotarians and guests gathered June 18, 1932, at Glacier Park Hotel to dedicate Waterton-Glacier International Peace Park, the first such park in the world. The program for the meeting included messages from U.S. President Herbert Hoover and Canadian Prime Minister R. B. Bennett. "It is my earnest hope," wrote Bennett, "that this great international peace park ... may forever remain a permanent memorial of all that neighbourly relations should be between adjoining nations." During the service, a bronze tablet "permanently commemorating the relationship of peace and good-will" between Canada and America was unveiled and dedicated by Middleton. Plans were made for a similar ceremony and cairn the following summer at the Prince of Wales Hotel, but it would not happen.

Dwindling tourism to Waterton was taking its toll on the balance sheet of the hotel. Business at the Prince of Wales Hotel had gone badly during the summer of 1932, with the railway taking "a large loss."[10] Over the following winter, the discussion in St. Paul was whether the hotel should be opened for the 1933 season. Working against the hotel was the long and costly route to bus American tourists from Glacier. It was 105 miles (169 km) from Glacier Park Hotel to the Prince of Wales Hotel—a four-hour drive over gravel roads. A round-trip ticket cost about $28 US and few tourists were willing to pay the price or make the long trip. Most other round trips in Glacier Park went for under $8; one of the most expensive being the $15 fare to travel the 106 miles (171 km) from Glacier Park Hotel to Many Glacier Hotel and back. "A shorter route to Waterton is necessary and the Kennedy Creek cutoff is seemingly our best plan," A. J. Binder, general manager of the Glacier Park Hotel Company, wrote Kenney.[11]

The Kennedy Creek cutoff—a direct route from where the Blackfeet Highway crosses Kennedy Creek just north of Babb to Waterton—was not a new idea. Even before the Prince of Wales Hotel was opened, Great Northern officials had discussed such a possibility as a way to avoid the long drive through Cardston and the then terrible condition of the Cardston-Waterton road.[12] The route would cut by more than one-third the 76-mile (122 km) trip from Many Glacier Hotel to the Prince of Wales Hotel. It would also make for a more scenic trip, with the road closer to the mountains. This was no small matter. Howard Hays, whose company operated the buses that carried the tourists, noted the "national park feeling" was lost during the drive onto the Prairie and through Cardston. "As a result, only about 10 per cent of (Great Northern) train passengers make the long trip to Waterton," he said, adding not all of those people enjoy the ride.[13]

Great Northern and Glacier Park Transport Company officials were convinced the Kennedy Creek cutoff was the only way to go and during 1931 lobbied intensely on both sides of the border to get funding for the road project. The first success came in August 1932 when the Canadian government gave the go-ahead for work to begin immediately on its portion of the road as a Depression relief measure.[14] Any elation was tempered by the fact Great Northern officials had about decided not to open the Prince of Wales Hotel the following year. That concerned Hays, who wondered what effect announcing closure of the hotel would have on the approval of funding for the project. He was also worried about "dampening the enthusiasm" of the Montana highways commissioner to start roadwork on the American side of the border.[15] Kenney knew keeping the hotel open would only increase "our already large loss," but he didn't want to compromise the highway project either.[16] Before decid-

A decline in visitation to Waterton during the Depression caused the Prince of Wales Hotel to be boarded up for three summers, 1933-35. Courtesy Jack Oland, author's collection.

A wrangler serves hot coffee during a lunch break for dudes on a saddle horse tour near Hanging Glacier. T. J. Hileman photo, Great Northern Railway publicity and advertising department, Minnesota Historical Society.

ing what to do, Great Northern contacted the superintendent of Glacier National Park for his opinion. E. T. Scoyen said closing the Prince of Wales Hotel would not affect the status of funding for the Kennedy Creek cutoff on the U.S. side. And, he added, Canadian officials would be "shortening their sails" when it came to spending, which would make a convenient excuse for closure.[17] With that assurance, Kenney decided not to open the Prince of Wales Hotel for the 1933 season.[18]

The announcement was a blow to the Rotarians who had hoped to repeat their peace park ceremony at the hotel that summer. Undeterred, they held their meeting at another hotel in Waterton, but decided to forego renewing their peace park vows until the Prince of Wales Hotel reopened.[19] The Rotarians would have to wait three summers, until 1936.

While the Kennedy Creek cutoff road was under construction on both sides of

the border, the Prince of Wales Hotel remained shuttered and closed to guests. Even Louis Hill did not seem interested in visiting the hotel or his cottage in the park, although he had more time on his hands since stepping down as chairman of the board of Great Northern in 1929. In his absence, Fred and Grace Udell and their family permanently occupied Hill's Waterton cottage, Carthew Lodge. The Udells were asked to reside in the house after RCMP had found two vagrants in the empty premises.[20] Rather than leave the property vacant, it was agreed a lodger would deter further incidents.[21] Fred (Slim) Udell had helped to build the Prince of Wales Hotel and after construction was hired as head of security. The Udells would live in the lodge year-round for nearly two decades.

Not all Great Northern's facilities in Waterton were forced to close because of the Depression. The *Motor Vessel International* remained in operation and, ironically, experienced some of its best years ever.

To keep the *International* running during the Depression took some adapting. When the Prince of Wales Hotel closed its doors, Ab Cahoon, the customs inspector, found himself without an office from which to work. Fortunately, he and his wife operated a grocery store in Waterton and he simply set up shop there, splitting his day between tending the store and keeping track of customers taking the three daily trips up and down the lake. To spare Cahoon from having to change into his dark blue customs uniform, leave his post at the store and walk to the dock when there was no need of his services, he and the captain of the *International* devised a system of signals. "If the captain picked up someone at Goat Haunt,

five to seven minutes before docking in Waterton, he'd give three long whistles," said Cam McKay, a cohort of Cahoon's and former customs inspector. "One clear whistle meant 'Nobody's here; you don't have to come down.'"[22]

Finding customers in Depression-plagued southern Alberta willing to pay $1.50 for a round-trip ride on the *International* was no easy feat. In three short summers ridership had fallen to nearly half—from 13,700 in 1929 to 7,525 in 1931.[23] Capt. Peter Primrose came up with a brilliant idea to counteract sliding sales when he hired Mart Kenney's seven-piece dance band to perform for special cruises. Mart Kenney and His Western Gentlemen had been based in Vancouver but came east in 1932 in search of bookings. They ended up spending the entire summer performing on weekends at Dave and Pat MacLean's dance pavilion in Waterton.[24] To augment the money the band was paid, Kenney struck a deal to perform on the

International Sunday evenings at what became known as "midnight frolics."[25]

The idea behind the midnight frolics was to skirt Alberta's strict "blue laws," which prohibited dancing and drinking on Sundays. The proximity of the U.S.-Canada border provided an easy out. Late

Tom Westgard was second in command of the International and would later pilot the vessel, after Capt. Primrose retired.
Courtesy Ann Harrison, author's collection.

On occasion, the customs inspector and one of Waterton's RCMP officers would enjoy a trip on the International. The group at the stern of the International consists of Prince of Wales Hotel employees.
Courtesy Ann Harrison, author's collection.

Capt. Peter Primrose and his wife operated the Motor Vessel International during the 1930s, even when the Prince of Wales Hotel was closed. It was Primrose who came up with the idea for the popular midnight frolics.
Courtesy Ann Harrison, author's collection.

Mart Kenney, leader of the seven-piece band Mart Kenney and his Western Gentlemen. Author's collection.

Sunday evenings during July and August, the band and partygoers would board the *International* and head to Goat Haunt, the band playing tunes on the way. At Goat Haunt, the passengers and band crowded into the rustic chalet, where the dance would begin. The dancing parties sometimes became such enthusiastic affairs that when the *International* docked around midnight upon its return to Waterton, the party would still be going strong. "We'd disembark and, with the whole band playing, we'd lead the revellers up Main Street like the Pied Piper of Hamelin, and directly into the (dance) hall," Mart Kenney recalled in his memoirs.[26] The midnight frolics were an instant hit and anticipated eagerly each season by park residents and visitors. They would last but three summers, until 1934, after which bigger opportunities beckoned for Mart Kenney and his band.[27] For Great Northern, the excursions proved exceptionally profitable. In 1932 alone, almost a quarter of all of the revenue the *International* earned came from the midnight frolics.[28]

Adding to the appeal of the outings was a general flouting of liquor laws on both sides of the border. Although Alberta law forced bars to close on Sundays and Prohibition in the U.S. remained in effect until December 1933, passengers ignored these rules and would often pack along alcoholic spirits to keep the mood going. Great Northern helped stoke the atmosphere by ensuring there was an adequate supply of beer at Goathaunt Chalet. Once when it appeared the beer shipment might be delayed, Mrs. Primrose, wife of the captain of the *International*, dashed off a note to inquire about the holdup. "Please hurry the beer to Goathaunt. Hope it will be here by Sunday as there are lots (of people) hoping to go down for it," she wrote.[29] For their part, the National Park Service rangers at Goat Haunt turned a blind eye to what was going on. Isolated as they were, they no doubt appreciated the weekly entertainment—and liquid refreshments.

There was more than a bit of irony in these midnight frolics. The *International* had been built in part to haul thirsty

Goathaunt Chalet in Montana was a respite from Alberta's 'blue laws,' which prohibited drinking and dancing on Sundays. When the Sunday midnight frolics were instituted in the 1930s, southern Albertans flocked to Waterton to get tickets for the cruises to Goat Haunt, where they could dance to Mart Kenney's orchestra and flout Alberta liquor laws. Author's collection.

Americans tourists in Prohibition-bound Montana from Goat Haunt to Waterton, where they could drink legally in Alberta. With the closure of the Prince of Wales Hotel because of the Depression, the vessel was now taking thirsty Canadians to the U.S. The situation took a further twist in 1934, by which time the Volstead Act had been repealed in America. The whole point of Great Northern having a hotel in Canada was removed with the end of Prohibition in the U.S. and the railway now had a very expensive white elephant on its hands. Whether they liked it or not, Great Northern officials were not about to abandon the resort, although the temptation was strong given its original purpose was no longer there and the building was losing money.

The resolve of railway officials to keep the Prince of Wales Hotel was tested in August 1935 during one of the worst forest fires in Waterton's history. Lightning along Boundary Creek, some five miles (8 km) south of Waterton townsite, touched off the blaze. Fire crews quickly reached the fire and kept it in check, but on August 9 high winds took it over control lines and it spread north, across the border.[30] Scoyen, the superintendent of Glacier Park, drove to Waterton and chartered the *International* to ferry 50 American Civilian Conservation Corps men and their equipment to the fire lines, which were on the American side of the border.[31] Dense brown smoke obscured the sky as the blaze grew steadily.

Then on Saturday, August 10, driven by southwest winds, the fire took on new life. A spur spread from the main fire near Boundary Bay and swept over Mount Richards; a "raging inferno" racing north toward Waterton townsite. The unexpected direction of the blaze caught firefighters off guard, trapping 75 men for a short while. In another instance, men had to jump 100 feet (30 m) from rocks into Upper Waterton Lake to escape the fast-moving flames.[32] "Get word to the people of Waterton if they don't want to take their own chances to move out of town as the fire is out of control," the fire marshal said in a radio-telegram sent to Pop Harwood, Waterton's postmaster.[33]

Billowing reddish-black smoke from a fire along Boundary Creek filled Upper Waterton Valley in August 1935. When the blaze jumped fireguards and began racing northward along the west shore of the valley, Waterton residents were put on evacuation alert. The fire came within a mile of the townsite before being contained. Author's collection.

E. T. Scoyen, superintendent of Glacier National Park. Courtesy Glacier National Park.

William P. Kenney was president of Great Northern Railway in the 1930s. Author's collection.

Scoyen put in a request for more CCC men while the RCMP and Canadian park officials began rounding up civilian volunteers and government employees to fight the fire.[34] By that afternoon, the conflagration was just a mile and a half from the townsite. Impenetrable clouds of reddish-black smoke filled the sky, sparks flew and the roar of burning wood could at times be distinctly heard from the townsite.[35] Residents and business people were warned to leave the park.[36] Some didn't wait for an official evacuation notice; family and friends of Waterton residents had raced with trucks that morning to the park to remove belongings and loved ones.[37]

Despite being closed, the Prince of Wales Hotel, because of its location, was selected as a safe haven for Waterton residents and their personal effects. "The Prince of Wales Hotel is so well equipped with fire guard appliances that a damaging blaze is practically impossible," the *Lethbridge Herald* reported. Great Northern officials weren't taking any chances; they sent a crew of five men, headed by Ray Sleeger, to keep watch over their half-million dollar investment, as the usual

complement of trained summer staff was not on hand. The hotel, with its own water system and exterior rooftop sprinklers, was thoroughly soaked as a precaution against wind-born embers.[38]

Fate took a turn in favour of the townsite and hotel when the prevailing south wind shifted and temperatures cooled. "By the grace of providence the wind changed for a short time from southwest to northwest, and a sprinkling of rain fell in the townsite for a few minutes," Waterton superintendent Herbert Knight recounted later. "This short change in direction of the wind was our salvation. ... Men were rushed close up to the fire at once and fireguards were thrown up and in spite of the worst conditions under which fire can be fought, with the wind whipping round again to the southwest and forcing the fire back on this line of fireguards, this line was held intact, and from that time not one yard was lost."[39]

In the aftermath of the blaze, Sleeger wired St. Paul: "I've saved the hotel."[40] "Why?" replied Kenney.[41] It was a telling comment. The temptation to collect the fire

The Motor Vessel International was chartered to carry men and equipment to fight the 1935 fire on Boundary Creek. Author's collection.

insurance money on the hotel must have been great. Despite Kenney's flippant tone, Great Northern was always gravely concerned whenever there was a forest fire threat anywhere in Waterton or Glacier parks. Company officials took the precaution of encrypting all messages and telegrams related to fires. "We know from past experiences publicity concerning fires or fire prevention in Glacier reacts unfavourably on hotel reservations and rail ticket issues," an internal memo noted.[42] Sleeger and his men had ensured the hotel's safety, but Great Northern was not about to tout their feat. The railway preferred unsung heroes; it was better for tourism.

But there would be no tourists at the Prince of Wales Hotel that season. For the third summer in a row, the railway had opted not to open the hotel, waiting for the completion of the Kennedy Creek cutoff road. Each winter, Great Northern officials had gone through the same discussion about whether to reopen the hotel or wait until the road was finished. And every time the answer was the same. "There's no justification in opening the Prince of Wales Hotel until the highway is completed and (bus fares are) lowered," wrote A. J. Dickinson, passenger traffic manager for Great Northern.[43] A year later, Dickinson said: "(Ticket agents) from the East get as much business for Glacier with or without the Prince of Wales Hotel."[44]

Following the 1935 fire, Great Northern officials again took stock. It was obvious Chief Mountain International Highway, as Kennedy Creek cutoff was officially named, would be completed the following year and there would be no excuse not to open the Prince of Wales Hotel. In anticipation of reopening the hotel, Great Northern sent Thomas McMahon, the hotel's architect, to Waterton to in-

spect the building. His report was not encouraging. The hotel had suffered badly from the elements and was in dire need of repair. Rain and snow had weathered away exterior paint to bare wood. "Water has soaked into the wood and decay has started," McMahon added. "The hotel should be painted (immediately) to prevent further damage."[45]

It was a familiar refrain. As early as 1931 the resident manager had reported the paint was weathering quickly and wood was distorting.[46] The problem was not the fault of poor workmanship on the part of Oland and Scott's workers, who had completed the hotel a scant four years before. Rather, it was the result of exposure to the elements, situated as the hotel is on a promontory with no natural shelter from the weather.

In March 1932, four days of driving rain led to further problems. Owing to shrinkage and cracking of lumber, "water came in everywhere," the caretaker said. The roof leaked and dropped water six stories to the lobby floor; rain seeped around the lobby and dining room windows, warping the floor. As well, in one bedroom the wind blew rainwater between the ceiling and the floor of the room above it, causing the plasterboard to become soaked and eventually collapse.[47] The estimate for painting in 1931 came to $8,600—$1,700 for the roof and $6,900 for the rest of the building.[48] Short of cash, Kenney said the work could wait until next summer.[49] It would wait even longer, until the spring of 1936, and cost even more.

McMahon's report on the state of the hotel and the cost of putting it right was met with anger in St. Paul. Perhaps the railway could sell the building for salvage, accountant Charles Jenks suggested.[50] Dickinson said it might be possible to dis-

Ann Harrison stands on a two story-high snow drift near the gift shop windows of the Prince of Wales Hotel. Her husband, Victor Harrison, was the winter caretaker at the hotel and it would have been his job to remove snow on the gift shop roof to prevent the possibility of it collapsing. Courtesy Ann Harrison, author's collection.

pose of the hotel "to other interests." Even with the new road, "it can only operate at a heavy loss," Dickinson added. Kenney bemoaned the fact nearly $700,000 had ever been spent to build the hotel and related facilities, that it had sat idle for three of the last nine summers and now, with the end of Prohibition in the U.S., the whole reason for the hotel's existence had passed. "We must rid ourselves of all these parasites as quickly as possible," Kenney wrote.[51] It was a harsh criticism, but one that could be said more openly now that Hill was no longer in control of Great Northern. Nonetheless, the repairs were made—most in time for the 1936 season. Kenney reasoned it was best to paint the hotel to maintain it "for further disposal."

Keeping watch on the hotel during the closure had been resident caretaker Victor Harrison. His task was a test of endurance. Waterton is a harsh environment in the winter, with driving winds and a snowfall that averages 226 inches (574 cm) annually.[52] Harrison experienced the worst the elements could muster and there was a period when it wasn't certain whether he'd

make it to see the hotel reopen again. His weekly reports to St. Paul provide insight into his job and how he and his wife, Ann, persevered as they maintained their vigil over the hotel.

"The weather has been severely cold with a keen north wind most of the time," Harrison wrote in a February 1936 report. "Several days the temperature was between 30 and 40 below. We had to move out of our bedroom into one big room and get up twice a night to keep the fires going."[53] A week later, Harrison reported: "With our coal just about out and cord wood impossible to get, we are in a jam if it doesn't moderate in the next few days."[54] Fortunately, the cold snap ended shortly afterward and Harrison was able to get the needed coal.

Within a week, Waterton was hit with heavy snowfalls. "Three days of snow have piled up over three feet on the level and snowshoes have to be used to move around," he reported.[55] "The roofs over the private dining room, newsstand and beer parlour piled five feet with wet snow and had to be cleaned off," Harrison noted, adding: "Ten-foot drifts on north side of dormitories were cut through to make an entrance and to stop water from running in."[56] Harrison fortunately made it through the winter, possibly the toughest he ever faced as caretaker.

The doors of the Prince of Wales Hotel were finally reopened on June 28, 1936. There was a palpable air of optimism among staff and Waterton business owners as the park's premier man-made attraction was back in operation. Tourism to Waterton had been on the upswing during the past two seasons, with visitation in 1935 hitting 47,777—nearly matching the pre-Depression high of 48,592 set in 1929.[57] Many of the tourists who arrived at the hotel came via the new Chief Mountain Highway, which had opened for traffic 13 days earlier. Although surfacing on the highway had yet to be completed, the route was a great time saver for tourists travelling between Waterton and Glacier parks.[58] It was also more scenic than the former route through Cardston, with the 9,000-foot (2,700 m) Chief Mountain—a sacred site for Blood and Blackfeet people—dominating the view.

Hays was enthusiastic about the 29 mile-long (47 km) highway: "This road is an outstanding, scenic route far more than just a short cut and I consider it second to none in either Glacier or Waterton parks. It materially contributes to the increase in park traffic. We expect traffic through Waterton and Glacier national parks this season to be heavy, twice as heavy as has been in previous summers," he said in a newspaper interview.[59] Hays was so encouraged by this new road and the opening three years earlier of Going-to-the-Sun Highway, his Glacier Park Transport Company bought 18 new 14-passenger buses. Custom-designed and built by the White Motor Company, they were a vast improvement over the existing fleet, most of which dated from 1927.[60]

The opening of Chief Mountain International Highway in 1936 provided a direct connection between Waterton and Glacier parks and was a crucial factor in deciding to reopen the Prince of Wales Hotel after a drop in business earlier in the Depression forced the hotel's closure for three summers. Glacier Park Transport Company purchased new 14-passenger White buses to use on this route and Going-to-the-Sun Highway. Great Northern Railway publicity and advertising department, Minnesota Historical Society.

Howard Hays Sr., president of Glacier Park Transport Company.
Courtesy William Hays, author's collection.

Even with Chief Mountain Highway open, the Prince of Wales Hotel continued to operate at a loss for several years—although it was considerably less than before the road had been built.[61]

The reopening of the Prince of Wales Hotel allowed members of the Rotary Club to complete the task they'd started in 1931 with the international peace park proposal. On Saturday, July 4, 1936, Rotarians from Alberta and Montana gathered to unveil a plaque on a cairn to the north of the hotel, mirroring the cairn set up at Glacier Park Hotel in 1932. With Middleton and Mitchell on hand, the Rotarians rededicated themselves to the task of maintaining peace and goodwill between Canada and the U.S.[62]

Peace, unfortunately, was not on the mind of Nazi leader Adolf Hitler and his Italian cohort Benito Mussolini. Within three years, much of Europe was caught up in the Second World War. The Prince of Wales Hotel was able to operate relatively unburdened for the first few years by the food and fuel rationing that followed and a drop in Canadian tourists owing to travel restrictions. Filling the rooms Canadians would have taken were visitors from the United States, which had not yet joined the war. They continued to arrive at Glacier and Waterton on tours. The conflict finally caught up to the hotel in 1942 when the Canadian government put restrictions on fuel oil. Using the influence of their old friend Senator Buchanan of Lethbridge, Great Northern officials attempted to obtain an exemption.[63] The alternative would have been to convert the boilers to use coal, a cost of $2,000 the railway was unprepared to pay.[64] Great Northern officials were so certain they'd receive an exemption that they sent the hotel manager and his wife, Harley and Anna Boswell, to Waterton to prepare for the arrival of staff.[65] Great Northern's exemption request was refused, however, and the railway decided not to open the hotel that year.[66] The hotels in Glacier Park were also eventually closed, in 1943, owing to the war effort. All remained shuttered until the summer of 1946.

Passengers on Glacier Park Transport Company buses were waived through the Canadian customs port on Chief Mountain Highway and instead were checked by the resident customs inspector at the Prince of Wales Hotel. Author's collection.

Years of Change

The post-Second World War era has been one of great change—no less so for the Prince of Wales Hotel. North American society went through social, technological and economic upheavals as the old order gave way to a new world. On the social front, wartime prosperity laid the groundwork for an ever-burgeoning middle class, which quickly became a dominant economic and political force in society. The Second World War proved to be the last hurrah for trains as a form of economical mass transit, hauling troops from one end of the continent to the other. This 19th century technology made way for more modern forms of personal transportation: buses, cars and airplanes. North American railroads found a niche in the new economic order by specializing in the hauling of freight. Each of these changes would have an impact on the Prince of Wales Hotel in major and minor ways.

When Great Northern reopened its Waterton and Glacier hotels in 1946, railway officials planned to pick up where they had left off before the war had forced closure of the facilities. That was certainly the case at the Prince of Wales Hotel, where a sea-soned visitor would have noticed little amiss upon reopening. The familiar surroundings were made more so by familiar faces; many of the hotel's top staff had returned after the four-year hiatus.

Chief among those familiar faces was manager Harley Boswell. There was hardly a returning guest who did not recognize "Mr. Boswell." A professional hotel man

These picnickers at Two Medicine Lake represented a new wave in Glacier visitors, auto-tourists, who by the 1950s were the dominant force in the park, far outstripping the number of people who arrived on Great Northern's trains. T. J. Hileman photo, Great Northern Railway publicity and advertising department, Minnesota Historical Society.

from his earliest days, Boswell made it his business to know hotel patrons and, when possible, greet them personally each summer.[1] He had been doing so at the hotel since 1930. His presence ensured continuity and the same high standard of service from hotel staff whatever the circumstances in the outside world.

Change, though, was occurring steadily in the world around the Prince of Wales Hotel and would continue unabated. Taking a lead in post-war rail travel, Great Northern spent thousands of dollars to introduce a revised Empire Builder in 1947. The first-class train featured new locomotive power, diesel, and all-new rolling stock—coaches, dining cars and sleepers. It was a valiant but ultimately unsuccessful attempt to re-establish rail passenger travel as the glorious and profitable venture it had been in the 1920s. For two decades, an ever-increasing number of North Americans had been foregoing trains for private cars and buses. That trend acceler-

ated after the war.[2] A new and growing competition to railways for long-distance travel came from airlines. Like the Great War before it, the Second World War had created a surfeit of trained pilots looking for work. Some found it, initially flying war surplus equipment and later planes tailored specifically for commercial needs as they soared past railways to dominate the long-distance travel market.

The effect of these changes in transportation trends was evident in tourism to Glacier. The number of visitors to the park skyrocketed, from 201,000 in 1946 to nearly three-quarters of a million in 1960, but those arriving by train became an ever-smaller percentage.[3] Only once between 1946 and 1960 did rail arrivals at Glacier Park exceed the pre-war high of 10,182 set in 1929.[4] The well-heeled guests, who had been a mainstay of the Prince of Wales Hotel and Great Northern's other hotels, arriving by train and staying for a week or weeks at a time, were quickly replaced. Filling their seats in the lobby and dining room were travellers who had arrived by private car or in tour groups on tight budgets and equally tight schedules.

The Park Saddle Horse Company was the first business to feel the consequences. It was a victim of the Depression as much as the changing nature of tourism. Park visitors could no longer afford the time or expense of an extended and guided saddle horse tour. Nor did they want to or have to.[5] Going-to-the-Sun Highway, completed in 1933, opened to motorists the interior of Glacier that had been previously only accessible to hikers or by horseback. At one time the largest outfit of its kind in the world with over 900 horses and numerous permanent camps throughout Glacier, the Park Saddle Horse Company didn't make it through the Second World War. The

Noffsinger family ceased operations in 1942 and the company was never revived. The virtual monopoly Park Saddle Horse Company had had on the saddle horse concession in Glacier was replaced after the war with several smaller concessioners offering primarily day trips.

With the demise of Park Saddle Horse Company went the permanent camps it had operated and chalets it had used throughout Glacier. Lack of funds and business meant little was invested for upkeep of the chalets and camps during the Depression and, by the end of the war many were in such a serious state of decay they couldn't be economically rehabilitated. Among those razed were Goathaunt Chalet, St. Mary Chalets, Fifty Mountain Camp, Crossley Lake Camp, Cut Bank Chalets and Going-to-the-Sun Chalets.

The closure and eventual destruction of Goathaunt Chalet in the 1950s ended a 20-year association with the Prince of Wales Hotel. The chalet was the halfway point on one of the most popular long saddle horse trips in Glacier—the North Circle Tour. A side trip from Goat Haunt to the Prince of Wales Hotel was meant to be a break from camp conditions for riders on the usually five-day trek. The *Motor Vessel International* was an integral part of this arrangement, hauling riders to and from Goat Haunt. Razing the chalet meant an end to visits from trail riders and the closing of a popular place for southern Albertans to party on midnight frolics and other occasions.

Glacier Park Transport Company also suffered as a result of the rising trend of personal motorcar touring. The privately owned company had always worked in conjunction with Great Northern, using its red buses to haul tourists from one railway hotel or chalet to another throughout Glacier on posted schedules. It also fiercely maintained its independence, selling its own Glacier tour packages quite separately from Great Northern. The ever-increasing number of auto tourists and the rise of and reliance on charter tours by the hotels saw Glacier Park Transport Company become little more than an arm of the hotel operations, a glorified shuttle service. No longer could the bus company count on attracting a major portion of its business from individual travellers on pre-arranged tours. In 1955, the operation was sold to Glacier Park Company, the renamed Great Northern subsidiary then running its Glacier and Waterton hotels.

Great Northern had witnessed the rise in this new class of automobile tourists and tried to react to it prior to the war. The perception was the railway looked with disdain on these new visitors. Critics, like W. C. Whipps, reminded the National Park Service that Glacier was a "playground for ALL the American people, not simply ... for the sole benefit of the Great Northern Railway company or a few rangers and white pants dudes."[6] Prompted by the National Park Service, Glacier Park Hotel Company extended its facilities with the

With the demise of the Park Saddle Horse Company during the Second World War, Goathaunt Chalet fell into disrepair from lack of use. Like several other chalets in Glacier Park, it was razed. Elmer Fladmark photo, courtesy National Park Service, GLAC-9505.

GREAT DOME COACHES, TOO!

Empire Builder coach passengers can enjoy Western scenic thrills, too—from their vantage point on the upper deck of the coach domes. On the lower deck they ride in superb comfort—in reserved reclining seats with individual leg rests. No extra fare. It's great!

Connections in Seattle and Portland to and from California

In an attempt to rebuild passenger train travel, in 1947 Great Northern launched a new Empire Builder, using diesel locomotives pulling all new rolling stock. Advertising for Glacier and Waterton was incorporated into the train by giving dining cars, sleeping cars, lounge observation cars and coffee shop cars the names of park locations, like GN 1140 Waterton Lake, GN 1151 Lake McDonald, GN1160 Gunsight Pass and GN 1172 Grinnell Glacier. Author's collection.

Great Northern's Rocky mascot was given a new, leaner look in the 1950s and used to advertise travel to Waterton and Glacier on the railway's new second-class train, the Western Star. Author's collection.

Great places to stay

construction of the Swift Current Auto Cabins in 1934 near Many Glacier Hotel and, in 1940, what became the Rising Sun motel-cabin complex near Going-to-the-Sun Chalets. The success of the cabins was cause for serious discussion at Great Northern's headquarters in St. Paul, Minn. The cabins were inexpensive to build and maintain compared to the now 30-year old hotels and chalets—and they were cheaper to rent.[7] Railway executives felt caught between a combination of corporate pride and duty to Louis Hill to keep and maintain the older facilities or follow the new trend. Their indecision would ultimately take its toll at Sun Point and Two Medicine Lake. Bypassed by motorists going over Logan Pass, Going-to-the-Sun Chalets were razed in 1948, as were St. Mary Chalets, which had been superceded by private entrepreneurs who built competing and less expensive facilities just outside the park at St. Mary village. Two Medicine Chalets survived into the 1950s, when all but the main lodge was destroyed.

Interestingly, no one thought to revive the idea of auto-cabins at the Prince of Wales Hotel that had been proposed by Hill. During the Depression, of course, the hotel had been closed and it was a marginal proposition when it was reopened, only to close again in 1942. At the time, Great Northern officials couldn't see the value of pouring any more money into Waterton. The decision not to compete more fiercely for auto-tourists paved the way for more cabins and motels in Waterton village after the war, with the Prince of Wales Hotel's share of the market becoming increasingly smaller.

The Empire Builder

The Empire Builder, named in honour of Great Northern founder James Jerome Hill, began operating daily service between Chicago and the Pacific Coast in 1929. In 1947 and again in 1951, the name passed to a fleet of new transcontinental streamliners. The addition of 22 colourful "Great Domes" in 1955, shown here, further embellished its long-standing reputation as one of the finest trains in the United States.

Carthew Lodge, Louis Hill's house in Waterton, was sold in 1949, the year after Hill's death, converted into guest rental accommodation and renamed Northland Lodge. Ray Djuff photo, author's collection.

That the cottage proposal for the Prince of Wales Hotel does not show up anywhere in Great Northern records after construction was owing in part to the fact Hill had long since quit being a major force in the running of Great Northern Railway. Hill had maintained an interest in railway operations, and particularly his beloved Glacier, after his retirement as chairman of Great Northern in 1929, but his influence had dwindled over the years, although he remained a railway board member. Louis Hill died in 1948.

Just before his death, Hill took steps to sever his personal connection with Waterton. Hill approached Hugh Black about buying Carthew Lodge, the house he had had built for himself in Waterton but never occupied.[8] Black was one of the new breed of entrepreneur attracted to Glacier Park. In the 1930s, he reacted when Great Northern dallied, building St. Mary Lodge and Resort just outside the park boundary to cater to auto tourists. Although the business Hugh and his wife Margaret founded

ultimately sealed the fate of St. Mary Chalets and, to a lesser extent, Going-to-the-Sun Chalets, Hill never harboured any ill will toward the Blacks. Whenever Hill was in the region, he would always stop to say hello, Margaret Black recalled.[9]

Although Hill died before a deal could be completed, Hill's wishes were followed and Hugh Black eventually bought Carthew Lodge for $6,000.[10] Black's plan was to turn it into a hotel and to do so he went into partnership with Cardston garage operator Earl Hacking.[11] The two jointly owned and operated the Northland Lodge, as it was renamed, as a summer resort until the early 1960s, when Black sold his interest to Hacking.[12]

The death of Hill and sale of Carthew Lodge were harbingers of things to come. Hill had been the driving force behind Great Northern's involvement in Glacier Park and his genius lay in its promotion. His vision had created the Prince of Wales Hotel, but the heady days of the 1920s were over and Hill was now gone. During the decade of the 1940s, Great Northern lost $1.4 million on its operations in Glacier Park alone.[13] The railway was now in the hands of a new generation of executives who were not about to keep the Glacier facilities out of sentiment and did not want to be stuck with money-losing ventures.

John Budd, who became president of Great Northern in May 1951, epitomized this change in philosophy.[14] The son of Ralph Budd, railway president from 1919 to 1931, John Budd had spent many summers in Glacier and personally knew its splendour and appeal.[15] As much as it tugged at his heart to abandon Glacier, Budd was ruled by his head. "From a practical standpoint, the first consideration of anyone interested in the operation will be the operating figures and balance sheet," he said when asked about how he intended to handle the railway's Glacier Park holdings.[16] Budd set a clear course: Great Northern could no longer afford to dabble in enterprises outside its main business of hauling freight.[17]

The new direction was evident in Great Northern's refusal to take out long-term leases for its operations in Glacier Park, instead going from one year to the next.[18] Railway officials made no bones about the fact they wanted out of the hotel concession business. In reply to a U.S. government suggestion that Great Northern spend $7.9 million to improve its Glacier Park holdings, the railway's president said he'd rather spend the money to modernize rolling stock and reduce operating costs.[19]

Great Northern took a miserly approach to its Waterton and Glacier holdings. What was the point of spending money to maintain them if they were going to be sold anyway? Whether it liked it or not, the railway found it couldn't always scrimp on some things. Such was the case with the roof of the Prince of Wales Hotel and upgrades to the *International*.

The problem with the roof of the hotel was its colour. Since the 1930s, Canadian park officials had been insisting the shingles be stained green so the roof would conform to the recommended park colour scheme.[20] The hotel was no moneymaker during the Depression and Great Northern balked at the estimated $1,700 cost.[21] Railway officials argued the roof should be left unpainted, as it was meant to be. The shingles were specially selected vertical grain cedar cut from live wood and put on with zinc-coated nails. The roof was made to last 50 years, during which time it was supposed to take on a weathered, grey colour.[22] Great Northern got through the Depression and war without painting the roof, but by 1950 the Parks Branch had run out

Four brave young ladies dive off the stern of the Motor Vessel International into the glacier and snow-fed water of Upper Waterton Lake. This is a publicity shot that was probably staged by the photographer using Prince of Wales Hotel employees. T. J. Hileman photo, Great Northern Railway publicity and advertising department, Minnesota Historical Society.

of patience. Much to the chagrin of later owners of the hotel who would have preferred the lower maintenance of the original design, the railway relented and painted the hotel's roof green.[23]

In the case of the *International*, it was Mother Nature who forced the railway to make unanticipated expenditures. In 1953, Great Northern commissioned a long-overdue major refit of the vessel to improve safety and operating economy. The twin Sterling gasoline engines were replaced with twin Detroit diesels, a smokestack was added and the boat's upper canopy removed. At the same time, the rocks that had been used as ballast to keep the stern in the water were removed.[24] The following winter, a record snowfall at Goat Haunt collapsed the roof of the boathouse in which the *International* is stored, pushing the new smokestack into the keel. Further repairs were made to the *International* and the boathouse was rebuilt as an A-frame to prevent a repeat incident.

Repeated expenditures of these types re-inforced why Great Northern wanted out of the parks and spurred on the search to find someone to take over the Waterton and Glacier operations. It was with a sense of optimism that Great Northern signed an agreement in 1956 with Donald T. Knutson to have him manage the facilities. The three-year deal (1957-59) turned the hotels and related facilities over to Knutson, who ran a construction company in Min neapolis and also owned hotels in Minnesota and North Dakota.[25] Although the railway made a commitment to spend $3 million over a three-year period to renovate the entire chain, officials maintained the idea of eventually selling the lot.[26]

Knutson's first move was to greatly increase room rates and then draw up a grandiose scheme of renovations and improvements that became known as the "dream list." All the guestrooms were refurbished at the Prince of Wales Hotel, the east wing of the lobby revamped so the gift shop could be enlarged, and several large rooms, including the Dominion Suite on the third floor, created out of smaller ones.[27]

A second set of renovations at the Prince of Wales hotel was approved for 1959. They included modernization of the kitchen, upgraded electrical service, new fire escapes, installation of a fire-suppression sprinkler system and further expansion of the gift shop.[28] The expansion of the gift shop saw the end of a venerable institution at the hotel—the beer parlour. It had been the reason Great Northern ventured into Canada to construct the hotel. Even after Prohibition ended in the U.S., the bar remained a popular place with hotel guests and Waterton residents. It was not uncommon to see dusty riders fresh off the trail wetting their whistles beside a group of locals enjoying a cold brew. The bar was where social classes mixed. Knutson ended all that by abandoning the beer parlour and creating an upscale bar, a cocktail lounge called the Maple Leaf Room, in what had formerly been the dining room annex. Beer was no longer available on tap, only in more expensive bottles. And unlike the beer parlour, which had a door to the outside, the only access to the Maple Leaf Room was through the hotel lobby. Few townspeople were willing to make the daunting journey, which took them directly past the staring eyes of front desk staff, into the rarefied atmosphere of a cocktail lounge. The Maple Leaf Room became the exclusive domain of hotel guests.

The Maple Leaf Room lasted only a year as a cocktail lounge. In 1960 it was reverted to again be a dining room annex and was replaced by the Windsor Lounge. The Windsor Room had been fashioned out of the east wing of the lobby the previous year by cutting away part of the grand staircase and framing in what was left as a convention meeting room.[29] To incorporate the lobby fireplace into the Windsor Room, the hearth was reduced in size and the original stone work was redone in a more modern style.

Another piece of the original hotel disappeared with these renovations. For years, Indian pictographs decorated the lobby walls and lanterns hung at various heights from the ceiling, fascinating visitors. They were a visual reminder of a people who had frequented Waterton before the arrival of European settlers. They were also a link between the Bloods and the hotel's namesake, Edward, Prince of Wales, who in 1919 was the first person to be in-

During the late 1950s, the east wing of the lobby was closed to create a convention facility called the Windsor Room. It was later converted into the Windsor cocktail lounge. The renovations included remodelling the fireplace and enclosing in the once grand staircase. Ray Djuff photos, author's collection.

ducted into the tribe as an honourary Kainai chief.[30] In the 1950s, Great Northern began playing down the native theme it had used for decades to promote travel to Glacier and Waterton, eventually dropping it from all advertising.[31]

The pictographs and lanterns harkened back to an earlier time, exactly the opposite approach Knutson was taking in mod-

The Kilmorey Lodge, like other motels in Waterton townsite, thrived on auto-tourism to the park. In a bid to capture more of that market, Donald Knutson proposed that Great Northern build its own motel. The railway sold the Prince of Wales Hotel before the proposal could be acted upon. Postcard, author's collection.

ernizing the building. The pictographs were removed and replaced with wallpaper.[32] The decision to eliminate the lanterns was based on new fire and electrical codes that discouraged their use.[33] In their place was installed a three-tiered chandelier made from aluminum.[34] After 30 years, any connection at the hotel to the heritage of Alberta's Blood tribe was gone.

For all the work undertaken by Knutson, Great Northern officials deemed the effort a failure. They desperately wanted out of the Glacier-Waterton hotel business, but did not think Knutson was the man to take over the railway's legacy. Serious questions had been raised about the economic feasibility of Knutson's renovations and his proposed expansion plans.[35] One of those plans was for a 138-unit, two-story motel Knutson wanted to build overlooking Upper Waterton Lake that would have cost $1 million.[36] There was also a question about whether the U.S. National Park Service would approve of any sale to Knutson, for the service saw in him a high level of commercialism that ran contrary to what

the government was trying to achieve in the park.[37] The management agreement expired in 1959 and was not renewed. The search for a buyer started anew.

At one point Great Northern's bosses considered splitting up the properties and selling them separately, entering into negotiations with Brewster Transport of Banff to buy the Prince of Wales Hotel and Glacier Park Transport Company. The talks failed, however, because Brewster was only willing to pay $250,000 for the hotel and $125,000 for the bus company, while the railway wanted $400,000 each, unrealistic sums in view of the later sale price for the whole hotel chain.[38]

In 1960, the railway approached Don Hummel about buying the hotels. "His name came to our attention," said Robert Downing, executive-vice president of Great Northern. "Running a hotel in a national park is different because July and August are months to raise money (through operations) and June and September are break-even months. He had the ability to take hotel reservations, too. We thought if we got an established operator, this off-season overhead could be carried."[39]

Hummel was an excellent candidate. A lawyer and former mayor of Tucson, Ariz., he had built the first concessions in Lassen Volcanic National Park in California, in 1933-34, and later operated in Mount McKinley in Alaska and Yosemite National Park in California. Hummel and a group of associates formed Glacier Park Inc. and, in December 1960, the Waterton and Glacier properties changed hands. The sale price was $1.4 million.[40]

The sale of the Prince of Wales Hotel and *International* ended many long-term ties that had been established between workers Great Northern had rehired season after season and Waterton's residents. Over three decades, Waterton townsfolk had built relationships with longtime management and staff, such as manager Harley Boswell, accountant Henry Healey and Victor Harrison, head bellman during the summer and winter caretaker. The cozy familiarity started to fall apart when the hotel was leased to Knutson's company, which brought its own management personnel and made renovations, like those to the beer parlour, that severed contact with local people.[41] And now Hummel brought in a new crop of senior people.

The distance between the two groups was swept away in June 1964 when a flood hit the Waterton townsite. Torrential rains combined with warm weather to melt the heavy snowpack in the mountains. Cameron Creek, swollen by runoff, burst its banks. The level of Upper Waterton Lake rose five feet (1.5 m) on June 7.[42] The only road into the park lay under water.[43]

Residents were evacuated to high ground, seeking refuge at the Prince of Wales Hotel, where rooms were provided free of charge. Equipped with a separate water and sewage system and auxiliary power plant, the hotel was a

A heavy winter snowpack in the mountains combined with a warm, wet spring in 1975 to raise the level of Upper Waterton Lake, flooding parts of the townsite. It was the second flood in a decade, both times forcing town residents to seek shelter at the Prince of Wales Hotel. Ray Djuff photo, author's collection.

safe haven. It remained home for some 130 townspeople for the next week, until water levels subsided and people could return to their homes and businesses.[44] The Prince of Wales Hotel was one of the only hotels among Hummel's holdings in Waterton-Glacier that did not sustain serious damage.[45]

In 1967, Glacier Park Inc. announced plans to undertake $500,000 worth of improvements to the hotel, to include a major updating of the interior of the building, the addition of 30 rooms, and construction of a massive underground convention hall and banquet facility capable of handling 400 guests.[46] The feature attraction of the underground facilities would have been huge picture windows cut into the south face of the hill so conventioneers could take in the vista. The expansion died on the order table before it could ever take place, however. It was done in by a change in national park property leasing regulations that stated commercial leaseholders would not receive compensation for improvements constructed on the property when the lease expired and there was no assurance the leaseholder would be able to renew the contract when it expired. With the 42-year lease on the Prince of Wales Hotel about to end in five years, Hummel couldn't see the feasibility of pouring $500,000 into the hotel with little guarantee of recouping the investment. "Stability of investment is absolutely essential if you are going to build a secure financial organization," Hummel said. "When you undermine the stability of investment, you run into all kinds of problems."[47] Rather than take a risk, Glacier Park Inc. shelved the idea.

It was not the first time Hummel's plans had been grounded. While Hummel was respected as an astute businessman and leader among concession operators in the United States, his ideas were often seen as contrary to the goals of the national parks. Hummel wanted park concessions to be profitable and sought approval for developments that would achieve that end. He ended up time and again butting heads with National Park Service officials who saw Hummel's schemes as being more exploitive than complementary.[48]

After failing repeatedly to get the types of commitments he wanted from the government, Hummel became disillusioned and started to entertain thoughts of getting out of the concession business.[49] His disenchantment, combined with the marginal profitability of the hotel operations, sometimes meant little money was put into upkeep of the buildings. The exterior of the Prince of Wales Hotel, which faces extreme exposure to the elements because of its prominent location, suffered badly, and began showing signs of weathering, such as peeling paint.

Fred Weatherup cottoned on to such details. The Lethbridge businessman had a plan to buy the hotel and make himself its saviour. The "Prince," Weatherup said, had fallen into a bad state of disrepair and was being mismanaged under Hummel's ownership. Glacier Park Inc. devoted itself solely to American tourists, making Canadians feel unwelcome at the hotel, Weatherup charged, adding lack of maintenance since being taken over from Great Northern had seen the guestrooms fall to "third-rate" status.[50] Under his Canadian ownership, Weatherup said, he would restore the hotel to its former glory and make it accessible to everyone, not just American tour groups.

Weatherup was sailing on a swelling tide of Canadian nationalism that was prevalent at the time, and he got a great deal of sympathy from the media. During the summer of 1974, Glacier Park Inc. had been severely criticized in newspaper stories over the way it apparently shunned Canadians trying to make reservations at the Prince of Wales Hotel.[51] The reports were based on misunderstandings about the way Glacier Park Inc. handled bookings and attempts were made to explain the situation, but the perception remained that the hotel was aloof to taking reservations from Canadians.[52]

Unfortunately, there had been other examples of apparent deference to American tourists that didn't help the cause of hotel staff and management trying to elicit understanding about Glacier Park Inc. operations and how booking mix-ups could occur. One summer in the 1960s, for example, the Prince of Wales Hotel was operated on daylight saving time, which was being used in Montana at the other hotels, while Alberta was on standard time. The idea was to make it easier to co-ordinate tours on both sides of the border, ensuring that guests arriving by bus from the U.S. wouldn't miss mealtimes. A Calgary family that had not been informed of the practice showed up at the hotel only to find they'd missed lunch because of the time discrepancy.[53] It was not an isolated incident.

Weatherup's criticism of the way Glacier Park Inc. was handling the property and his appeal to Canadian nationalism got him nowhere. After two unsuccessful offers to make a deal for the Prince of Wales Hotel, Weatherup eventually had to satisfy himself with buying Kootenai Lodge in Waterton, which he later sold. But Weatherup had been right in sensing the Prince of Wales Hotel was for sale; he was simply premature and couldn't put together the right offer.

That was not the case with Arthur Burch, an excursion boat operator in Glacier Park. In 1975, Hummel sold the *International* to Burch, who owned Glacier Park Boat Company. The boat company had a long history in Glacier Park, having operated there since 1938. Although ownership of the Prince of Wales Hotel and vessel were now independent, Burch maintained ties with Glacier Park Inc., co-ordinating operations for the benefit of group tours at the hotel.

Just as Don Hummel, who was in his early 70s, was tiring of the work involved in running Glacier Park Inc., his son Clifford stepped on to the scene. Clifford had grown up around the hotels and had worked his way through most departments. In 1976, Don felt his son was ready to become a senior manager in the firm and handed Clifford the reins of the Prince of Wales Hotel. For the next two years, Clifford struggled to prove himself worthy. As well as running the hotel in the summer, Clifford spent months before and after each summer season undertaking large and small repairs to the building, including fire-safety improvements such as the installation of smoke detectors and additional fire escapes. His initiative and drive mirrored his father's, as did his sometimes brusque manner with staff, and it appeared as if Clifford might succeed his father—until a falling out between the two in 1978.[54] During a visit to Waterton, Don learned Clifford was planning to convert one of the staff dormitories into a year-round lodge and had already partially gutted the building for remodelling. Don, who had not been informed of the project, was incensed and in a not uncharacteristic blowup with Clifford, fired his son on the spot. The project was abandoned and the dormitory restored.

Don Hummel. Joseph Sheaffer photo, author's collection.

Sunset highlights Vimy Peak and the Prince of Wales Hotel. Ray Djuff photo, author's collection.

The end of the road for Don Hummel came in March 1981 when Glacier Park Inc., including the Prince of Wales Hotel, was sold to Greyhound Food Management Company, Inc. of Phoenix, Ariz. Although there had been signs Hummel was ready to sell for years, he claims the U.S. National Park Service pushed him into it.[55]

Under new ownership, the Prince of Wales Hotel came in for another series of renovations, including updating of the lobby, replacement of the furniture in guestrooms, installation of new windows throughout the building, and construction of a new roof over the old shingles. Yet another bit of the original hotel was lost in the exercise. The boilers, which had been such a struggle to get to the park, were decommissioned, replaced by an electrical heating system for hotel rooms. No longer does the clanking of pipes awaken guests as steam hisses while working its way through the hotel in the early morning.

While the boilers sit idle, some related equipment soldiers on at the Lethbridge Regional Hospital. When Ken Manning, director of plant operations at the hospital, heard the two steam pumps at the Prince of Wales Hotel might be scrapped, he persuaded the hotel's owners to donate them to the hospital. Refurbished, one pump now supplies steam heating to the entire hospital while the other pumps steam to the hospital's laundry, kitchen, heat therapy pools and sterilizing equipment. "They worked for 60 years at the hotel and will probably last another 60 years here," said Manning, who was once a Prince of Wales Hotel employee.[56] It is a testament to the durability of the work of the designers and builders of the hotel and an indication that there would appear to be no end in sight for the Prince of Wales Hotel.

11 A Motto of Service

The motto of England's Prince of Wales is "Ich Dien"—I serve. It also fits as a motto for the staff at his namesake hotel. Without dedicated employees, the Prince of Wales Hotel would not have lasted as long as it has or created the following of loyal guests who return year after year. There is little margin for error when it comes to service at a summer resort. Its continuity, like other hotels in the chain, is based on satisfied patrons and maintaining its reputation. But the potential for error is great, staffed as the hotels are by college and university students with only a handful of professionals to guide them. Fortunately, the Prince of Wales Hotel has been blessed with caring workers, benevolent managers and understanding guests. The result has been a success story that spans more than seven decades.

From the outset, Great Northern made it clear to the staff it expected the utmost dedication to duty and spelled out exactly what that meant. "The ideal of this organization is ... to please and satisfy our guests ... and to let no guest depart feeling that everything and more was not done to make his visit with us something to look back upon with pleasure."[1] Anything less was grounds for dismissal.

The staff for the hotel has always been drawn from the ranks of students at Canada's universities, colleges and technical schools. It is not unusual to find all 10 provinces and the territories represented among the staff. U.S. citizens, unless they have authorization, are restricted by Canadian employment laws from working at the hotel. Staff members are not necessarily hired on the basis of what individuals are studying at school—only a handful might be in hotel management or culinary

There were strict rules of conduct for bellmen and page boys. Ensuring compliance with these rules was head bellman, Victor Harrison, at right. Courtesy Betty Baker, author's collection.

The costumes and hairstyles have changed, but the spirit that pervades the dining room of the Prince of Wales Hotel remains the same. Ray Djuff photo, author's collection.

arts—but rather for their enthusiasm and ability to adapt to ever-changing situations.

"If you have been told by a former Waterton visitor or employee that the work is easy, we warn you from the start that the information is based on a misunderstanding of actual conditions. THE WORK IS HARD," a pamphlet to potential employees warned. "Our service is so informal and elastic that it is certain at one time or another during the season you will be asked to perform tasks not specified in your classification."[2]

The lack of specific job skills usually shows up during the first weeks after opening, as newcomers are learning the

ropes. One young waitress, her first day on the job, was told by a customer that the french onion soup was too salty. The cook assured the waitress that this was impossible and, pointing to the steam table, said: "The soup hasn't been put out yet." The waitress had served brackish water from the steam table.[3]

The students generally settle in quickly, although some take longer than others. One waitress was so anxious about doing a good job that she used to have nightmares. Her roommates would hear her rushing around her dorm room in the middle of the night "sleep-waiting."[4]

Forgiving guests go a long way to ease the pressure on new and seasoned employees. That is particularly so of repeat patrons, who come to learn from the staff the trials of working at a summer resort and make accommodations for them. Employees tend to pamper repeat customers, but that doesn't always ensure perfect service. Waitress Sally Pike recalled how dining room employees "always grovelled" to one New York couple that returned year after year. "One summer after I had finished working there, I was visiting the (couple) in the dining room. She confided to me that the food wasn't always very good and secretively showed me the container of Lawry's Seasoning Salt she carried to augment her food."[5]

The dining room isn't the only area of the hotel subject to the close scrutiny of guests. In its time, the hotel was on par with all but the most elegant establishments. While the exterior presents a timeless charm and the lobby of the hotel has been updated periodically, the bedrooms have not changed substantially since the building was constructed. As the years have passed, some guests think they've entered a time warp when they walk into their rooms and balk at seeing 1927 amenities. Most get into the spirit of the place and see the sink in the bedroom, a tub but no shower, water sprinkler pipes conspicuous on the ceiling and lack of a television or radio in the rooms as quaint. Others are not so forgiving, expecting substantially more for their money. It is on such occasions employees show their mettle by working out guest concerns and at the same time explaining the history of building.

Hotel patrons are also often surprised when they hop in the elevator and then look around blankly for a button to press to hurry them to their floor. It can take several minutes to realize the Otis elevator, original to the building, must be manually operated by a bellman.

One area where the hotel was slow to grasp modern ways was in accepting credit cards. During the 1960s and 1970s, Don Hummel steadfastly refused to allow their use to pay for rooms and meals. The profit from operating a summer resort was slim enough without having to pay credit card handling fees, he argued. Some guests were caught short when told they would have to pay their bill with cash or a cheque. It was a frustrating policy for staff to enforce and for guests to endure, leading to a few rows at the front desk.

Some challenges to hotel staff are predictable. Every second year, employees gird for an invasion of Rotarians from Alberta, Saskatchewan and Montana. In keeping with the promise made when they established Waterton-Glacier International Peace Park in 1932, Rotarians have attempted to meet annually in the parks ever since to renew their vow "to foster all international relationships." It is the longest-standing convention held in the parks, alternating between the Prince of Wales Hotel and Glacier Park Lodge. It's a never-to-be-forgotten experience for those involved.

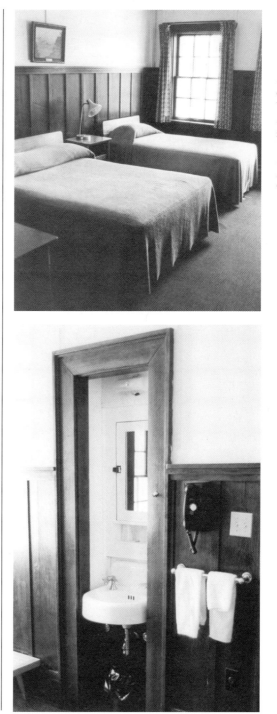

Bedroom furnishings have been replaced and modernized over the years, but there is no hiding the 1920's design features in hotel rooms, like wall phones and old-fashioned sinks in the bedroom rather than washroom. It can be disconcerting for first-time guests to the hotel who wonder if they've been transported through a time warp to an earlier era. Ray Djuff photos, author's collection.

From the time it opened until the 1950s, horses were always available for rent at the hotel, offering everything from hourly services to guided tours for staff and guests. In the early years, the concession was operated by the Morris brothers. In the 1950s, grizzly bear expert and wildlife author Andy Russell, who owns a ranch just north of Waterton, offered guide services. T. J. Hileman photo, Great Northern Railway publicity and advertising department, Minnesota Historical Society.

Hiking has always been a popular pastime with hotel staff. In the early days, female staff could expect to be chaperoned by the dorm matron or another older staff member during outings. Courtesy Betty Baker, author's collection.

The three-day convention makes use of just about every resource in the hotel, with delegates meeting continuously at different venues. From the registration of delegates and the opening cocktail party to signing out, it's one long, mad dash for the staff. The highlight of the convention is a dinner the final evening for delegates and their spouses that takes over the lobby, the only room in the hotel big enough to accommodate all the guests. For this event, just about everyone on staff is pressed into service as a waiter, waitress, to bus tables or work in the kitchen. A special liquor licence is obtained for the occasion, so drinking is permitted anywhere in the building. The morning after can be a headache for both the staff and guests, none of whom looks forward to rousing and getting back to business too quickly.

After a demanding episode like the Rotary convention, the staff needs to blow off steam. When the employees are 100 or so college students, it's a surefire recipe for high jinks. The students generally manage to keep their high spirits in check until off duty, but that isn't always the case. One summer, a waiter made up an elaborate story to answer the frequently asked question of why Upper Waterton Lake is so blue. Staff will usually describe how light reflecting off suspended particles in the water, known as glacial flour, gives the lake a range of colours. But this mischievous waiter offered a slightly less nature-based answer. Appearing to answer in all sincerity, he explained to a table of elderly ladies how each spring the mountain streams were blocked so the lake could be drained. Then, the waiter continued, the park service hired a crew—including some hotel staff—to paint the lake bottom blue.

Another question answered often by front-desk staff is the location of the hotel's washrooms. It is not an unusual request as many tourists arrive after a lengthy trip and the washrooms are not readily found; the men's room is in the basement and the ladies' room is up two flights of stairs. One front desk clerk, having heard and answered the question hundreds of time, came up with a unique, if silly response. With his hands on the countertop as if he were playing the piano, the clerk pranced back and forth behind the front desk chanting: "Up the stairs, half a flight, second landing, on the right." His reply startled not only the lady who asked the question, but his co-workers.

After the initial thrill of working at a summer resort has worn off, employees have to look for creative ways to keep up their spirits. A form of self-deprecating humour can arise. It's at such times the staff begins to refer to themselves as PoWs, an acronym created from the initials Prince of Wales but meaning "prisoner of war."

Bruce Kerr, right, and a friend climbed Bear's Hump on their hands and knees to while away a free summer day. Ray Djuff photo, author's collection.

Others find new thrills in Waterton's many recreational opportunities, like hiking, sailboarding and mountain-bike riding.

Not infrequently, competition develops among staff to see who hikes the greatest number of trails or scales the most peaks. These rivalries can also be over more ridiculous things. In the 1960s, one employee made a macho display of hiking in moccasins while the rest of his compatriots wore boots or running shoes. At the end of the season, an elaborate "burial" ceremony off the stern of the *International* was planned for the dilapidated moccasins. The occasion was complete with music and on-lookers toasting the event with ginger ale.[6]

A decade later, a pair of employees put another twist on hiking when they decided to while away an afternoon crawling to the top of Bear's Hump on their hands and knees. The trail is only three-quarters of a mile (1.2 km) in length, but it is steep and takes about 40 minutes one way. With potato sacks and pieces of carpet tied to their hands and knees, it took the two little more than an hour to get to the top. After taking in the panorama, they rewarded themselves by walking down the trail upright.

A trio playing light classical arrangements was once a fixture in the hotel lobby, providing dinner music and, later in the evening, a concert. The trio was often the rallying point for performances showcasing the talents of other hotel staff. Courtesy Robert Trapp, author's collection.

members themselves, requiring great effort and countless hours outside of time on the job. A trio of musicians, which was a staple in the lobby during the evenings for many years, usually acted as the catalyst, arranging performances by interested students and providing accompaniment. One summer in the 1960s an especially energetic group produced and performed *Oklahoma!* An attempt by Knutson to mandate staff variety shows failed miserably and created nothing but resentment.[8]

Variety shows not only entertain but also act as a relief valve for employees. This ditty, sung to the tune of the Coca-Cola song, *It's the Real Thing*, illustrates the sentiment.

> *We'd like to teach you folks to laugh*
> *At all of our mistakes*
> *Like spilling drinks and leaky sinks*
> *And burning your beef steak*
>
> *We'd like to show we're having fun*
> *While looking after you,*
> *We work all day and play all night*
> *And make our money, too!*
>
> *It's a real drag, work is*
> *In the middle of August*
> *When the heat is on*
> *And you want to relax/Oh, yeah*
> *It's a real drag*[9]

Attending dances at the pavilion was a Saturday night ritual for hotel employees for many decades. The pavilion featured a live band and jitney dance, with patrons paying 10 cents a dance or three for 25 cents. Initially, there was an attempt to keep male and female hotel staff apart during off-hours unless accompanied by a chaperone. The dances were one of the few times the sexes could mix freely. "There was a sort of housemother over the girls and curfew was 10 o'clock, with a special of 12 o'clock on dance nights," recalled Helen Graham of Lethbridge, who worked in the linen and laundry room at the hotel in 1927. "It could be arranged, however, to have a friend let you in if you were going to be extra late!"[7]

Not all pastimes are frivolous. The students often channel their exuberance into more entertaining ventures, such as creating variety shows and musicals. Participation in such shows is voluntary and almost always initiated by the staff

Overseeing and trying to direct all this collegiate energy is the hotel's manager. The Prince of Wales Hotel has had the good fortune of having three outstanding managers who set and maintained a tradition of excellence in service that carries on to this day: Capt. Rodden Stanley Harrison, Harley H. Boswell and Robert Hayes. With two brief exceptions, they managed the hotel for its first 40 years.

Capt. Harrison was the hotel's first manager. Like Boswell and Hayes, he came with an extensive resume, including having owned his own hotel. Some employees thought Harrison's tweedy, English manner was pompous and out of place in the remote wilderness of Waterton. "(He was) a real Colonel Blimp type," recalled bellhop Ainslie Pankhurst. "He kept a horse and went riding in the accepted togs of Hyde Park every morning at 7."[10] Regardless of the staff opinion of his personal style, Harrison was universally respected for his knowledge of the business and the high standard he set for himself and his employees.

Every season, the manager and staff take the hotel "out of winter mothballs." Harrison faced a unique set of problems in 1927. Most managers rely on a corps of returning staff and department managers to set the tone and train newcomers, who comprise anywhere from one-half to two-thirds of the complement. That first summer, Harrison had one employee with Glacier Park Hotel Company experience, his assistant manager Fred Slack, and only a handful of professionals. Everyone else had to learn his job on the fly.

Added to this difficulty was the fact that when Harrison and his staff showed up, construction on the hotel had not yet been completed. Rob Armstrong was the elevator operator in 1927: "I recall that prior to opening, the staff was engaged in setting up the rooms and in cleaning paint and varnish from the millions of small panes of glass that make up the windows in the rooms. The latter was my job and it seemed to go on forever. While this was going on … carpenters, painters, etc. of Oland's construction crew were swarming around putting on the finishing touches."[11]

The job of preparing the hotel for opening each spring not only makes the build-ing habitable, but also benefits the staff. The shared experience of hard work forges a bond between staff members as they learn about the hotel and each other. Brought together from all over the country, this diverse group of people learns to work and act in unison.

Harrison moulded that cohesive force with a series of strict rules about staff conduct. The rules were not without precedent. Every employee was expected to read the *Service Regulations and Information for Employees* handbook and know its contents by heart. It advised bellboys and porters to "be quiet and orderly on the bench and when you are 'front,' stand with your arms folded or at attention." They were also to "never allow a guest to put on his coat in your presence without offering to assist, or to pick up anything he may drop." Dining room employees were told: "Take pride in the appearance of your tables. Provide them daily with fresh wild

Capt. Rodden Stanley Harrison was the first manager of the Prince of Wales Hotel. He was a grandfatherly type, stern but not rash to make judgments with hotel employees. Courtesy Ann Harrison, author's collection.

Hotel manager Capt. R. Stanley Harrison knew he was in for a busy time whenever one of these large Glacier Park Transport Company touring sedans pulled up. It usually carried railway officials or VIPs who would require more than the usual amount of attention as hotel guests. T. J. Hileman, J. J. Hill Library, LH 2818.

flowers which you will find in profusion not far from any hotel in the park."[12]

One day while dining with Harrison, Canon Middleton questioned the practice of picking wild flowers. A conservationist, Middleton argued the flowers should be left for all to enjoy. "The important people come to the Prince and that is where they can see the flowers," Harrison replied haughtily.[13]

Lest anyone forget the rules, periodic visits and reminders from Howard Noble, general manager of Glacier Park Hotel Company, helped reinforce collective memories. "Last year … finger bowl service was quite frequently neglected," Noble noted in a letter to his hotel managers. "And when (guests) leave the door, the girl could say a word, 'I hope you enjoyed your meal.' I notice this is the method in the most successful up-to-date cafes."[14]

Harrison was considered such a success after his first season at the Prince of Wales Hotel there was talk at Great Northern's headquarters of him replacing Noble, who was nearing retirement.[15] At the

end of the 1927 season, Harrison was given a grand tour of all Glacier Park Hotel Company's facilities. After two more successful seasons, he was invited to St. Paul to meet the railway's top brass. Harrison left St. Paul in the belief he was to succeed Noble, so it "was certainly a great surprise" when he received a notice from the railway his services were no longer required.[16] Exactly what transpired has been lost to history.

Harley Boswell followed Harrison. Like Harrison, Boswell had a thorough grounding in the hotel business. Born in 1888 in Illinois, Boswell started his career in the hospitality industry at the tender age of 10, taking a job as a bellboy at a hotel in Peoria to help his mother make ends meet. A drunk had murdered his father, a farmer, in 1892.[17] When he grew older, Harley and his younger brother Elmer got summer jobs in the Rockies. They both did stints at the Banff Springs Hotel and Chateau Lake Louise. Harley's girlfriend and later wife, Anna, joined them in seeking work at mountain resorts. Elmer and Harley tried farming in Idaho during the First World War, but gave it up after several years. They found themselves more suited to a cosmopolitan life and headed for Chicago, where Harley eventually landed a job at the prestigious Palmer House.[18]

Harley and Anna couldn't get the lure of the Rockies out of their blood. By means they never disclosed, Harley was able to arrange with his employers at the Palmer House to take each summer off so he and Anna could visit and work "in their beloved mountains."[19] Their travels took them through Glacier and Waterton parks. Being so closely associated with the Rockies and hotel industry, Harley was well placed to hear about any job openings suited to an up-and-coming assistant manager. When the manager's job for the Prince of Wales Hotel became available in 1930, he jumped at it.

Harley and Anna Boswell were opposites when it came to personality type and dealings with staff, but in the end they both achieved the same goal: Winning the loyalty of their employees and making guests feel welcome and relaxed. Harley was an extrovert, always ready to flash a smile, extend a hand in greeting and engage a stranger to the hotel in conversation. He was a member of a club of hotel managers known as the "Greeters" and used the skills he learned at meetings to great effect at the Prince of Wales Hotel, showing a special interest in hotel patrons.[20] He wanted to be notified about returning guests so he could greet them personally, and they were sure to be invited to dine at the Boswells' table at least once during their stay. As well, returning guests would often find fresh flowers in their rooms and, if they imbibed, "Boswell's bottle"—the guest's preferred alcoholic beverage.[21]

Harley Boswell's ability to remember the names of guests and staff, even after a lapse of many years, was notable. "I can recall that after I left Waterton in the fall of 1932, I never returned till about 25 years," said bellhop Ainslie Pankhurst. "I walked into the hotel in the summer and Mr. Boswell was at the front desk. He said: How are you Ainslie? I nearly flipped. I was so surprised that he would remember my name after all those years. He must have dealt with hundreds of employees in those years. ... A great hotel man. He had a way with guests."[22]

Anna Boswell was more introverted but no less forceful in her way. Her duties as housekeeper kept her upstairs and away from public view, requiring "unceasing attention to maintaining the high standards

Harley Boswell. Courtesy Frances Bellucci.

During the winter months, Harley Boswell was an assistant manager at Chicago's prestigious Palmer House. Postcard, author's collection.

Top left: A recognition of Harley Boswell's renown came in 1952 when he was featured on the cover of American Hotel Journal. Courtesy Frances Bellucci, author's collection.

she and the hotel demanded," said Mary Weber Fuller, a niece. "I'm afraid she was a bit of a perfectionist, which endeared her to the clients but not always to the help."[23] Most younger people found Anna "intimidating" upon first meeting her, but warmed up to her once they got to know the gentle person under the tough facade.[24]

The governor general of Canada, the Viscount Alexander of Tunis, was particularly impressed by the Boswells. He stayed at the hotel for three days in August 1951 prior to being inducted as an honourary chief into the Blood tribe.[25] "I must tell you that (the governor general) was specially impressed by the quiet dignity and ease of manner displayed by Mr. and Mrs. Boswell," said Middleton, who helped or-

ganize the vice-regal visit. "He asked that I personally express his deep appreciation for the kind courtesy and generosity thus extended," Middleton said in a letter to Great Northern headquarters in St. Paul.[26] Later, the governor general sent a signed photograph to the Boswells "in appreciation of a delightful stay."[27]

The attention the Boswells showed their guests was irrespective of rank. They paid just as much attention to a vice-regal party as they did to Waterton's longtime residents, who could expect an annual invitation to dine at the Prince of Wales Hotel. It was a small gesture to show townsfolk they were always welcome and to never feel the hotel was off limits. These dinners provided a second service unknown to the guest, said Sophie Allison, who was sometimes a guest along with her father, Canon Middleton. It gave the Boswells an opportunity to watch the performance of their dining room staff. "Woe be the person who slipped up or was out of line," Allison said. "You could be sure the indiscretion would be noted and addressed later."[28]

For all their vigilance, the Boswells could not be everywhere and all seeing. Like other managers in the hotel chain, Harley Boswell could expect a memo pointing out some laxness in his operation from time to time. "The vice-president (of the company), on a recent trip to the Prince of Wales Hotel, states that he observed one of the girls working behind the counter in the gift shop smoking cigarettes while displaying merchandise to one of the guests. … I wish you would have this practice stopped immediately. You have probably noted that each employee's contract plainly states that smoking is not permitted in the lobbies or any place where they are in contact with guests while on duty."[29]

When Great Northern turned over management of its hotels to Knutson in 1957, Boswell, then 68 years old, decided it was time to retire. He knew it would be best for Knutson and his management team if they had free rein to operate the Prince of Wales Hotel as they pleased. Boswell's health, which had been a cause of concern for several years, was also a factor in his decision to step aside.[30] What followed were five summers during which there was a change of manager almost annually, including one year when Boswell was brought out of retirement.

A sense of continuity returned in 1963 when Robert Hayes, an experienced hotelier from Florida, became manager. Like Boswell and Harrison before him, Hayes was a disciplinarian who expected no less of his staff than he did of himself. In the swinging 1960s, Hayes strictly upheld the staff dress code: No sideburns or hair over the ears for men, and skirt lengths at or just below the knee for women. Just as Harrison had maintained a curfew for staff, so did Hayes, although by the 1960s it had been pushed from 11 p.m. to 1 a.m.

While Hayes ruled the roost, there was one tiny corner in the basement of the east wing of the hotel he left alone: The office of the resident customs inspector, a holdover from when the hotel first opened. For three decades Ab Cahoon, a school teacher and Waterton businessman, held the summer position.[31] When not on duty, Cahoon made a point of inviting returning guests, favoured staff and select town residents to his basement office for a drink. He kept an informal guest registry signed by those who sampled his refreshments. Cahoon's hospitality was renowned, prompting one visitor to comment in the guest book, "It's not the customs office— it's the office customs we appreciate." Cahoon tried to ensure, until the last few years, that his office refreshments remained something of a secret; it would not have gone over well with Hayes.[32] Visits to Cahoon's office ended on September 7, 1968, when he packed up for the last time. "Am I the end?" his wife Lucille wrote in the book. She was. Her name and comment are the last entry. The customs office in the hotel was closed with Cahoon's retirement, and his duties transferred to the Chief Mountain border crossing.

All managers need to periodically escape the pressure and daily routine of their job and Hayes and Boswell were no exception. Like Harrison before him, Boswell loved to ride horses.[33] During their 23 seasons at the Prince of Wales Hotel, Harley and Anna explored every trail in Waterton Park on horseback. Harley also liked to get away on his own. He would sometimes ride to the rolling, glacier-formed hills to the east where he would dismount

Maids on a break soak up some sunshine on a porch near the staff cafeteria. There would be no dawdling for these young ladies; buses would be arriving from Many Glacier Hotel before noon with a new group of tourists and the maids had to ensure the rooms were ready. *Courtesy Betty Baker, author's collection.*

With their exotic American dialects and youthful good looks, Glacier Park Transport Company bus drivers, or gearjammers as they were nicknamed, were considered a prize date or boyfriend by eligible Waterton girls. *Ann Harrison, author's collection.*

for a nap while his horse grazed, said Bea Armstrong, a Waterton cottager. Boswell chose this manner of escape because "he could be sure of a rest," Armstrong said. "There are no telephones on the plains, he used to say."[34]

Hayes found rest fleeing to his fifth-floor hotel room, where he would take a daily nap. Unlike Boswell, Hayes was not worried about being bothered by telephone calls—it was understood he was only to be disturbed if there was an emergency. Seldom was there a matter of sufficient merit to disturb Hayes' period of rest. One occasion when Hayes was awakened was in 1967 when the dining room staff threatened to strike because the hostess had fired a busboy for what the staff thought was an inappropriate reason. A call was placed to Hayes' room, but he refused to negotiate during his naptime. Hayes did agree to meet with the disgruntled staff later, when hot heads had cooled and he was rested.

The busboy was eventually reinstated, the hostess chastened and a crisis averted.[35]

Handling guests can pose as much of a challenge for the manager of the Prince of Wales Hotel as sorting out staff issues. One remarkable incident took place in the 1960s when a group of well-meaning tourists tried to assist police. The fracas started when the tourists saw the hotel's elderly gardener using a broom to shoo away a deer decapitating his carefully tended flowers. Hoping to make a case of animal cruelty against him for hitting the deer, several tourists grabbed the gardener and dragged him to the front desk where they asked a clerk to call the RCMP. Meanwhile, another group of tourists tried to wrangle the deer into the hotel lobby to hold the animal as physical evidence. For several minutes, pandemonium reigned until the deer escaped and the gardener, after dressing down the tourists in an explosion of Chinese, stormed off leaving Hayes to deal with the well-meaning citizens. No charges were ever laid in the incident.

Visitors to the hotel have stood out for other reasons, and employees go home each season with a new crop of stories. It can be but an offhand comment that sets one patron apart from the many. A tourist once walked up to the front desk and asked: "Where are the seals?"

"There aren't any," the clerk replied, somewhat puzzled.

"Why did the sign say 'Seal guns here'?" the tourist said, referring to the sign at the park entrance requiring anyone carrying weapons to secure them while visiting Waterton.[36]

Then there was the tourist who asked his waitress: "How much does that mountain weigh?" Quite calmly the waitress replied: "Is that with or without trees, sir?" Alternate answers over the years include:

"Is that with or without snow?" and "Is that with or without animals?"

Alberta's liquor laws, combined with religion, created a custom in the dining room that puzzled hotel patrons no end. When it became legal to serve liquor in dining rooms, some of the waitresses and waiters balked. The reluctant servers were Mormons, whose faith prohibits anything to do with alcohol. To circumvent forcing the Mormons to handle liquor, the bartender was required to serve all drinks and wine in the dining room. Guests found it odd when their server refused to take liquor orders, instead referring them to the bartender. And it was equally odd to have to pay for the beverages separately from the meal.

The wind in Waterton is frequently the subject of comment by visitors, and not without reason. The average speed of the wind off the lake is 20 miles per hour (32 km/h), and hurricane force blasts of 100 miles per hour (161 km/h) are not unknown.[37] The rejoinder by tour bus guides when asked about the wind in Waterton is that it sometimes blows so hard there are whitecaps in the toilets at the Prince of Wales Hotel. This always brings a hearty laugh, but is often forgotten as the day wears on. In the evening, the tour guide's remark begins to take on meaning. As hotel guests try to settle in for a night's rest, some find sleep eludes them. The wind can create a racket as it whistles through sliver-size joints or cracks where the wood has dried and shrunk over the decades. In extreme situations, windows may rattle in their jambs and screen doors slam if not hooked shut. Finally, a swaying motion sets in as the wooden hotel flexes and rocks back and forth on its foundation. In ones and twos, guests descend to the lobby in search of steady ground. The next morning over breakfast, guests regale each other with stories about the ferocity of the wind. The tour guide's colourful remark will be a prized memory shared with friends for years to come.

The wind isn't the only thing to shake up guests at the hotel. With a building as old as the Prince, it's not surprising there should be a ghost story about it. According to the tale, in the early years of the hotel, a chambermaid named Sara was spurned by her lover. Disheartened, she is said to have leaped to her death from the fourth floor mezzanine to the lobby below. Her spirit reportedly haunts the hotel by "rattling liquor bottles and exhaling icy sneezes down the necks of wary guests."[38]

This ghost story bears an uncanny resemblance to a true but tragic incident that occurred at the hotel in 1977, which explains why the legend of Sara didn't begin until the 1980s. A gift shop worker committed suicide by jumping from a sixth-story window onto the flagstone patio in front of the hotel.[39] The exact motive and circumstances that led up to the suicide can not be irrefutably established, but it is

Linnet Lake, just north of the hotel, was a popular swimming hole for hotel staff and park visitors, with its sandy beach and nearby bathhouse for changing. Courtesy Ann Harrison, author's collection.

While Hollywood stars, like Clark Gable, and other luminaries were invited by Great Northern to visit Glacier Park, the railway seldom showed these guests the northern half of the peace park or the Prince of Wales Hotel. In an August 1937 stop at Glacier Park Hotel, Gable meets Middle Calf, left, and Theodore Last Star. Great Northern Railway publicity and advertising department, Minnesota Historical Society.

enlist or entice notable people to visit Glacier Park. So while Clark Gable, U.S. President Franklin Roosevelt, FBI director J. Edgar Hoover and Crown Prince Olaf and Princess Martha of Norway saw the beauty of Glacier, little effort was made to show them the Canadian half of Waterton-Glacier International Peace Park.[40] Rather, it seems, noteworthy people—like other tourists—discover Waterton by accident. For the staff of the Prince of Wales Hotel, it's a momentary thrill to have such visitors. For a highly recognized public figure, it's a treasure to discover an out-of-the-way place where their fame doesn't detract from their enjoyment of the park.

Newspaper columnist and author Ernie Pyle arrived in Waterton on foot in the 1940s, having hiked 50 miles (80 km) in four days from Going-to-the-Sun Highway via Granite Park Chalets and Fifty Mountain Camp.[41] Steve McQueen and his family pulled up to the Prince of Wales Hotel in 1967 in a huge motorhome while making their way to Alaska on a family vacation.[42] Clint Eastwood and his wife popped in during a break from filming the movie *Thunderbolt and Lightfoot* in Montana. Likewise William Shatner (*Star Trek*), Linda Blair (*The Exorcist*) and Alicia Silverstone (*Clueless*) stopped in while filming movies in southern Alberta.

Although times have changed greatly since the Prince of Wales Hotel opened, the pledge of hotel staff to serve guests remains constant. Employees are ever-vigilant to carry on the legacy of those who came before them, ensuring the future of the hotel and many more stories about managers, staff and patrons.

known the woman had a crush on the young and handsome hotel manager, Clifford Hummel.

Unlike the Banff Springs Hotel, the Prince of Wales Hotel has not been a magnet for personalities or Hollywood stars. Great Northern Railway would sometimes

Epilogue

No work of history is carved in stone or, in the case of the Prince of Wales Hotel, wood. As long as the building remains standing, its story will continue to unfold.

Carthew Lodge, the home Louis Hill had built in Waterton, continues to operate as Northland Lodge under the ownership and management of the Hacking family. Fire nearly destroyed the lodge on May 17, 1989. The heat from the early morning blaze was so intense the windows exploded, waking the park warden who alerted the fire department. The damage was repaired but the suspected arsonist was never found.

In 1986, Waterton Inter-Nation Shoreline Cruises Co. purchased the *Motor Vessel International*. The owners have invested substantial sums to renovate the vessel, ensuring its continued safe operation for many years to come.

The international peace park concept, initiated and promoted by Rotarians, has been copied around the world. The natural beauty and diversity of Waterton-Glacier park was singled out in 1995 as a World Heritage Site, one of only 500 such sites in the world having "outstanding universal value." At the time, it was the only World Heritage Site consisting of two adjoining parks in different countries.

In the unending world of corporate reorganization and name changes, the company that owns the Prince of Wales Hotel, Glacier Park Inc., has a new master, Viad Corp. In a bold attempt to lengthen the summer tourist season, the Prince of Wales Hotel, along with its corporate sister Glacier Park Lodge, is now open from mid-May to late-September. This was first tried experimentally once in the 1970s and proved, because of poor planning, to be an economic disaster. Glacier Park Inc. is using discount prices to entice tourists to the hotels early and late in the season, a promotion that has, initially, met with good success.

Since the mid 1990s, Glacier Park Inc. has had ongoing discussions with park officials about a proposal to expand the hotel. The initial design for the expansion was based on sketches drawn in 1927 by architect Roy Childs Jones with Toltz, King and Day of St. Paul, Minn. Glacier Park Inc's. expansion proposal is the most serious since Great Northern opened the hotel. Whatever the outcome, it will be a new chapter in the unfolding story of the Prince of Wales Hotel.

Appendices

Hikers struggle up the forested slope of Mount Crandell for a better view of the Prince of Wales Hotel and Upper Waterton Lake. Canadian Government Travel Bureau photo, author's collection. CGTB 9-1405.

Hotel Plans Impress
Waterton Hostelry To Be Fully Modern

(From Our Own Correspondent)

WATERTON NATIONAL PARK–

Aug. 25.–Every feature of a modern hotel, including a rotunda, lounge, dining room, stores, barbershop, and mezzanine, all in a four storey, 64-room Swiss chalet type building, measuring 212 ft. (63.6 m) by 88 ft. (26.4 m) exclusive of wide flanking terraces is shown in final Great Northern hotel plans which arrived yesterday.

Provision is made for additional dormitory wings and an enlarged lobby and dining room.

Distinctive points are a large rotunda of four-storey heighth, and an immense fireplace with an exterior stone chimney rising 61 feet (18.3 m).

The ground floor includes the lobby, lounge, dining room, shops, manager's office, kitchen, help's dining room and two terraces adjoining the lobby.

Three shops and lounge measuring 56 feet by 40 feet (16.8 m by 12 m), with a stone fireplace are in the east wing. The dining room measuring 56 feet by 40 feet (16.8 m by 12 m), kitchen, etc., are in the west wing.

Rotunda

The rotunda or lobby which is in the centre measures 52 feet, 9 in. by 82 feet (17.9 m by 24.6 m). Balconies for each storey level go up in tiers around it. On the south side, overlooking the lake, a mezzanine covers part of the lobby. Here, up for two stories, a few huge windows light up the interior. Bedrooms flank the rotunda balconies for the next two stories.

The windows on the ground floor measure 12 feet wide by 9 feet high (3.6 m by 2.7 m) each, and those on the second floor, 12 feet by 8 feet (3.6 m by 2.4 m). They are of plate glass divided into regular rectangular sections that can be opened to the outside air on calm days.

Entrance is afforded from the drive-way by a 54 feet by 18 feet (16.2 m by 5.5 m) flagstone terrace. From the other end of the rotunda, a larger 110 feet by 20 feet (33 m by 6 m) terrace looks out on the lake below.

Another doorway is through an entrance corridor adjacent to the shops and lounge. It is separated from the latter by two most artistic [sic]

This exit leads to what will be a lawn and gardens.

Handsome Touch

The fireplace and chimney is a very distinctive piece of architecture. The stonework in the lounge is 14 feet wide (4.2 m) over all. The hearth is 6 feet wide (1.8 m) and the opening 6 feet high (1.95 m). The 61 foot (18.3 m) chimney is enclosed for the first floor but rises above the east entrance hall and against the main building for the rest of its height. It is supported by buttresses for part of its length.

The bedroom corridors in the east wing end against the chimney wall. Here for three stories, windows and [sic] pierced through the stone with the flue is to one side. This produces a most pleasing effect on the exterior of the stack.

Underneath the ground floor is a partially excavated basement. Below the east wing is a barbershop, photographer's studio, and mens' [sic] lavatories. A storeroom is beneath the kitchen.

The kitchen and help's dining room are built out of the dining room. No bedrooms are above them. The kitchen is 31 feet by 37 feet (9.3 m by 11.1 m).

Second Floor

The second floor has a mezzanine reading room already mentioned. This takes up the south section immediately over a portion of the rotunda. From the balconies overlooking the rest of the rotunda; 18 bedrooms extend into the east and west wings, also flank the balconies to the north.

The next floor has 23 bed chambers.

The increase is because rooms are now in the space a reading room took on the mezzanine floor. The fourth and last floor is precisely similar to the one below it.

Each of the 64 bed rooms has a bath, and are all outside rooms. The majority of them have small rustic projecting balconies. Each room is an exact duplicate of the others. They are 16 feet by 10 feet (4.8 m by 3 m). Finishes are in wood panelled wainscoting with some kind of fireproof plasterboard above.

The interior decoration of the whole building is rather similar. Wood panels, stone and rough finishes are used entirely to produce a most harmonizing rustic impression.

Exterior drawings show a most delightful Swiss chalet type of building with picturesquely carved eaves, and barge-boards, balconies and harmonizing wooden fire-escapes all produce this effect.

High stone-faced foundations and wooden sidings above further heighten it. Then there is the stone chimney already mentioned.

Most distinctive is a slight indentation in the top centre of the front of the hotel. Overhanging it is a modified gable with artistic barge-boards and eaves.

As stated allowance is made for future construction, two diagonal dormitory wings will run northeast and southeast from the end of the east wing.

The lobby can be extended to include the present dining room and it replaced by a larger one continued from the west wing.

Layout of the grounds is not shown. Neither are plans of the outlying buildings.

However, it is known that the servants' sleeping quarters will be on the wooded slope of the hill to the west of the hotel site. Construction of that building will be commenced very soon.

The following article from the Lethbridge Herald, August 27, 1926, was the first account to describe in detail Great Northern Railway's proposed hotel in Waterton Lakes National Park. The design, from which the Prince of Wales Hotel originated, is based on Many Glacier Hotel in Glacier National Park, Mont.

The following is from an April 2, 1927, article in the Lethbridge Herald. The description shows how the design of the Prince of Wales Hotel changed in the months since it was first publicly announced (see description on previous page).

Waterton National Park is Tourist Lodestone

NEW ERA OF PROSPERITY COMES TO SOUTHWEST ALBERTA RESORT WITH ERECTION OF G.N.R. HOTEL

Enormous Increase in Tourist Traffic from U.S. May be Expected When "Prince of Wales" Hotel Opens in June—Total expenditure Planned is Over a Million Dollars, Opening All Points in Park to tourists—Details of Hotel Structure

(From Our Own Correspondent)

WATERTON NATIONAL PARK April 1—The new hotel under construction here is rather unique in that it differs materially from the usual style of architecture followed by the Great Northern in their hotel buildings, it being of the latest Swiss chalet style with deep pitched high roofs and extremes in outside finishing along attractive lines.

The structure which is built in four wings extending north, south, east and west is surmounted in the centre by a 40 foot (12 m) observation tower, access to which is gained by a winding stairway to an observation chamber of comfortable dimensions. ...

A Charming Interior

The present structure has 90 guest chambers, each with private bathroom, etc., and with private outside doors leading to hanging balconies on the exterior walls.

These 90 bedrooms are distributed over seven different floor levels, the east and west wings being five storeys in height, while the centre and main sections have seven floors which follow around the outside walls only, leaving the centre open from ceiling to rotunda floor, a height of 70 feet (21 m).

From each floor mezzanine floors extend around the lobby, giving clear views of the large rotunda beneath.

This is all finished in huge square timbers of different designs, while the ceiling is supported underneath and open to view by immense trusses built of 14 x 20 square (35.5 cm by 10.1 cm) timbers, strengthened with large iron butterfly hinges and plates.

The ceiling itself is of narrow matched lumber nailed diagonally in different panels which makes a very artistic finish.

The mezzanine floors are all edged with fancy scroll work railings three feet in height. The front of the main rotunda and facing the upper lake view is all finished plate glass doors and windows affording exceptionally good light and unobstructed view.

This rotunda extends east over the entire floor space of the bottom of the east wing and includes the lounge room, which has an immense big stone fireplace at one end, the rock chimney from which extends clear over the peak of the roof, being 75 feet (22.5 m) in height.

The lounge room end of the rotunda also has practically all glass front. From this room a stairway leads down into the basement where the photo studio, barber shops, beauty parlour, etc., are located.

The north wing up to the first floor is built on large pillars open underneath, which constitutes the driveway to the main hotel entrance and where the big busses [sic] will unload their passengers.

This end is finished in fancy glass as a contrast to the plate glass on the opposite side. On the north side and facing the entrance will be large parking space for cars, hitching rails for saddle ponies, etc., while on the south side a large open flagstone terrace is being built surrounded by a three foot stone wall.

Immediately west of the rotunda is the dining room which has large clear glass windows on both north and south sides. In this spacious room several adze finished pillars in rustic design support the floors above and add materially to the appearance of the room itself.

West of this is the kitchen, which is built against the hotel but practically an independent section from the main building, it being of low cottage style roof with large stone chimneys and has full sized basement underneath.

Built into the corner between the north and west wings is the manager's office which connects with the registry and cashiers' desks in the rotunda. Opposite these on the east side of these doors is the passenger elevator which runs from the basement to the fifth floor rooms.

Interior Finish

Inside finishing is of all plaster board, with the rotunda finished in mural paintings of local scenes. A long addition with flat sloping roof and long overhanging eaves, supported by fancy brackets houses the baggage and check rooms.

On the outside of the building shows a rock race for several feet to the first floor line. From here it is stucco and pebble dash to the third floor and then matched and dipped siding laid in panels of different designs, all the window casings and eave boards of fancy scroll work with huge timber brackets hung from the gable ends and following the slope of the roof.

With all this contrasting finish outside, the hanging balconies from every floor and on all sides and ends with supports of fancy cut brackets, the scroll work around the windows and along the eaves, etc., a most striking and pleasing effect is obtained in exterior finishing.

Water Supply

The water supply is taken care of by a pumping station on the lakes shore below the Narrows from where water is piped up the hill to the hotel and west to a knoll some 300 yards from the hotel itself, into a 100,000-gallon (450,000 litre) steel water tank which rests on a 100-foot (30 m) steel tower. This tank is for fire protection, in addition to which sprinkler pipes four inches (15.6 cm) in diameter are laid along the peaks of the roof, which allows for immediate sprinkling of the entire top of the building in case of fire or for cooling purposes in case of excessive heat.

A power house built beneath the hill on the west and directly below the water tower has engines and boilers installed sufficiently large to meet the heating and lighting requirements of a 600-room hotel if necessary.

A large garage is also to be built here for the accommodation not only of the visiting motorists but for the fleet of transportation busses [sic] belonging to the company, which will be used to transport the thousands of tourists to the hotel from Glacier Park hotels and from Banff on the north.

INDIANS MAKE DECORATIONS FOR NEW HOTEL

[By O. J. McGillis]

The building of the Prince of Wales hotel in the Canadian Rockies abutting the north boundary of Glacier National Park, will adequately relieve the pressure which has been felt in Glacier Park for added de luxe accommodations, and it will at the same time provide these superior creature comforts at a location from which not only the famous beauty spots of the Canadian Rockies will be accessible by easy motor, launch and saddlehorse trips, but from which the hitherto almost unapproachable but stupendous grandeur of the north country of Glacier Park can be seen in the same easy way. ...

Swiss Architecture

The architecture of the hotel is Swiss. The building with its high gabled roofs and dormers, its carved beams and ornamented balconies seems to add charm to its lovely Alpine setting.

It consists of a high gabled central section and gabled wings extending from either side. Three graceful dormers on each side of the two wings break the monotony of the high-pitched roofs.

Within the main section of the building is the lobby, an open well five stories high. It is supported by heavy carved posts, beams and trusses. At the north and south side of this main section above the second first floor are sleeping rooms.

The outlook from the lobby at both ends is through plate glass windows that extend high from the ground. The main entrance is on the north end of the lobby section, and the lobby is 54 feet wide by 82 feet long (16.2 m by 24.6 m).

As the lobby is entered the hotel office is on the right, and on the opposite side an office is provided for the convenience of patrons in arranging for tours, saddlehorse trips and train reservations.

On this side also is an elevator and a broad stairway leading to the upper floors. The first floor of the east wing contains a large lounge room along one side of which will be hotel shops, and at the far end of the room there will be a mammoth fireplace.

The ground floor of the other wing will contain, at the far end, a modern hotel kitchen off the lobby. In this wing will be the dining room with a seating capacity of 250 guests.

Blood Indians Make Friezes

Friezes around the walls of the lobby and lounge rooms are being made by the Blood Indians, one of the Blackfeet [sic] Confederacy tribes which is settled on a reservation in Canada a short distance from the new hotel.

These Indians, like their confederates, the Peigans and Blackfeet, had no written language.

Their traditions and legions were handed down generation after generation by word of mouth. In some instances records were made of tribal exploits by picture writing on skins, and they became quite adept in the making of pictographs.

The friezes which will decorate the lobby and lounge of the Prince of Wales Hotel will portray in vividly-colored pictographs the significant and heroic events in the lives of the present Blood Chiefs and of a few who are remembered out of the dim past for their achievements.

Coats of Arms Appear

The dining room frieze will consist of reproductions on canvas panels of some of the outstanding scenic views of both Glacier and Waterton Lakes National Parks. A panel above the north or main entrance of the hotel will be embellished with the coats of arms of the Dominion of Canada and the provinces of British Columbia, Alberta, Saskatchewan and Manitoba.

Plate glass windows extending the entire height of the first floor will provide an alluring outlook from both sides of the lounge room and dining room.

One of the striking features of the interior decoration will be the lighting fixtures. They are unique and original in design; great and small pendant lanterns covered with parchment and decorated with pictographs by the Blood Indians.

All of the space above the first floors in the east and west wings of the Prince of Wales hotel is given over to sleeping rooms. In all there will be 90 bedrooms, arranged to comfortably accommodate each two persons.

A few of the rooms on the top floor will not have private baths, but 80 out of the total of 90 rooms in the hotel will have private baths.

The hotel structure was so planned that additions can easily be made, and the plan is to eventually have accommodation for from 400 to 500 guests, and dining room capacity for the same or a larger number.

The accommodations which will be available when the present unit of the hotel is completed will be as fine as are to be found in any of the better class resort hotels in the country.

The hotel, of course, will be steam heated, electric lighted, and there will be hot and cold running water throughout.

The following is from a July 9, 1927, article in the Lethbridge Herald. The evolution of the design of the hotel is evident from the first two news stories. It also provides a good description of the interior finish of the hotel.

Bibliography

Interviews

Allison, Sophie	Waterton Park, Alta.	August 10, 1975
Annand, George	Waterton Park, Alta.	August 5, 1974
Armstrong, Barbara	Waterton Park, Alta.	August 14, 1974
Baker, Betty	Waterton Park, Alta.	August 3, 1974
Black, Margaret	St. Mary, Mont.	November 20, 1997
Downing, Robert	St. Paul, Minn.	March 14, 1995
Friesen, Helen	Waterton Park, Alta.	July 16, 1975
Hacking, George	Provo, Utah	August 19, 1996
Harrison, Ann	Victoria, B.C.	September 1, 1976
Haug, Ernie	Waterton Park, Alta.	August 18, 1974
Meklusik, Anne	Waterton Park, Alta.	August 6, 1974
Montalbetti, Eugene	Waterton Park, Alta.	August 6, 1974
O'Brien, Mary	Marshall, Minn.	December 1, 1990
Oland, Jack	Calgary, Alta.	January 8, 1975
Oland, Jr., Doug	Waterton Park, Alta.	September 9, 1990
Reeves, Jim	Lethbridge, Alta.	August 21, 1975
Sterrett, Bill	Balzac, Alta.	July 24, 1996
Tangren, Joan	Waterton Park, Alta.	September 9, 1990
Thompson, Andy	Lethbridge, Alta.	April 29, 1975

Correspondence

Armstrong, R. J.	Penticton, B.C.		
Currie, Gertrude	Lethbridge, Alta.	Oland, Mary R.	Lethbridge, Alta.
French, Bessie	Hill Spring, Alta.	Pankhurst, Ainslie	Lethbridge, Alta.
Graham, Helen	Lethbridge, Alta.	Pike, Sally	Vancouver, B.C.
Graham, Magde	Lethbridge, Alta.	Platt, Margaret	Maple Ridge, B.C.
Haug, Lillian	Fort Macleod, Alta.	Potter, Jessie	Vancouver, B.C.
Higgins, Don	Lethbridge, Alta.	Routledge, H. E.	Lethbridge, Alta.
Jones, A. T.	Edmonton, Alta.	Taylor, George	Magrath, Alta.
LaFlamme, Irene	Tucson, Ariz.		
Meech, V. E.	Del Mar, Calif.		

Commercial Opportunities in Waterton Lakes National Park Townsite. A study prepared for Parks Canada by Hu Harries and Associates Ltd., 1977.

Development Plan for Waterton Townsite, Waterton Lakes National Park. Prepared for Parks Canada by the planning division of Underwood, McLellan and Associates Ltd., 1970.

Djuff Fond, Ray. M8259. Glenbow Museum archive. Collection of papers, photographs and blueprints on the Prince of Wales Hotel donated by former hotel employee.

Eastcott, Doug, editor. *The Holyroyd Journals—Chronicles of a Park Warden 1919-1947.* Parks Canada. n.d.

Getty, Ian. *The History of Human Settlement in Waterton Lakes National Park 1800-1937.* A research paper prepared for the Historic Parks Branch. Calgary, Alta.: Parks Canada, 1971.

Hays, Sr., Howard H., and Noble, H. A. *Drivers' Manual.* 8th edition. East Glacier, Mont.: Glacier Park Transport Company, 1949.

Hill, Sr., Louis Warren. Business and personal papers in the possession of the James Jerome Hill Reference Library in St. Paul, Minn.

Middleton, The Venerable Archdeadon Samuel H. A collection of letters, notes and clippings in the possession of his daughter, Sophie Allison of Pincher Creek, Alta.

Great Northern Railway president's subject files:

File 11.677	Glacier and Waterton Lakes Parks: Power plants 1924-59.
File 11.732	Waterton Lakes Park: Prince of Wales Hotel construction and operation 1925-60.
File 11.866	Canadian Rockies Hotel Company 1926-40.
File 11.866 A	Canadian Rockies Hotel Company: Prince of Wales Hotel.
File 12.094	Prince of Wales Hotel Co.: Boat for Waterton Lake 1926-55.
File 12.506	Waterton Lakes Park: Proposed golf course.
File 13.638	Glacier Park Hotel Co., Canadian Rockies Hotel Company: AFEs and RFAs 1932-58.
File 13.657	Glacier Park Hotel Co., Canadian Rockies Hotel Company: Claims against Taymond and Whitcomb Co. 1932-34.
File 13.760	Waterton Lakes Park: Bar and liquor licence for Prince of Wales Hotel.
File 14.476	Glacier Park Company and Prince of Wales Hotel company: Force and organization. 193?-61.
File 4697	Glacier Park Hotel and Station 1911-17.
File 6456	Glacier Park Transport Company 1935-37.

Great Northern Railway records, Glacier Park Company:

Box 22.F.11.9B	Glacier Park Co., Canadian division.
Box 22.F.8.5B	Glacier Park Co., Canadian exchange rates.
	Launches and Docks. International 1929-60.
Box 22.F.8.6F	Glacier Park Co., Prince of Wales Hotel correspondence 1950-60.
	Glacier Park Co., Prince of Wales Hotel newsstand 1932-36, 1949.
Box 22.F.9.1B	Glacier Park Co., Indian historical paintings
	Instructions and bulletins
	Caretaker reports
	Roads and trails
	Waitress uniforms

Box 22.F.9.6F	Glacier Park Co., Forest fires 1919-45.
Box 22.F.9.7B	Glacier Park Co., *M.V. International* construction 1926-27.
Box 22.F.11.1B	Glacier Park Co., *M.V. International* operations 1922-57.
Box 17.C.7.5B	Glacier Park Co., Photographs
Box 133.F.2.12F	Glacier Park Co., Photographs
Box 133.F.2.13B	Glacier Park Co., Photographs
Box 22.F.11.10F	Glacier Park Co., Canadian division
Box 22.F.12.1B	Glacier Park Co., Licences, beer 1927-60
	Construction materials inventory
Box 132.F.19.5B	Glacier Park Co., Barber shop leases, Beauty shop leases
	Prince of Wales Hotel construction, employee injuries

General correspondence

Oland, Sr., Douglas. Unpublished memoirs written in September 1963 in Lethbridge, Alta.

Toltz, King, Duvall, Anderson and Associates, St. Paul, Minn. Architectural drawings and sketches and photographs made by employees in 1926-27 for the Great Northern Railway for a hotel in Waterton Lakes National Park, Alta.

Vickers, J. Roderick. *Alberta Plains Prehistory: A review.* Archeological Survey of Alberta. Occasional Paper No. 27. Edmonton, Alta: Alberta Culture, Historical Resources Division, 1986.

Official publications and records

Beals, Dr. Ralph L. *History of Glacier National Park with Particular Emphasis on the Northern Developments.* Berkeley, Calif.: U.S. Department of the Interior, National Park Service, 1935.

Canada, Orders in council.   May 30, 1895.
June 8, 1911.
June 24, 1914.

Interior, Department of the. *Reports of the Park Superintendents.* Ottawa, Ont.: King's Printer, 1911-30.

Interior, Department of the. *Waterton Lakes National Park: Lakes Amid the Mountains.* Ottawa, Ont.: King's Printer, 1928.

Mines and Resources, Department of. *Waterton Lakes National Park, Alberta.* Ottawa, Ont.: King's Printer, 1939.

Mines and Technical Surveys, Department of. Baird, D. M. *Waterton Lakes National Park: Lakes Amid the Mountains.* Ottawa, Ont.: Queen's Printer, 1971.

Newspapers

Calgary Herald
Cardston News
Edmonton Journal
Fort Macleod Gazette
Fort McMurray Today
Hungry Horse News
The Lethbridge Herald
New York World
Pincher Creek Echo
Red Deer Advocate
St. Paul Dispatch
Toronto Globe and Mail

Aldington, Richard. *The Strange Life of Charles Waterton*. New York: Duell, Sloan and Pearce, 1949.

Anderson, Frank W. *Frontier Guide to Waterton: Land of Leisure*. Calgary, Alta.: Frontiers Unlimited, 1968.

Bloch, Michael, editor. *Wallis and Edward, Letters 1931-1937*. New York: Summit Books, 1986.

Bloch, Michael. *The Secret File of the Duke of Windsor*. London: Bantam Press, 1988.

Borne, Lawrence R. *Dude Ranching—A Complete History*. Albuquerque, N.M.: University of New Mexico Press, 1983.

Brumley, Laurie Milne. *The Narrows Site in Waterton Lakes National Park, Alberta*. Unpublished MA thesis, University of Calgary, 1971.

Buchholtz, C.W. *Man in Glacier*. 2nd edition. West Glacier, Mont.: Glacier Natural History Association, 1993.

Byfield, Ted, editor. *Brownlee and the Triumph of Populism*. Volume 5 of *Alberta in the 20th Century—A Journalistic History of the Province in Twelve Volumes*. Edmonton, Alta.: United Western Communications Ltd., 1996.

Canon (Samuel H. Middleton). *Waterton-Glacier International Peace Park*. (Published by the author, 1947).

Cashman, Tony. *The Alberta Motor Association—A History*. Edmonton, Alta.: Alberta Motor Association, 1967.

Chief Mountain Country—A History of Cardston and District, Vol. 1. Calgary, Alta.: Cardston and District Historical Society, 1978.

Christopherson, Edmund. *Adventure Among the Glaciers*. Missoula, Mont.: Earthquake Press, 1966.

Creese, Walter L. *The Crowning of the American Landscape—Eight Great Spaces and Their Buildings*. Princeton, N.J.: Princeton University Press, 1985.

Cruise, David and Griffiths, Alison. *Lords of the Line—The Men Who Built the CPR*. Markham, Ont.: Penguin Books of Canada, 1988.

Deittert, Gerald A. *Grinnell's Glacier—George Bird Grinnell and Glacier National Park*. Missoula, Mont.: Mountain Press Publishing Company, 1992.

Dempsey, Hugh. *Indian Tribes of Alberta*. Calgary, Alta.: Glenbow Museum, 1979.

Dempsey, Hugh A. *The Gentle Persuader. A Biography of James Gladstone, Indian Senator*. Saskatoon, Sask.: Western Producer Prairie Books, 1986.

Donzel, Catherine, Gregory, Alexis and Walter, Marc. *Grand Hotels of North America*. Toronto, Ont.: McClelland & Stewart, 1989.

Downs, Art, editor. *Waterton National Park—Land of the Shining Mountains*. Frontier Series No. 15. Surrey, B.C.: Frontier Books, 1980.

Evans, Simon. *Prince Charming Goes West—The Story of the E. P. Ranch*. Calgary, Alta.: University of Calgary Press, 1993.

Forsberg, Roberta J. *He Who Shoots the Stars—The Story of Canon Middleton*. Whittier, Calif., Historical Society of Alberta, 1964.

Gladstone, G. L. *A History of Waterton Lakes National Park, Waterton Park, Alberta*. (n.p.) 1961.

Gordy, P. L., Frey, F. R. and Norris, D. K., compiled by. *Geological Guide for the CSPG 1977 Waterton-Glacier Park Field Conference*. Calgary, Alta.: Canadian Society of Petroleum Geologists, 1977.

Gray, James H. *Booze—The Impact of Whisky on the Prairie West*. Scarborough, Ont.: The New American Library of Canada Limited, 1974.

Gray, James H. *The Roar of the Twenties*. Toronto, Ont.: Macmillan of Canada, 1975.

Gray, James H. *Bacchanalia Revisited—Western Canada's Boozy Skid to Social Disaster*. Saskatoon, Sask.: Western Producer Prairie Books, 1982.

Hagen, John. *A History of Many Glacier Hotel*. Minneapolis, Minn.: Glacier Park Foundation Inc., 1985.

Hanna, Warren L. *Montana's Many-Splendored Glacierland*. Seattle, Wash.: Superior Publishing Company, 1976.

Hart, E. J. *Diamond Hitch—The Early Outfitters and Guides of Banff and Jasper*. Banff, Alta.: Summer Thought Ltd., 1979.

Hart, E. J. *The Selling of Canada—The CPR and the Beginning of Canadian Tourism*. Banff, Alta.: Altitude Publishing Ltd., 1983.

Hart, Edward John. *The Brewster Story: From Pack Train to Tour Bus*. Banff, Alta.: Brewster Transport Company Ltd., 1981.

Hidy, Ralph W., Hidy, Muriel E. and Scott, Roy V., with Hofsommer, Don L. *The Great Northern Railway—A History*. Boston, Mass.: Harvard Business School Press, 1988.

Hitchcock, Anthony and Lindgren, Jean. *Country Inns, Lodges and Historic Hotels of Canada*. Fifth edition. New York: Burt Franklin and Company, 1985.

Holbrook, Stewart. *The Story of American Railroads*. New York: Crown Publishers, 1947.

Holbrook, Stewart H. *James J. Hill—A Great Life in Brief*. New York: Alfred A. Knopf, 1955.

Huddleston, Fred M. *A History of the Settlement and Building Up of the Area in S.W. Alberta bordering Waterton Park on the North, from 1889*. (By the author.) Circa 1969.

Hummel, Don. *Wake Up, America! The Environmentalists are Stealing the National Parks—The Destruction of Concessions and Public Access*. Bellevue, Wash.: The Free Enterprise Press, 1987.

Hungry Wolf, Beverly. *Daughters of the Buffalo Women—Maintaining the Tribal Faith*. Standoff, Alta.: Canadian Caboose Press, 1996.

Kalman, Harold D. *The Railway Hotels and the Development of the Chateau Style in Canada*. No. 1 of *Studies in Architectural History*. Victoria, B.C.: University of Victoria Maltwood Museum, 1968.

Kenney, Mart. *Mart Kenney and His Western Gentlemen*. Saskatoon, Sask.: Western Producer Prairie Books, 1981.

Klein, Aaron. *Encyclopedia of North American Railroads*. New York: Bison Book Corporation, 1985.

Lane, Harold Francis, editor. *The Biographical Directory of the Railway Officials of America*. 1913 edition. New York: Simmons-Boardman Publishing Co., 1913.

Liddell, Ken. *Alberta Revisited*. Toronto, Ont.: Ryerson Press, 1960.

Liddell, Ken. *Roamin' Empire of Southern Alberta*. Frontier book No. 6 Calgary, Alta.: Frontiers Unlimited, n.d.

Lothian, W. F. *A Brief History of Canada's National Parks*. Ottawa, Ont.: Department of the Environment, 1987.

MacGregor, James A. *A History of Alberta*. Edmonton, Alta.: Hurtig Publishers, 1972.

Malone, Michael. *James J. Hill, Empire Builder of the Northwest*. Oklahoma City, Okla.: University of Oklahoma Press, 1996.

Martin, Albro. *James J. Hill and the Opening of the Northwest*. New York: Oxford University Press, 1976.

Matthews, Henry. "Kirtland Cutter: Spokane's Architect," in *Spokane & The Inland Empire—An Interior Pacific Northwest Anthology*. Edited by David H. Stratton. Pullman, Wash.: Washington State University Press, 1991.

Matthews, Henry. "The Search for a Northwest Vernacular: Kirtland Cutter and the Rustic Picturesque 1888-1920," in *Art and the National Dream—The Search for Vernacular Expression in Turn-of-the-Century Design*. Edited by Nicola Gordon Bowe. Dublin, Ireland: Irish Academic Press, 1993.

McCarter, Steve. With an essay by Dale Martin. *Guide to The Milwaukee Road in Montana*. Helena, Mont.: Montana Historical Society Press, 1992.

McKee, Bill and Klassen, Georgeen. *Trail of Iron—The CPR and the Birth of the West, 1880-1930*. Vancouver, B.C.: Douglas & McIntyre Ltd., 1983.

Ober, Michael J. "Enmity and Alliance: Park Service-Concessioner Relations in Glacier National Park, 1892-1961." Unpublished MA thesis, University of Montana, 1973.

Panati, Charles. *Panati's Parade of Fads, Follies and Manias—The Origin of Our Most Cherished Obsessions.* New York: Harper Perennial, 1991.

Patton, Brian, editor. *Tales from the Canadian Rockies.* Edmonton, Alta.: Hurtig Publishers, 1984.

Picture Writing by the Blackfeet Indians of Glacier National Park, Montana. Interpretations by Chief Eagle Calf and Chief Heavy Breast. St. Paul, Minn.: Great Northern Railway, circa 1923.

Pomeroy, Earl. *In Search of the Golden West: The Tourist in Western America.* New York: Alfred A. Knopf, 1957.

Pringle, Heather. *A Guide to Waterton Lakes National Park.* Vancouver, B.C.: Douglas and McIntyre Ltd., 1986.

Pyle, Ernie. *Home Country.* New York: William Sloane Associates, 1947.

Raczka, Paul. *Winold Reiss—Portraits of the Races.* Great Falls, Mont.: C. M. Russell Museum, 1986.

Reeves, Dr. Brian. *An Archeological Resources Inventory of Waterton Lakes National Park.* Calgary, Alta.: University of Calgary, 1970.

Reiss, Winold and Linderman, F. B. *Blackfeet Indians.* St. Paul, Minn.: Great Northern Railway, 1935.

Rinehart, Mary Roberts. *Call of the Mountains.* St. Paul, Minn.: Great Northern Railway, 1927.

Robinson, Donald H. *Through the Years in Glacier National Park.* West Glacier, Mont.: Glacier Natural History Association, 1960.

Rodney, William. *Kootenai Brown: His Life and Times 1839-1916.* Sydney, B.C.: Gray's Publishing Ltd., 1969.

Sann, Paul. *The Lawless Decade—A Pictorial History of a Great American Transition: From the World War I. Armistice and Prohibition to Repeal and the New Deal.* Greenwich, Conn.: Fawcett Publications, 1971.

Scace, Robert C. *An Initial Bibliography of Waterton Lakes National Park.* Calgary, Alta.: National Historic Parks Branch, 1972.

Scharff, Robert. *Glacier National Park and Waterton Lakes National Park.* New York: David McKay Company, 1967.

Schultz, James Willard. *Recently Discovered Tales of Life Among the Indians.* Compiled and edited by Warren L. Hanna. Missoula, Mont.: Mountain Press Publishing Company, 1988.

Shankland, Robert. *Steve Mather of the National Parks.* New York: Alfred A. Knopf, 1970.

Spry, Irene M., editor. *The Papers of the Palliser Expedition 1857-1860.* Toronto, Ont.: The Champlain Society, 1968.

Steele, C. Frank. *Prairie Editor—The Life and Times of Buchanan of Lethbridge.* Toronto, Ont.: The Ryerson Press, 1961.

Thorsell, James W. "Recreational Use in Waterton Lakes National Park." Unpublished MA thesis, University of Western Ontario, 1967.

Van Kirk, Sylvia M. "The Development of National Park Policy in Canada's Mountain National Parks 1885-1930." Unpublished MA thesis, University of Alberta, 1969.

Watkins, T. H. *Righteous Pilgrim—The Life and Times of Harold Ickes, 1874-1952.* New York: Henry Holt and Company, 1990.

Whilt, Jim. *Giggles from Glacier Guides.* Kalispell, Mont.: O'Neil Print, 1935.

Williams, M. B. *Waterton Lakes National Park, Alberta, Canada.* Ottawa, Ont.: F. A. Acland—King's Printer, 1928.

Windsor, H.R.H. Edward, Duke of. *A King's Story: The Memoirs of the Duke of Windsor.* Toronto, Ont.: Thomas Allan Ltd., 1951.

Wood, C. R. *Lines West: A Pictoral History of Great Northern Railway Operations 1887-1967.* Seattle, Wash.: Superior Publishing Company, 1967.

Wright, Janet. *Architecture of the Picturesque in Canada.* Ottawa, Ont.: National Historic Parks and Sites Branch, Parks Canada, Environment Canada, 1984.

Yandell, Michael D. Editor. *National Parkways—A Photographic and Comprehensive Guide to Glacier & Waterton Lakes National Parks.* Casper, Wy.: World-Wide Research and Publishing, 1974.

Yenne, William J. *Switchback—Bill Yenne's 50 Years in the Mountains of Montana and the West.* Kalispell, Mont.: WY Books, 1983.

Articles

Buchanon, Donald W. "The Mormons in Canada." *Canadian Geographical Journal.* March 1931.

Buchanon, Donald W. "Waterton Lakes National Park." *Canadian Geographical Journal.* February 1933.

Diehl-Taylor, Christiane. "Passengers, Profits and Prestige—The Glacier Park Hotel Company, 1914-1929." *Montana, The Magazine of Western History.* Summer 1997.

Duthie, Beth. "Reiss, Kihn, and Tailfeathers—They Painted the Indians." *Glenbow.* July/August 1985.

Edwards, G. J. and Edwards, G. T. "Langdon Kihn: Indian Portrait Artist." *The Beaver.* Winter 1984/85.

Flandrau, Grace. "The Story of Marias Pass." Great Northern Railway Historical Society reference sheet No. 263. June 1998.

Keyhoe, Donald E. "Seeing America with Lindbergh." *National Geographic Magazine.* January 1928.

Lambert, Kirby. "The Lure of the Parks." *Montana, The Magazine of Western History.* Spring 1996.

Lang, George W. "Many Splendored Glacier Land." *National Geographic.* May 1956.

McConnell, Malcolm. "The Rockies, Our Civilized Wilderness." *Reader's Digest.* August 1987.

Middleton, "Canon" S. "Legend and Folklore of the 'Inside Lakes.'" *Canadian Cattlemen.* August 1958.

Myres, M. T. (Tim). "Thomas W. Blakiston, Charles Waterton and John George Brown and their interconnected associations with Waterton Lakes National Park, Alberta." *Alberta Naturalist.* Spring 1986.

Oberdorf, Charles. "That Special Lodge in the Park." *Saturday Night.* July/August 1976.

Phillips, Alan. "Canadian Rockies, Lords of a Beckoning Land." *National Geographic.* September 1966.

Runte, Alfred. "Promoting Wonderland: Western Railroads and the Evolution of National Park Advertising." *Journal of the West.* January 1992.

Stutz, Leo. "The *Gertrude* and Waterton Mills." *Alberta History.* Spring 1984.

Tanner, Scott J. "A Biography of Winold Reiss: The man who created the Great Northern Railway's Blackfeet Indian portraits." Great Northern Railway Historical Society reference sheet No. 242. June 1996.

Walter, Dave. "Grandeur in Glacier: Lake McDonald Lodge." *Montana Magazine.* March/April 1997.

Endnotes

Chapter 1

1 David Cruise and Alison Griffiths. *Lords of the Line—The Men who Built the CPR* (Markham, Ont.: Penguin Books, 1989), p. 38.

Cruise and Griffiths indicate Hill figured an investment of $5.5 million would buy out the current bondholders and complete the railway line, purchasing a "staggering" $19 million in assets, including $11.4 million in tracks. The railroad's land grant alone had an estimated worth of $6.7 million.

2 Three of the founders of what would become Great Northern would, in 1880, be the driving force behind the syndicate commissioned by the Canadian government to build the Canadian Pacific Railway: J. J. Hill, Donald Smith and George Stephen. Hill's greatest contribution to the CPR was bringing the legendary William Van Horne into the fold as general manager, hoping to use his expertise on American railways to speed up construction of the western leg of the CPR to the Pacific Coast. Van Horne would later go on to become the CPR's president. Hill resigned from Canadian Pacific and sold all his stock in 1882, as he knew the railway would soon become a competitor to his own.

3 Later, the Chicago, Milwaukee & St. Paul Railway Company line (known as the Milwaukee Road) would thread through Montana to the West Coast, separating Great Northern from Northern Pacific. The Milwaukee Road was completed in 1909.

4 Marias Pass had long been known and used by the area's native people and some white trappers and traders, although it had never been committed to paper. Engineer John F. Stevens officially discovered it for Great Northern in December 1889. It is one of the lowest passes through the Rockies, at 5,216 feet (1,565 m). Stevens later went on to use his railway engineering prowess in a major way with the construction of the Panama Canal. A monument to Stevens was erected and dedicated at Marias Pass in 1925.

For more information on Stevens and Marias Pass, see "The Story of Marias Pass" by Grace Flandrau, Great Northern Railway Historical Society reference sheet No. 263, June 1998.

5 Michael Malone, *James J. Hill, Empire Builder of the Northwest* (Oklahoma City, Okla.: University of Oklahoma Press, 1996), p. 102.

6 Malone, *James J. Hill, Empire Builder*, p. 187.

7 Warren L. Hanna, *Montana's Many-Splendored Glacierland* (Seattle, Wash.: Superior Publishing Company, 1976), p. 112.

It is likely that Louis' brother James would have headed the railway had he not quit the business because of poor health in the early 1900s. Like Louis, James was a Yale graduate and worked his way up through the railway ranks. At age 27 he was managing Eastern Railway of Minnesota and in 1899 became vice-president of Great Northern. When James stepped aside, J. J. Hill turned to Louis as his natural successor.

Ralph W. Hidy, Muriel E. Hidy and Roy V. Scott with Don L. Hofsommer. *The Great Northern Railway: A History* (Boston, Mass.: Harvard Business School Press, 1988), p. 108.

8 Alfred Runte, "Promoting Wonderland—Western Railroads and the Evolution of National Park Advertising," *Journal of the West*, January 1992.

9 Hanna, *Montana's Many-Splendored Glacierland*, p. 112.

Louis Hill's collection of native artifacts later become the basis for major displays at three museums, including the Plains Indian Museum in Browning, Mont.

10 C. W. Buchholtz, *Man in Glacier* (West Glacier, Mont.: Glacier Natural History Association, Inc., 1993), pp. 46-49.

Also see Gerald A. Diettert, *Grinnell's Glacier—George Bird Grinnell and Glacier National Park* (Missoula, Mont.: Mountain Press Publishing Company, 1992), pp. 87-95.

11 Diettert, *Grinnell's Glacier*, p. 94.

12 Ibid.

While Buchholtz offers evidence of praise for Hill's effort, citing it as a key reason for the establishment of Glacier National Park, Diettert counters it, claiming Hill played a very small role in the founding of the park. After the legislation was signed, Diettert writes in *Grinnell's Glacier*, "Both Congressman Pray and Senator Carter sent letters congratulating Grinnell and thanking him for his efforts. No one acknowledged Louis W. Hill."

13 Howard H. Hays Sr. and H. A. Noble, *Drivers' Manual*. 8th ed. (East Glacier, Mont.: Glacier Park Transport Company, 1949), p. 57.

For details about the development of Glacier Park, see C. W. Buchholtz, *Man In Glacier* (West Glacier, Mont.: Glacier Natural History Association, 1976) and Donald H. Robinson, *Through the Years in Glacier National Park* (West Glacier, Mont.: Glacier Natural History Association, 1960).

14 Hanna, *Montana's Many-Splendored Glacierland*, p. 109.

15 Hays and Noble, *Drivers' Manual*, p. 58.

16 April 12, 1912, telegram from Louis Hill to Albert Hogeland, chief engineer for Great Northern Railway. Great Northern Railway president's subject files. Glacier Park Hotel and Station 1911-17. Great Northern Railway company records, Minnesota Historical Society archive, St. Paul, Minn.

17 September 16, 1911, letter from Louis Hill to William Harder of Portland, Oregon. Ibid.

    Hill ordered a set of blueprints of the Forestry Building so architect Samuel Bartlett could study them when designing Glacier Park Hotel.

18 "It was not until the late 19th century, when Americans were closer to achieving the conquest of the wilderness that they could see the pioneer cabin as a romantic source for their own architecture."

    Henry Matthews, "The Search for the Northwest Vernacular: Kirtland Cutter and the Rustic Picturesque 1888-1920" in *Art and the National Dream—The Search for Vernacular Expression in Turn-of-the-Century Design*, edited by Nicola Gordon Bowe (Dublin, Ireland: Irish Academic Press, 1993), p. 69.

19 Ibid.

20 Ibid., p 72.

21 Lake McDonald Lodge was not originally part of the Great Northern chain of hotels and chalets in Glacier. It was commissioned and built in 1913-14 for John Lewis, a private businessman from Columbia Falls who had been operating a hotel at Lake McDonald at that site since 1906. The lodge was acquired by Great Northern in 1930.

22 August 15, 1912, telegrams. Great Northern Railway president's subject files. Glacier Park Hotel and Station 1911-17. Great Northern Railway company records, Minnesota Historical Society.

23 Hanna, *Montana's Many-Splendored Glacierland*, p. 110.

24 Ralph Hidy et al., *The Great Northern Railway—A History*, p. 125.

25 Ibid., p. 109.

26 Michael J. Ober, *Enmity and Alliance: Park Service-Concessioner Relations in Glacier National Park, 1892-1961* (Unpublished MA thesis, University of Montana, 1973), p. 50.

    Also see Robert Shankland, *Steve Mather of the National Parks* (New York: Alfred A. Knopf, 1970), p. 134.

27 Ibid., p. 51.

28 *Chief Mountain Country—A History of Cardston and District*, Vol. 1 (Calgary, Alta.: Cardston and District Historical Society, 1978), p. 189.

    Also see Roberta J. Forsberg, *He Who Shoots the Stars—The Story of Canon Middleton* (Whittier, Calif.: The Historical Society of Alberta, 1964), pp. 4-6.

29 January 10, 1942, letter from Canon S. H. Middleton to O. J. McGillis, chief advertising agent for Great Northern Railway. Personal and business papers of the Venerable Archdeacon Samuel H. Middleton in the possession of his daughter, Sophie Allison of Pincher Creek, Alta.

30 Interview with Sophie Allison on August 10, 1975, in Waterton Park, Alta.

31 Department of the Interior, *Reports of the Park Superintendents* (Ottawa, Ont.: King's Printer, 1914), p. 91.

32 For an authoritative look at the life of Kootenai Brown, see William Rodney, *Kootenai Brown—His Life and Times 1839-1916* (Sidney, B.C.: Gray's Publishing Ltd., 1969).

33 W. F. Lothian, *A Brief History of Canada's National Parks* (Ottawa, Ont.: Environment Canada, 1987), p. 29.

34 Ibid., p. 46.

    The size of what is now Waterton Lakes National Park has varied dramatically over the years for a variety of administrative and legislative reasons. In 1911, it was reduced to a mere 13.5 square miles (35 sq. km) and, in 1914, was boosted to 423 square miles (1,096 sq. km). The park currently encompasses 203 square miles (526 sq. km), making it the smallest in the Canadian Rockies.

35 William Rodney, *Kootenai Brown*, p. 192.

Chapter 2

1 *Calgary Herald*, January 25, 1922.

    Also see Ian Getty, *The History of Human Settlement at Waterton Lakes National Park, 1800-1937* (Ottawa, Ont., Unpublished report for the Parks Branch, 1971), p. 112.

2 Heather Pringle, *A Guide to Waterton Lakes National Park* (Vancouver, B.C.: Douglas and McIntyre Ltd., 1986), p. 76.

3 Getty, *The History of Human Settlement at Waterton*, p. 139.

4 June 16, 1926, memo from Albert Hogeland to Ralph Budd for Louis Hill. Great Northern Railway president's subject files. Waterton Lakes Park: Prince of Wales Hotel construction

and operation 1925-60. Great Northern Railway company records, Minnesota Historical Society archive, St. Paul, Minn.

5 Getty, *The History of Human Settlement at Waterton*, p. 113.

    A complicating factor was the fact Upper Waterton Lake straddles the Canada-U.S. border and raising the lake level would, of necessity, have required American approval. Such approval was not forthcoming. Eventually, several dams for irrigation would be built, though many years later, well outside the park and away from the border. St. Mary's dam was opened in July 1951.

6 *The Lethbridge Herald*, May 4, 1926.

7 Ibid., July 8, 1926.

8 Ibid., May 20 and July 27, 1926.

9 Ibid., July 8, 1926.

10 Ibid., May 18, 1926.

11 Ibid., May 14 and July 7, 1926.

12 Ibid., August 25, 1927.

13 James H. Gray, *Bacchanalia Revisited – Western Canada's Boozy Skid to Social Disaster* (Saskatoon, Sask.: Western Producer Prairie Books, 1982), p. 35.

14 Ibid., p. 42.

15 Ibid., p. 42.

    For a complete description of Prohibition on the Prairies, see James Gray's *Booze – The Impact of Whisky on the Prairie West* (Scarborough, Ont.: The New American Library of Canada Limited, 1974).

16 *The Lethbridge Herald*, September 28, 1926.

17 Ibid., May 2, 1924.

18 Ibid., May 15, 1924.

19 Ibid., June 21, 1924.

20 A 42-year lease was issued February 1, 1926, on 10 acres (four hectares) on the knoll at a rate of $100 a year. Separate leases were issued for a dormitory ($25 per year) and an icehouse ($10 per year).

    February 1, 1926, lease. Great Northern Railway president's subject files. Great Northern Railway company records, Minnesota Historical Society.

21 Ibid.

    The letter indicates Hogeland received word from Ottawa on March 6, 1926. Stories appeared in New York newspapers on March 5.

22 *The New York Times*, March 5, 1926.

23 *The New York World*, March 5, 1926.

24 May 17, 1926, letter from Hoke Smith to Ralph Budd. Great Northern Railway president's subject files. Great Northern Railway company records, Minnesota Historical Society.

Smith even went as far as putting a Washington, D.C., placeline on the story so it would "appear as coming from government sources rather than any Great Northern source."

25 January 20, 1927, memo. Ibid.

26 January 20, 1927, letter from Albert Hogeland to Louis Hill. Louis Warren Hill Sr. papers, James Jerome Hill Reference Library, St. Paul, Minn.

27 *The Lethbridge Herald*, March 9, 1927.

Also see January 10, 1927, letter from F. G. Dorety to Ralph Budd. Louis Hill papers, J. J. Hill Library.

As soon as it was learned Great Northern was applying for a tavern licence, a couple of enterprising Lethbridge area men asked to sublet the beer parlour. Louis Hill politely turned down the offer over concern that "we could not control the place as well as if we ran it ourselves."

January 29, 1927, letter from Andrew Hogg, counsel for Canadian Rockies Hotel Company in Lethbridge, Alta., to F. L. Paetzold, secretary for Great Northern Railway, and February 2, 1927, letter from Louis Hill to Howard Noble. Louis Hill papers, J. J. Hill Library.

28 Ibid., July 13, 1927.

29 April 13, 1927, letter from Alex MacKay, vice-president of the Alberta Motor Association in Calgary, to Louis Hill. Louis Hill papers, J. J. Hill Library.

30 *The Lethbridge Herald*, March 14, 1927.

31 April 19, 1927, letter from Andrew Hogg to F. G. Dorety. Louis Hill papers, J. J. Hill Library.

32 *The Lethbridge Herald*, December 21, 1926.

33 April 29, 1927, letter from Ralph Budd to C. O. Jenks. Louis Hill papers, J. J. Hill Library.

34 Ibid.

35 *The Lethbridge Herald*, July 20, 1926.

36 Ibid., July 21, 1926.

37 Ibid., May 14, 1927.

38 Ibid., April 1, 1927.

39 July 22, 1935, letter from William Kenney, president of Great Northern Railway, to Howard Hays, president of Glacier Park Transport Company. Great Northern Railway president's subject files. Glacier Park Transport Company 1935-37. Great Northern Railway company records, Minnesota Historical Society.

40 November 25, 1935, letter from William Kenney to Howard Hays. Ibid.

Chapter 3

1 Albert Hogeland, chief engineer for Great Northern, met with Canadian parks commissioner James Harkin in Ottawa in December 1925. Hogeland returned to St. Paul with the promise of a lease from the Canadian government and temporary authority to begin work on a hotel.

December 8 and December 23, 1925, memos. Great Northern Railway president's subject files. Waterton Lakes Park: Prince of Wales Hotel construction and operation 1925-60. Great Northern Railway company records, Minnesota Historical Society archive, St. Paul, Minn.

2 Minutes of January 7, 1926, meeting of the Great Northern Railway board of governors. Ibid.

3 Ibid.

The calculation for the cost of building the hotel was based on the $490,000 price of the 240-room Glacier Park Hotel. The cost in Canada was thought to be 80 per cent greater than 1912-15, when Glacier Park Hotel was built, which would make its inflation-adjusted price $900,000, or $3,750 per room. Added to the cost of 118 rooms (at $3,750 each) was $125,000 for the lobby, dining room and kitchen, and $75,000 for road, sewage, grading, water supply and other incidentals, for a total of $642,500.

4 March 11, 1926, letter from Albert Hogeland to Louis Hill. Louis Warren Hill Sr. papers, James Jerome Hill Reference Library, St. Paul, Minn.

5 March 15, 1926, letter from the Grand Forks Builders and Traders Exchange, North Dakota. Great Northern Railway president's subject files. Waterton Lakes Park: Prince of Wales Hotel construction and operation 1925-60. Great Northern Railway company records, Minnesota Historical Society.

6 March 16, 1926, letter from the Lethbridge Board of Trade to Ralph Budd. Ibid.

7 March 31, 1926, letter from J. McDiarmid Company Ltd. of Winnipeg, Manitoba. Ibid.

8 April 5, 1926, letter from Morell and Nichols Inc. Ibid.

9 April 29, 1926, letter from Heintzman Piano Co. Ltd. of Calgary, Alberta, to Louis Hill. Louis Hill papers, J. J. Hill Library.

10 March 20, 1926, letter from Gregg and Aird, Inc. of New York. Great Northern Railway president's subject files. Waterton Lakes Park: Prince of Wales Hotel construction and operation 1925-60. Great Northern Railway company records, Minnesota Historical Society.

11 March 15, 1926, letter from the Grand Forks Builders and Traders Exchange, North Dakota. Ibid.

12 March 19, 1926, letter from Great Northern to the Grand Forks Builders and Traders Exchange, North Dakota. Ibid.

13 March 5, 1926, reports in the *New York Times*, *New York Telegram* and *New York Herald*.

14 December 31, 1925, memo from Louis Hill to Ralph Budd. Great Northern Railway president's subject files. Waterton Lakes Park: Prince of Wales Hotel construction and operation 1925-60. Great Northern Railway company records, Minnesota Historical Society.

15 May 7, 1926, letter from Albert Hogeland to Louis Hill. Louis Hill papers, J. J. Hill Library.

16 In 1927, Howard H. Hays Sr. of Riverside, Calif., took control of the bus company and renamed it Glacier Park Transport Company. Roe Emery remained in the picture as a shareholder and silent partner. Emery used his newfound freedom to devote more time to his other transportation concessions.

17 Louis Hill took the condition of roads in and around Glacier Park personally. The railway had millions of dollars invested in its tourist facilities in Glacier and Hill couldn't understand why federal authorities weren't ready to match, in some small measure, the financial commitment Great Northern had poured into the park. Particularly frustrating for Hill was the federal budget appropriation for Glacier Park. Established in 1910, the park's appropriation for 1911 was $15,000, raised to $69,200 in 1912 and remained at that level until it was increased to $100,000 in 1917. It was a paltry amount compared to the $1.5 million Great Northern had spent on accommodations and roads during the same period. It's no coincidence increases in appropriations for Glacier came after Hill lambasted the Secretary of the Interior in an eight-page telegram listing deficiencies in the way the park was being operated. "It is really an outrage to hundreds of tourists to advertise the park and have the government join in the advertising, as you did this year at the railroad's expense, and then not make good on the roads and trails," Hill's telegram stated.

18 May 29, 1926, letter from Louis Hill to G. W. Noffsinger. Great Northern Railway president's files. Waterton Lakes Park: Prince of Wales Hotel construction and operation 1925-60. Great Northern Railway company records, Minnesota Historical Society.

19 March 19, 1926, letter to Grand Forks Builders and Traders Exchange, North Dakota, from Ralph Budd. Ibid.

Also see March 8, 1926, letter to Dwight P. Robinson Co. Inc. from Ralph Budd. Ibid.

20 Undated (1926) and unsigned contract between Walter Butler Company of St. Paul, Minn., and the Canadian Rockies Hotel Company. Louis Hill papers, J. J. Hill Library.

21 June 16, 1926, memo from Ralph Budd to Louis Hill. Great Northern Railway president's subject files. Waterton Lakes Park: Prince of Wales Hotel construction and operation 1925-60. Great Northern Railway company records, Minnesota Historical Society.

22 May 28, 1926, memo from Louis Hill. Ibid.

23 June 10, 1926, letter from Albert Hogeland to Louis Hill. Ibid.

24 June 14, 1926, memo. Ibid.

25 June 24, 1926, memo. Ibid.

26 *The Lethbridge Herald*, April 8, 1926.

27 Ibid., May 4, 1926.

28 June 18, 1926, telegram from Louis Hill to Ralph Budd. Great Northern Railway president's subject files. Waterton Lakes Park: Prince of Wales Hotel construction and operation 1925-60. Great Northern Railway company records, Minnesota Historical Society.

29 February 1, 1926, lease. Ibid.

30 July 19, 1926, memo from Albert Hogeland to Ralph Budd. Ibid.

31 June 18, 1926, telegram from Louis Hill to Ralph Budd. Ibid.

32 Douglas Oland Sr. (Unpublished memoirs written in Lethbridge, Alta., in 1963), p. 23.

Floyd Parker was in Waterton on and off from mid-April to early May 1926. A Great Northern memo dated April 12, 1926, ordered Parker and a rodman to Waterton to survey the hotel site. A *Lethbridge Herald* report indicates Parker arrived about April 17. He was still in the park on May 15, in time for the opening of the Waterton dance pavilion.

33 Ibid.

34 June 16, 1926, memo from Ralph Budd to Louis Hill. Great Northern Railway president's subject files. Waterton Lakes Park: Prince of Wales Hotel construction and operation 1925-60. Great Northern Railway company records, Minnesota Historical Society.

35 Ibid.

36 Oland memoirs, p. 24.

37 Ibid.

38 Ibid., pp. 26-27.

39 Ibid., p. 21.

40 Ibid.

41 Ibid.

42 *Chief Mountain Country—A History of Cardston and District.* Vol. 1 (Calgary, Alta.: Cardston and District Historical Society, 1978), p. 462.

43 Oland memoirs, p. 22.

44 *The Lethbridge Herald*, July 12, 1926.

The newspaper reported that Oland and Scott had built 15 cottages in Waterton "in the past few years."

45 Oland memoirs, p. 23.

46 *The Lethbridge Herald*, May 14, 1926.

Waterton did not receive public electrical service until after the Second World War. Many local businesses had generators for lighting and power.

47 *The Lethbridge Herald*, May 18, 1926.

48 Ibid.

49 Ibid., May 14, 1926.

Chapter 4

1 Canadian Pacific used a Swiss theme for some of its lesser structures, such as Mount Stephen House at Field and Glacier House at Glacier, both in British Columbia. But the design of those CP structures differs from that used by Great Northern in Glacier National Park, Mont. Great Northern tended to rustic-looking chalets constructed around log frames and/or walls, while the CPR generally used cut and dimensioned lumber, not logs. CP's buildings also had other styling cues, often Elizabethan or Tudor, which set them apart from those of Great Northern.

2 October 16, 1913, letter from Ralph Budd, president of Great Northern Railway, to G. R. Martin, comptroller. Glacier Park Company, Glacier Park Division: Hotels and Camps, General correspondence 1912-13. Great Northern Railway company records, Minnesota Historical Society archive, St. Paul, Minn.

Cabins, in particular, were duplicated in several locations. An 18-foot by 18-foot design and another 28 feet by 28 feet were used at Two Medicine Chalets, Cut Bank Chalets, St. Mary Chalets, Going-to-the-Sun Camp and Many Glacier Camp.

3 April 17, 1926, letter from Louis Hill to Charles Jenks. Ibid.

4 April 26, 1926, memo from Louis Hill to Thomas McMahon. Canadian Rockies Hotel Company records in the Louis Warren Hill Sr. papers, James Jerome Hill Reference Library, St. Paul, Minn.

5 Ibid.

6 April 27, 1926, letter from Louis Hill to Thomas McMahon. Louis Hill papers, J. J. Hill Library.

7 *The Lethbridge Herald*, July 9, 1926.

8 Ibid., July 12, 1926.

9 Ibid., June 24, 1926.

The number of men hanging around the area waiting for work in Waterton became so great the local citizen's committee suggested in a newspaper report that no more labourers come to the park as there were more than enough people on hand for any work that could crop up.

10 Ibid., July 12 and 27, 1926.

11 Ibid., July 12, 1926.

12 Interviews with Andy Thompson on April 29, 1975, in Lethbridge, Alta., and with Jack Oland on January 8, 1975, in Calgary, Alta.

13 *The Lethbridge Herald*, July 27, 1926.

14 Ibid., July 31, 1926.

15 September 7, 1992, letter from Mary O'Brien to the author. Author's collection.

16 *The Lethbridge Herald*, July 29, 1926.

17 Interview with Mary O'Brien on December 1, 1990, in Marshall, Minn.

Also interviews with Jack Oland and Andy Thompson.

18 The depth of the foundations and footings is based on architectural blueprints for the Prince of Wales Hotel.

Also see *The Lethbridge Herald*, July 29, 1926.

19 *The Lethbridge Herald*, July 12, 1926.

20 Douglas Oland Sr. (Unpublished memoirs written in Lethbridge, Alta., in 1963), p. 28.

21 Ibid., p. 24.

22 *The Lethbridge Herald*, August 11, 1926.

23 Ibid., August 14, 1926.

24 August 16, 1926, letter from Ralph Budd to Louis Hill. Louis Hill papers, J. J. Hill Library.

25 *The Lethbridge Herald*, August 11 and 14, 1926.

For several months after the start of the Prince of Wales Hotel project, there seemed to be no end of letters from local speculators looking to make a dollar from Great Northern. A month after Budd's visit, Great Northern's on-site engineer wrote Budd to report that a local man had said the railway was thinking of building smaller hotels "near Waterton." The local man was proposing Great Northern consider Lee Lake Ranch as a potential site for a chalet and "model farm." Budd's curt reply was that the local entrepreneur was mistaken in what he'd heard.

In another letter, a hotel labourer wrote Great Northern to advise goat hunting season had opened and he had heard the railway wished a mounted goat to display in the hotel. When the would-be hunter indicated he wanted $500 to supply a mounted animal, a railway official replied that "we have other arrangements."

26 Ibid., August 17, 1926.

27 Ibid., August 14, 1926.

28 Ibid., August 11, 1927.

29 August 16, 1927, letter from Ralph Budd to Louis Hill. Louis Hill papers, J. J. Hill Library.

30 *The Lethbridge Herald*, August 18, 1926.

31 Ibid., August 19, 1926.

32 August 16, 1926, letter from Ralph Budd to Louis Hill. Louis Hill papers, J. J. Hill Library.

33 *The Lethbridge Herald*, July 12, 1926.

34 August 29, 1926, memo from Albert Hogeland to Ralph Budd. Great Northern Railway president's subject files. Waterton Lakes Park: Prince of Wales Hotel construction and operation 1925-60. Great Northern Railway company records, Minnesota Historical Society.

35 *The Lethbridge Herald*, September 7, 1926.

36 Oland memoirs, p. 28.

Oland says he paid a total of $80,000 in handling charges just to get material from Cardston to Waterton to build the hotel.

37 *The Lethbridge Herald*, September 27, 1926.

38 Ibid.

39 Ibid., October 19, 1926.

Also see October 9, 1926, letter from Ralph Budd to Doug Oland. Great Northern Railway president's subject files. Waterton Lakes Park: Prince of Wales Hotel construction and operation 1925-60. Great Northern Railway company records, Minnesota Historical Society.

40 September 14, 1926, letter from Louis Hill to Albert Hogeland. Great Northern Railway president's subject files. Waterton Lakes Park: Prince of Wales Hotel construction and operation 1925-60. Great Northern Railway company records, Minnesota Historical Society.

41 September 14, 1926, letter from Louis Hill to Ralph Budd, William Kenney and Charles Jenks. Louis Hill papers, J. J. Hill Library.

42 Ibid.

43 September 18, 1926, memo from Albert Hogeland to Ralph Budd and Louis Hill. Ibid.

44 October 13, 1926, letter from Louis Hill to Hugh Comstock, designer, in Carmel, Calif. Ibid.

Besides his home in St. Paul, a farm outside the city and a cabin in Glacier Park, Louis Hill also had a residence in Pebble Beach, Calif., only a few miles from Carmel.

45 September 14, 1926, letter from Louis Hill to Albert Hogeland. Ibid.

Max Toltz was no stranger in Great Northern circles. German-born Toltz, a civil engineer, had joined Great Northern in 1882, when it was known as the St. Paul, Minneapolis & Manitoba Railway. He worked his way up through the ranks to become assistant chief engineer. After a row with the fiery J. J. Hill, Toltz quit the railway, but was later persuaded by Louis Hill to rejoin Great Northern to work on electrification of the Cascade Tunnel. Toltz eventually set up his own firm in St. Paul in 1910, often doing original and consulting work for Great Northern.

Beaver Day was born in 1884 and attended the University of Pennsylvania, which was "the" school of architecture for many years. He joined Max Toltz and Wesley King in April 1919 to form Toltz, King and Day, where he was chief architect for the firm.

46 December 31, 1925, letter from Louis Hill to Ralph Budd. Great Northern Railway president's subject files. Waterton Lakes Park: Prince of Wales Hotel construction and operation 1925-60. Great Northern Railway records, Minnesota Historical Society.

47 September 25, 1926, letter from William Kenney to Ralph Budd. Great Northern Railway president's subject files. Prince of Wales Hotel Co. Boat for Waterton Lake 1926-55. Ibid.

Swanson, born in Pennsylvania in 1883, moved to Montana in 1906 and quickly established a reputation as a boat builder on Montana's Flathead Lake. When Glacier National Park was created in 1910, he soon found his services in need there. In 1911 he built the *Ethel*, a 71-foot (21.3 m) boat to carry passengers on Lake McDonald. He also built boats for Great Northern. In 1926 Swanson obtained his own tour boat concession in Glacier, forming Glacier Park Boat Company. In 1926 he built the 55-passenger *Little Chief*, now used on St. Mary Lake, and the *Sinopah*, now on Two Medicine Lake, and in 1928 the *DeSmet*, also still in service, on Lake McDonald.

48 November 22, 1926, memo from William Kenney to Ralph Budd. Ibid.

49 Great Northern's advertising department was not alone in its use of native themes to promote the railway. Native imagery was key to luring Eastern tourists to the West and all the major railways, including Canadian Pacific, Northern Pacific and the Santa Fe, to name but a few, capitalized on it. Natives had little hand in the use of their images, history or culture in these promotional efforts, usually being relegated to the role of employees or props in photographs. On the Blackfeet reservation, with its chronically high unemployment rate, Great Northern jobs were highly prized. Other enterprising Blackfeet people learned there was money to be made selling postcards and trinkets to tourists and posing for photographs when trains stopped at Glacier Park Station.

50 September 23, 1926, letter from Louis Hill to W. R. Mills. Louis Hill papers, J. J. Hill Library.

Also see January 6, 1927, letter from Louis Hill to W. R. Mills. Ibid.

"Picture writing" is an ancient art practised by North American Indians, in the absence of an alphabet, to record their deeds, exploits, legends and folklore.

Middleton's daughter, Sophie Allison, says the pigments used for the Prince of Wales Hotel canvases were natural and made by each artist. The artists obtained the colours from various natural sources, like vegetable colourings and minerals, and mixed the pigments with grease, Allison said. They were then applied with a sharp or pointed stick about the size of a pencil.

51 Despite being a leader in what is now considered the despised residential school system, where native people were taken from their homes and kept at schools run by

religious orders, Middleton and St. Paul's Anglican School appear to have survived public inquiries into abuses with their reputations relatively intact. In the 1920s and 1930s, Middleton introduced what were then viewed as progressive steps in teaching native people in a residential school setting, meant to integrate native people more fully into western culture. Middleton appears to have been able to maintain a fine balance between preparing native youths for integration into wider society while at the same time preserving a sense of pride in his charges for their history and culture, which he adapted into many aspects of the school's curriculum and activities.

He was not without his critics, though. Students have since complained that Middleton was no better than other residential school principals in forcing students to attend classes, even through then legal use of police intervention, despite the unwillingness on the part of both parents and children to be parted. He has also been chastised for attempting to keep more senior students away from what was considered the regressive influences of their home lives by having them stay with him at his Waterton summer camp.

Whatever the current opinion of him, Middleton was highly respected at the time by local native people. He earned their respect by proving his physical prowess at their games, studying their customs and learning to speak the Siksika language—"not just a working knowledge but the ability to speak it as fluently and as well as any Blood Indians. To do this he set aside all other duties for months to mingle in the camps and sit in the tepees listening to the old people tells stories of the past. It was a complete immersion course."

Chief Mountain Country—A History of Cardston and District, Vol. 1 (Calgary, Alta., Cardston and District Historical Society, 1978), p. 189.

Also see Roberta Forsberg, *He Who Shoots the Stars—The Story of Canon Middleton* (Whittier, Calif.: Historical Society of Alberta, 1964) and Beverly Hungry Wolf, *Daughters of the Buffalo Women—Maintaining the Tribal Faith* (Standoff, Alta.: Canadian Caboose Press, 1996).

52 November 1 to December 27, 1926, weekly reports filed by George Anderegg, field accountant at the hotel site, to J. C. Seiberlich, general accountant at Great Northern headquarters in St. Paul, Minn. Canadian Rockies Hotel Company: General correspondence. Great Northern Railway company records, Minnesota Historical Society.

53 Oland memoirs, p. 28.

54 October 25 and November 1, 1926, weekly reports filed by George Anderegg, field accountant at the hotel site, to J. C. Seiberlich. Canadian Rockies Hotel Company: General correspondence. Great Northern Railway company records, Minnesota Historical Society.

55 September 7, 1992, letter from Mary O'Brien to author. Author's collection.

56 Ibid.

Also see *The Lethbridge Herald*, December 15, 1926.

57 *The Lethbridge Herald*, December 2, 1926.

Also Jack Oland interview.

58 *The Lethbridge Herald*, October 19, 1926.

59 Ibid., November 2, 1926.

60 Ibid., November 25, 1926.

61 Deborah Witwicki, "The Car emerges as a necessity, the joy and bane of modern life" in *Brownlee and the Triumph of Populism*, Volume 5 of *Alberta in the 20th Century—A Journalistic History of the Province in Twelve Volumes*. Ted Byfield, editor (Edmonton, Alta., United Western Communications Ltd., 1996).

Also see James A. MacGregor, *A History of Alberta* (Edmonton, Alta.: Hurtig Publishers, 1972), p. 243.

62 For more on the founding and early years of the Alberta Motor Association see: Tony Cashman, *The Alberta Motor Association—A History* (Edmonton, Alta., Alberta Motor Association, 1967).

63 *The Lethbridge Herald*, April 27, 1927.

64 Ibid., April 28, 1927.

65 C. Frank Steele, *Prairie Editor—The Life and Times of Buchanan of Lethbridge* (Toronto, Ont.: The Ryerson Press, 1961), p. 120.

66 Ibid., p. 172.

67 The tower on the Prince of Wales Hotel is a curiosity, as it is the only one of Great Northern's hotels and chalets to have one. There are two possible sources for the design feature. The Hotel Lafayette on Lake Minnetonka, Minn., built in 1882 by the St. Paul, Minneapolis & Manitoba Railway, a J. J. Hill-operated predecessor company to Great Northern, featured numerous gables and a central tower not unlike the Prince of Wales Hotel. Also in Great Northern's architectural library was a blueprint submitted in 1914 by Spokane, Wash., architect Kirtland Cutter for Many Glacier Hotel. It features a tower, topped by a flagpole, over the lobby portion of the building. While the Hotel Lafayette had a steeply pitched roof, Cutter's plan for Many Glacier Hotel shows a low roofline more in keeping with Glacier Park Hotel. A vestige of Cutter's tower eventually showed up as a spire over the breezeway connecting the lobby of Many Glacier Hotel to Annex 2, constructed in 1917. A similar spire was used when a porte-cochere was added to the entrance of Many Glacier Hotel in the late 1950s.

68 Hill made it very clear that the revisions to the lobby section were simply that and no major changes were pending to his grand plan of a 300-room hotel with numerous annexes. "The plans should provide so that we can work present installations out in such a way as to fit in with the ultimate scheme," Hill wrote architect Thomas McMahon.

September 14, 1926, letter from Louis Hill to Thomas McMahon. Louis Hill papers, J. J. Hill Library.

69 *The Lethbridge Herald*, December 17, 1926.

By March 1927, every UFA member of the legislature south of Lethbridge would be behind Great Northern's request.

70 Ibid., December 4, 1926.

71 Interview with Mary O'Brien.

72 October 25, 1926, report from George Anderegg to J. C. Seiberlich. Canadian Rockies Hotel Company: General correspondence. Great Northern Railway company records, Minnesota Historical Society.

73 Oland memoirs, p. 29.

74 Ibid.

75 Henry Matthews, "The Search for the Northwest Vernacular: Kirtland Cutter and the Rustic Picturesque 1888-1920" in *Art and the National Dream—The Search for Vernacular Expression in Turn-of-the-Century Design*, edited by Nicola Gordon Bowe (Dublin, Ireland: Irish Academic Press Ltd., 1993), p. 77.

76 When the new blueprints arrived, George Anderegg revised his estimate of how far along construction had proceeded from 40 per cent to 30 per cent. The 40 per cent mark was not surpassed until Anderegg filed his December 14 report.

November 1 and December 14, 1926, reports from George Anderegg to J. C. Seiberlich. Canadian Rockies Hotel Company: General correspondence. Great Northern Railway company records, Minnesota Historical Society.

Chapter 5

1 February 21, 1927, report from George Anderegg to J. C. Seiberlich. Prince of Wales Hotel construction. Great Northern Railway company records, Minnesota Historical Society archive, St. Paul, Minn.

2 *The Lethbridge Herald*, February 26, 1927.

3 Ibid., February 1, 1927.

4 Douglas Oland Sr. (Unpublished memoirs written in Lethbridge, Alta., in 1963), p. 29.

5 December 11, 1926, memo from Floyd Parker to Albert Hogeland. Rocky Mountain Hotel Company records, Louis Warren Hill Sr. papers, James Jerome Hill Reference Library, St. Paul, Minn.

6 Ibid.

7 *The Lethbridge Herald*, December 16, 1926.

8 Ibid.

9 Ibid.

10 Ibid.

11 Ibid.

12 Ken Liddell's column, *Calgary Herald*, September 15, 1971.

13 December 11, 1926, memo from Floyd Parker to Albert Hogeland. Louis Hill papers, J. J. Hill Library.

14 *The Lethbridge Herald*, December 11, 1926.

15 Ibid.

16 Ken Liddell's column, *Calgary Herald*, September 15, 1971.

17 December 11, 1926, memo from Floyd Parker to Albert Hogeland. Louis Hill papers, J. J. Hill Library.

All of southern Alberta was hit hard by the storm. Trees were knocked down everywhere, blocking roads and snapping telephone and power lines. The snow drifted heavily and isolated rural towns for days. Church services were cancelled as the temperature plummeted from 33°F (1°C) on Saturday to 4°F (-13°C) on Sunday and –18°F (-27°C) by Monday morning. In Waterton, windows were smashed out of cars and some vehicles were blown off the road and into bushes. The entire front of a Waterton store was torn away and a large section of the roof with several windows smashed. The most incredible sight had to be that of Ellison's rooming house. It "was lifted bodily and blown clean over onto the street, where it now stands sideways," the *Lethbridge Herald* reported.

18 Ibid.

19 Ibid.

Information about the use of winches comes from an interview with Andy Thompson in Lethbridge, Alta., on April 29, 1975, and Ken Liddell's column, *Calgary Herald*, September 15, 1971.

20 Ibid.

21 Ibid.

22 *The Lethbridge Herald*, January 20, 1927.

23 Ibid., February 16, 1927.

24 Ibid., February 16, 1927.

25 Weekly reports from George Anderegg, field accountant at the Prince of Wales Hotel construction site, to J. C. Seiberlich, general accountant at Great Northern's headquarters in St. Paul, Minn., chart the progress of the building. In his December 14 report, Anderegg indicates 45 per cent of the hotel had been finished. By February 15, 62 per cent of the hotel had been built, with the total rising to 69 per cent as of March 15. Prince of Wales Hotel construction. Great Northern Railway company records, Minnesota Historical Society.

26 August 30, 1926, memo from Ralph Budd to Louis Hill. Great Northern Railway president's subject files. Waterton Lakes Park: Prince of Wales Hotel construction and operation 1925-60. Great Northern Railway company records, Minnesota Historical Society.

Budd favoured the name Boundary Hotel, being short and easy to remember. He went so far as to suggest that if Louis Hill liked the name, "I believe we could have the name of the large lake changed to Boundary Lake as the international boundary runs through it and the lower lake could well be left Waterton Lake, without any inconsistency." It was a brash statement, showing utter contempt for Canadian jurisdiction and name selection protocol. It was, however, representative of how much sway Great Northern Railway officials felt they had when it came to pulling the strings of government—on either side of the border.

27 December 9, 1926, letter from Edward Ward to Ralph Budd. Ibid.

28 December 24, 1926, memo from J. A. Lengby to W. R. Mills and December 29, 1926, reply from Mills. Ibid.

29 January 5, 1927, memo. Ibid.

30 January 7, 1927, memo from Ralph Budd to Louis Hill. Ibid.

31 January 10, 1927, letter from Ralph Budd to Edward Ward. Ibid.

32 Interview with Sophie Allison on August 10, 1975, in Waterton Park, Alta.

33 September 21, 1946, letter from Canon Samuel Middleton to J. S. Jeffries. From a collection of letters, notes and clippings of Samuel Middleton in the possession of his daughter, Sophie Allison of Pincher Creek, Alta.

34 Interview with Sophie Allison.

Middleton's loyalty to the Crown would be rewarded later in life. In 1936, King George V gave him the King's Jubilee Medal for community leadership. In recognition of his services as chaplain of the 18th Field Brigade, C.R.A., he was given the Efficiency Decoration Medal for Canada in 1937 and promoted in rank to major. And in June 1937 the governor general of Canada, at the command of the King, invested Middleton as an officer and companion of the Ancient Order of St. John of Jerusalem for Middleton's distinguished service toward the betterment of His Majesty's people.

Roberta Forsberg, *Chief Mountain—The Story of Canon Middleton* (Whittier, Calif.: Historical Society of Alberta, 1964), p. 79.

35 Roberta Forsberg, *Chief Mountain—The Story of Canon Middleton* (Whittier, Calif.: Historical Society of Alberta, 1964), p. 35.

36 November 24, 1926, memo from Ralph Budd to William Kenney. Great Northern Railway president's subject files. Waterton Lakes Park: Prince of Wales Hotel construction and operation 1925-60. Great Northern Railway company records, Minnesota Historical Society.

37 Oland memoirs, p. 21.

38 September 7, 1992, letter from Mary O'Brien to author. Author's collection.

39 December 18, 1926, memo from William Kenney to Ralph Budd. Prince of Wales Hotel Co.: Boat for Waterton Lake. Great Northern Railway company records, Minnesota Historical Society.

40 Oland memoirs, pp. 29 and 30.

Also see Ken Liddell's column, *Calgary Herald*, September 15, 1971.

41 *The Lethbridge Herald*, March 18 and July 9, 1927.

42 Interviews with George Annand on August 5, 1974, in Waterton Park, Alta., and Ernie Haug on August 18, 1974, in Waterton Park, Alta.

43 April 12 and 18, 1927, reports from George Anderegg to J. C. Seiberlich. Prince of Wales Hotel construction. Great Northern Railway company records, Minnesota Historical Society.

44 *The Lethbridge Herald*, March 12, 1927.

45 Ibid., March 16, 1927.

   The budget estimates showed $1,729,000 was spent on highways in 1926 and $246,442 on market roads, while the province was proposing to spend only $1 million for highways and $400,000 for market roads in 1927. The estimates showed the province expected to collect $1.259 million under the Highway Traffic Act.

46 April 6, 1927, telegram from Ralph Budd to Louis Hill.

   Also see May 20, 1927, memo from Albert Hogeland to Louis Hill. Louis Hill papers, J. J. Hill Library.

47 April 6, 1927, telegram from Ralph Budd to Louis Hill. Ibid.

48 May 30, 1927, letter from Albert Hogeland to J. A. Lengby. Ibid.

49 "I agree with you we should not take Canadian province [sic] bonds and waive interest. Also think it important to get our government authorities to co-operate with Canadian Park and provincial authorities on location of new and shorter road as suggested by Mr. Kenney."

   April 7, 1927, telegram from Louis Hill to Ralph Budd. Ibid.

50 April 6, 1927, telegram from Ralph Budd to Louis Hill. Ibid.

51 *The Lethbridge Herald*, February 1, 1927.

52 The workforce rose from 60 in mid-January 1927 to 125 by mid-April, reaching its peak in late June at 230.

   January 11, April 5 and June 27, 1927, reports from George Anderegg to general accountant, Great Northern Railway. Prince of Wales Hotel construction. Great Northern Railway company records, Minnesota Historical Society.

53 March 5, 1927, memo from Floyd Parker to Albert Hogeland. Great Northern Railway president's subject files. Waterton Lakes Park: Prince of Wales Hotel construction and operation 1925-60. Great Northern Railway company records, Minnesota Historical Society.

54 Oland memoirs, p. 29.

55 May 24, 1927, letter from Albert Hogeland to Louis Hill. Louis Hill papers, J. J. Hill Library.

56 *The Lethbridge Herald*, June 2, 1927.

57 Ibid., May 16, 1927.

58 May 24, 1927, letter from Albert Hogeland to Louis Hill. Louis Hill papers, J. J. Hill Library.

59 May 20, 1927, memo from Albert Hogeland to Louis Hill. Ibid.

60 May 21, 1927, memo from Louis Hill. Ibid.

61 May 26, 1927, telegram from Alberta Senator W. A. Buchanan to Ralph Budd. Ibid.

62 June 5, 1927, telegram from Howard Noble to William Kenney. Ibid.

63 June 3, 1927, letter from Howard Noble to William Kenney. Ibid.

64 June 7, 1927, letter from F. G. Dorety, general counsel for Great Northern Railway, to Louis Hill. Ibid.

65 May 21, 1927, Great Northern Railway "day letter" from J. A. Lengby to Ralph Budd. Ibid.

66 Ibid.

67 *The Lethbridge Herald*, May 16, 1927.

68 Ibid., June 9, 1927.

69 December 20, 1955, letter from Canon Samuel Middleton to Howard Hays. Canon Middleton papers.

70 *The Lethbridge Herald*, June 2, 1927.

71 June 9, 1927, memorandum. Louis Hill papers, J. J. Hill Library.

   Also see *The Lethbridge Herald*, June 14, 1927.

72 *The Lethbridge Herald*, June 22 and 28, 1927.

73 June 24, 1927, letter from Howard Noble to William Kenney. Glacier Park Co.: Roads and trails. Great Northern Railway company records, Minnesota Historical Society.

74 The water supply system started with a pump house to the east of the hotel on Middle Waterton Lake, which drew water from the lake and sent it to the 100,000-gallon (450,000 litre) water tank atop a 100 foot-high (30 m) steel tower. The tank supplied hotel drinking water, a rooftop sprinkler system and the boilers. The boilers were housed in a multi-purpose building called the "powerhouse," located west of the hotel and just below the water tower. The powerhouse also contained the hotel laundry and the generators that provided the hotel with electricity. Used water ended up in a septic tank 500 yards (450 m) north of the hotel, which then drained into a leach field.

75 April 12, 18 and June 13, 1927, weekly reports from George Anderegg to W. G. Read, accountant, Great Northern Railway. Glacier Park Company: General correspondence, Great Northern Railway company records, Minnesota Historical Society.

76 *The Lethbridge Herald*, November 6, 1926.

77 Ibid., May 30 and 31, 1927.

78 The inscription on photographs taken at the time indicates 32 horses were used, but a count of the steeds in most pictures shows only 28 horses—24 in front and four behind. A June 2 *Lethbridge Herald* article puts the team at 36 horses, as does a July 12, 1927, letter from William Fisher to Howard Noble. It's possible some of the team had been unhitched by the time the photos were taken.

79 *The Lethbridge Herald*, June 2, 1927, and dates on photographs of the event.

80 Chinook is a native word for "snow-eater." The strong, warm, dry wind blows off the mountains of southern Alberta and can raise temperatures from –20°F (-29°C) to 70°F (20°C) in a matter of hours.

81 *The Lethbridge Herald*, June 2, 1927, and interview with Andy Thompson.

82 The opening date of the hotel was set arbitrarily by William Kenney when he couldn't reach an agreement with hotel manager Capt. Harrison and Oland. "They were fooling around with (the opening date) and did not have it ready, and I felt that if we did not set an arbitrary date, they would not open this season."

   August 20, 1927, letter from William Kenney to Louis Hill. Louis Hill papers, J. J. Hill Library.

83 July 6, 1927, letter from William Kenney to Louis Hill. Ibid.

84 Oland memoirs, p. 39.

85 Ibid.

Chapter 6

1 *The Lethbridge Herald*, June 3, 1927.

2 Ibid., August 11, 1926.

3 Ibid., August 24, 1926.

4 Ibid., July 17, 1926.

5 Ibid., May 2, 1927.

6 Douglas Oland Sr. (Unpublished memoirs written in Lethbridge, Alta., in 1963), p. 36.

7 *The Lethbridge Herald*, May 16, 1927.

8 Ibid., August 31, 1926.

9 Interview with George Annand on August 5, 1974, in Waterton Park, Alta.

   Also see *The Lethbridge Herald*, September 7, 1926.

10 *The Lethbridge Herald*, May 16, 1927.

11 Trustees called for tenders for construction of a new school in May 1927.

12 *The Lethbridge Herald*, March 28, 1927.

13 Ibid., March 28, 1927.

14 Ibid., July 25, 1927.

15 Ibid., May 20 and June 3, 1927.

16 Ibid., July 19, 1927.

17 Ibid., August 25, 1927.

18 Ibid., June 21 and July 4, 1927.

19 Ibid., April 12 and July 4, 1927.

20 Ibid.

Calgary Power began providing electrical service to Waterton in 1947.

21 Ibid., April 26, 1927.

22 Ibid., July 27, 1927.

23 Ibid., April 11, 1927.

24 Ibid., July 4, 1927.

25 Ibid., July 2, 1927.

26 Ibid., August 6, 1927.

27 Ibid., March 9 and August 27, 1927.

28 Following his return to America, Lindbergh went on a 20,000-mile (32,200 km), 82-stop, cross-continental tour of the U.S. for the "Promotion of Aeronautics," sponsored by the Daniel Guggenheim Foundation. The trip, which Lindbergh made at the controls of his famous *Spirit of St. Louis*, was to emphasize the safety and durability of modern aircraft and how they could be used reliably for civil aviation. The tour took Lindbergh to Montana, over Glacier National Park and within view of Waterton.

See "Seeing America with Lindbergh," *National Geographic Magazine*, January 1928.

29 *The Lethbridge Herald*, May 16, 1927.

30 Ibid., April 12, 1927.

31 Ibid., July 9, 1927.

32 Ibid., August 2, 1927.

33 Ibid., July 28, 1927.

34 Ibid., May 2 and July 14, 1927.

35 Ibid., July 14, 1927.

36 Ibid., May 2, 1927.

37 H.R.H. Edward, Duke of Windsor. *A King's Story: The Memoirs of the Duke of Windsor* (Toronto, Ont.: Thomas Allen Limited, 1951), p. 152.

38 Ibid.

39 May 9, 1927, memo from Louis Hill. Great Northern Railway president's subject files. Waterton Lakes Park: Prince of Wales Hotel construction and operation 1925-60. Great Northern Railway company records, Minnesota Historical Society archive, St. Paul, Minn.

40 *The Lethbridge Herald*, June 8, 1927.

Chapter 7

1 *The Lethbridge Herald*, July 26, 1927.

Among those present were: Howard Hays Sr. of Glacier Park Transport Company; George Noffsinger, president of Park Saddle Horse Company; Howard Noble, general manager of Glacier Park Hotel Company; L. H. Jelliff, local MP; Albert Hogeland, chief engineer for Great Northern; W. Brewster of Brewster Transport in Banff; R. J. Dinning, the Alberta liquor commissioner; and Canon Samuel Middleton.

2 Ibid.

3 May 25, 1927, letter from Howard Noble, general manager of Glacier Park Hotel Company, to William Kenney, vice-president of Great Northern Railway. Glacier Park Co.: Roads and Trails. Great Northern Railway company records, Minnesota Historical Society archive, St. Paul, Minn.

4 July 26, 1927, telegram from William Kenney to Louis Hill. Louis Warren Hill Sr. papers, James Jerome Hill Reference Library, St. Paul, Minn.

5 Douglas Oland Sr. (Unpublished memoirs written in Lethbridge, Alta., in 1963), p. 28.

6 Oland memoirs, p. 32.

7 Interview with Mary O'Brien on December 1, 1990, in Marshall, Minn.

8 July 25, 1927, report from George Anderegg to W. G. Read, accountant, Great Northern Railway. Canadian Division: Prince of Wales Hotel construction. Great Northern Railway company records, Minnesota Historical Society.

9 August 8, 1927, report from George Anderegg to W. G. Read. Ibid.

10 August 3, 1927, report from George Anderegg to W. G. Read. Ibid.

Also see *The Lethbridge Herald*, July 27, 1927.

11 *The Lethbridge Herald*, July 18, 1927.

12 Ibid., May 2, 1927.

13 Ibid., June 13, 1927.

14 Ibid., May 20, 1927.

15 Undated letter (circa 1975) from former Prince of Wales Hotel bellhop Ainslie Pankhurst of Lethbridge, Alta., to author. Author's collection.

16 May 13, 1927, letter from R. H. Webb to Howard Noble, general manager of Glacier Park Hotel Company and Canadian Rockies Hotel Company. Great Northern Railway president's subject files. Waterton Lakes Park: Prince of Wales Hotel construction and operation 1925-60. Great Northern Railway company records, Minnesota Historical Society.

17 July 6, 1927, letter from William Kenney to Louis Hill. Louis Hill papers, J. J. Hill Library.

18 *The Lethbridge Herald*, July 11 and 13, 1927.

19 July 6, 1927, letter from William Kenney to Louis Hill. Louis Hill papers, J. J. Hill Library.

20 October 22, 1976, letter from Irene LaFlamme to author. Author's collection.

21 Ibid.

22 *The Lethbridge Herald*, July 14, 1927.

23 Interview with Mary O'Brien.

See also interview with Betty Baker on August 3, 1974, in Waterton Park, Alta.

24 Interview with Andy Thompson on April 29, 1975, in Lethbridge, Alta.

See also Oland memoirs, p. 32.

25 Interview with Betty Baker.

26 September 8, 1927, letter from Albert Hogeland to Louis Hill. Louis Hill papers, J. J. Hill Library.

The wooden water pipes have since been replaced.

27 *The Lethbridge Herald*, June 28, 1927.

28 October 22, 1976, letter from Irene LaFlamme to author. Author's collection.

29 *The Lethbridge Herald*, August 23, 1927.

30 May 31, 1927, letter from F. G. Dorety to Louis Hill. Louis Hill papers, J. J. Hill Library.

31 February 14, 1927, letter from F. G. Dorety to Albert Hogeland and February 17, 1927, letter from Albert Hogeland to F. G. Dorety. Ibid.

Also see *The Lethbridge Herald*, May 16, 1927.

"It is not the intention to locate the beer sales room in the main hotel," Hogeland wrote. "It is planned to erect a separate three-story frame building about 40 feet by 86 feet (12 m by 25.8 m) in which the beer sales room will be on the ground floor."

32 *The Lethbridge Herald*, August 10, 1927.

33 Letter from Ainslie Pankhurst.

34 *The Lethbridge Herald*, August 17 and 24, 1927.

36 Ibid., July 11, 1927.

37 Ibid., July 27, 1927.

38 Scott J. Tanner, "A Biography of Winold Reiss: The man who created the Great Northern Railway's Blackfeet Indian portraits." Great Northern Railway Historical Society reference sheet No. 242. June 1996.

Also see Paul Raczka, *Winold Reiss, Portraits of the Races—Art Has No Prejudice* (Great Falls, Mont.: C. M. Russell Museum, 1986).

39 *The Lethbridge Herald*, August 13, 1927.

40 Ibid., August 15, 1927.

41 Ibid., August 15, 1927.

42 Ibid., August 18, 1927.

43 Ibid., September 2, 1927.

44 Ibid., August 17 and 29, 1927.

45 Ibid., August 5, 1927.

    From 1932 to 1972 Beil produced bronze sculptures for the Calgary Stampede's rodeo and chuckwagon champions.

46 Ibid., September 6, 1927.

47 Ibid., September 1, 1927.

48 Ibid., August 25, 1927.

49 Ibid., August 13, 1927.

50 Ibid., August 4, 1927.

51 December 31, 1927, year-end report for the Canadian Rockies Hotel Company Limited. Louis Hill papers, J. J. Hill Library.

52 *Wall Street Journal*, August 2, 1927.

53 *The Lethbridge Herald*, September 3, 1927.

    While the number of visitors that year was less than the previous year, the 6,012 people who came to Waterton in August 1927 was almost double the 3,847 for the same month in 1926.

54 December 31, 1927, year-end report of the Canadian Rockies Hotel Company Limited. Louis Hill papers, J. J. Hill Library.

Chapter 8

1 As he had done for the Prince of Wales Hotel, Louis Hill chose the name for the *Motor Vessel International*. Howard Noble, general manager of Glacier Park Hotel Company, had three suggested names for the boat, including Mountain View, Mokowan (Siksika for Big Belly) and Pitaska. In April 1927, the matter was taken to Hill, who rejected Noble's ideas and christened the vessel *International*. The name is appropriate, given the boat crosses the Canada-U.S. border each time it plies Upper Waterton Lake.

   The name *International* had been used at least once before, for a steamboat that operated on the Mississippi and Red rivers out of St. Paul. Originally owned by the Hudson's Bay Company, it was sold to Norman Kittson, who would later be a partner with J. J. Hill in founding Great Northern Railway.

2 January 11, 1927, authorization for expenditure. Canadian Rockies Hotel Company. Great Northern Railway company records, Minnesota Historical Society archive, St. Paul, Minn.

3 May 9, 1927, memo from Howard Noble to William Kenney. Ibid.

4 *The Lethbridge Herald*, August 6, 1927.

   Also see May 25, 1927, memo from Howard Noble to F. G. Dorety. Great Northern Railway company records, Minnesota Historical Society.

5 May 7, 1927, memo. Louis Warren Hill Sr. papers, James Jerome Hill Reference Library, St. Paul, Minn.

   See also *The Lethbridge Herald*, May 2, 1927.

6 *The Lethbridge Herald*, June 2, 1927.

7 August 25, 1926, letter from E. S. Busby, chief inspector for the Department of Customs and Excise in Canada to Howard Noble, general manager of Glacier Park Hotel Company. Great Northern Railway president's subject files. Prince of Wales Hotel Co.: Boat for Waterton Lake 1926-55. Great Northern Railway company records, Minnesota Historical Society.

8 June 17, 1927, memo from Howard Noble to F. G. Dorety. Canadian Rockies Hotel Company. Ibid.

9 *The Lethbridge Herald*, June 21, 1927.

10 Ibid., August 18, 1927.

11 Ibid., September 17, 1927.

    The current owner of the vessel claims that it was less than ready when first launched. "When it was built … (Swanson) knew how hard the wind could blow out on the lake," said Rod Kretz, whose family business now owns the *International*. "He put the big gas Sterling motors in the front of the boat, along with the fuel tanks. The idea was to get as much weight up there as possible," Kretz said. "When it was launched, the rudder was sticking out of the water. … Before taking it to town, he had the rear of the boat loaded down with rocks to balance it out."

12 July 13, 1927, letter from Andrew Hogg to F. G. Dorety. Canadian Rockies Hotel Company. Great Northern Railway company records, Minnesota Historical Society.

13 Scott J. Tanner, "A Biography of Winold Reiss: The man who created the Great Northern Railway's Blackfeet Indian portraits." Great Northern Railway Historical Society reference sheet No. 242. June 1996.

14 Paul Raczka, *Winold Reiss, Portraits of the Races—Art Has No Prejudice*, (Great Falls, Mont.: C. M. Russell Museum, 1986), p. 27.

15 The images were also used on postcards, Great Northern Christmas cards, Great Northern playing cards, the menu covers in the dining cars of its trains, and in portfolios of 24 prints prepared by the railway and made available for direct sale or through bookstores. Winold Reiss's portraits became as much associated with Glacier Park and Great Northern as Rocky, the railway's mountain goat logo.

    In the 1930s, Reiss would establish an art school at St. Mary Chalets. One of his students was a young Blood, Gerald Tailfeathers, who went on to become a renowned artist in his own right.

16 *The Lethbridge Herald*, July 8, 1927.

17 Ibid., August 1, 1927.

18 Ibid., August 23, 1927.

19 Interview with Anne Harrison on September 1, 1976, in Victoria, B.C.

20 Interview with Betty Baker on August 3, 1974, in Waterton Park, Alta.

21 July 9, 1927, letter from Louis Hill to Albert Hogeland. Louis Hill papers, J. J. Hill Library.

22 Roy Childs Jones attended Purdue University and the University of Pennsylvania, where he earned his master's degree in architecture in 1914. Besides being chief designer at Toltz, King and Day from 1919 to 1928, Jones was also on the faculty of the school of architecture at the University of Minnesota. He was named head of the school in 1937 and held that position until his retirement in 1953.

23 *The Lethbridge Herald*, August 23, 1927.

24 These sketches of the Prince of Wales Hotel are in the possession of Toltz, King, Duvall, Anderson and Associates of St. Paul, Minn. There is a seventh sketch for expansion, but it does not contain a proposed floor plan like the other six and differs markedly, showing a much larger variety of additions.

25 Jones likely didn't realize it was illegal then in Alberta to drink and dance in the same room and would not become possible until three decades later when alcohol could, for the first time, be served in dining rooms that also had dance floors.

26 *The Lethbridge Herald*, September 6, 1927.

27 Ibid.

28 Hill's remarks to *The Lethbridge Herald* about extending Akamina Highway to link with Glacier were an attempt at boosterism—one that Hill realized would not come about soon, if at all, although he was not averse to trying. Little more than a month later he admitted in a letter that a loop road was an unlikely prospect. Hill wrote: "I (am not) keen about the prospect of an auto road from Lake McDonald north to the Prince of Wales Hotel."

November 15, 1927, letter from Louis Hill to Charles Jenks, vice-president Glacier Park Hotel Company. Louis Hill papers, J. J. Hill Library.

29 August 20, 1927, letter from Ralph Budd to Louis Hill. Great Northern Railway president's subject files. Waterton Lakes Park: Prince of Wales Hotel construction and operation 1925-60. Great Northern Railway company records, Minnesota Historical Society.

30 Ibid.

31 Ibid.

32 Douglas Oland Sr. (Unpublished memoirs written in Lethbridge, Alta., in 1963), p. 31.

33 Ibid.

34 Ibid., p. 32.

35 March 13, 1928, letter from J. R. Mills of Stanley Thompson and Co. Ltd. to Ralph Budd. Great Northern Railway president's subject files. Waterton Lakes Park: Prince of Wales Hotel construction and operation 1925-60. Great Northern Railway company records, Minnesota Historical Society.

36 March 15, 1928, letter from Ralph Budd to Louis Hill. Ibid.

37 March 17, 1928, letter from Ralph Budd to J. R. Mills of Stanley Thompson and Co. Ltd. of Toronto. Ibid.

  Stanley Thompson would eventually design expansion of the Waterton golf course to 18 holes.

38 September 6, 1927, telegram from Louis Hill to William Tucker. Louis Hill papers. J. J. Hill Library.

39 *The Lethbridge Herald*, August 26, 1948.

40 Oland memoirs, p. 42.

  Also see June 2, 1928, letter from Doug Oland to Louis Hill. Louis Hill papers, J. J. Hill Library.

41 Ibid.

42 March 11, 1992, letter from Mary O'Brien to author. Author's collection.

43 June 2, 1928, letter from Doug Oland to Louis Hill. Louis Hill papers, J. J. Hill Library.

44 Ibid.

45 June 4, 1928, letter from Howard Noble, general manager of Glacier Park Hotel Company, to Oland and Scott. Ibid.

46 June 8, 1928, letter from Doug Oland to Louis Hill. Ibid.

47 June 15, 1928, letter from Louis Hill to Oland and Scott. Ibid.

48 Ibid.

49 August 30, 1928, letter from Doug Oland to Louis Hill. Ibid.

50 September 12, 1928, letter from Doug Oland to Louis Hill. Ibid.

51 Ibid.

52 Oland memoirs, p. 44.

  Also see *Calgary Herald*, October 15, 1971.

53 Ibid.

54 Ibid.

55 October 4, 1928, letter from Albert Hogeland to George Anderegg. Prince of Wales Hotel Construction: General correspondence. Great Northern Railway company records, Minnesota Historical Society.

56 November 14, 1928, letter from George Anderegg to Albert Hogeland. Ibid.

Chapter 9

1 Parks Canada attendance figures for Waterton Lakes National Park.

2 Donald Robinson, *Through the Years in Glacier National Park* (West Glacier, Mont.: Glacier Natural History Association, 1960), p. 127.

3 Parks Canada attendance figures for Waterton Lakes National Park.

4 Ibid.

5 July 17, 1931, letter from William Kenney to Horace M. Albright, director of the National Park Service, Washington, D.C. Glacier Park Co.: Roads and trails. Great Northern Railway company records, Minnesota Historical Society archive, St. Paul, Minn.

6 Canon (Samuel Middleton), *Waterton-Glacier International Peace Park* (Published by the author, 1947).

7 Roberta Forsberg, *Chief Mountain—The Story of Canon Middleton* (Whittier, Calif.: Historical Society of Alberta, 1964), p. 55.

8 Department of the Interior, *Reports of the Commissioner of Canadian National Parks 1904-1911*, (Ottawa, Ont.: King's Printer, 1911), p. 63.

9 Ibid.

10 December 19, 1932, memo from William Kenney to H. H. Brown. Great Northern president's subject files. Waterton Lakes Park: Prince of Wales Hotel construction and operation 1925-60. Great Northern Railway company records, Minnesota Historical Society.

  Net revenue from operations for the Canadian Rockies Hotel Company was in the red that

summer to the tune of $27,000, an increase from the $19,000 loss racked up the previous year.

11 February 3, 1932, letter from A. J. Binder to William Kenney. Glacier Park Co.: Roads and trails. Ibid.

12 *The Lethbridge Herald*, September 27, 1926.

13 July 16, 1932, letter from Howard Hays, president of Glacier Park Transport Company, to Ralph W. Greenway, president of the Lethbridge Board of Trade. Glacier Park Co.: Roads and trails. Great Northern Railway company records, Minnesota Historical Society.

14 *The Lethbridge Herald*, October 24, 1932.

15 December 1932, letter from Howard Hays to A. J. Binder. Great Northern president's subject files. Waterton Lakes Park: Prince of Wales Hotel construction and operation 1925-60. Great Northern Railway company records, Minnesota Historical Society.

16 January 27, 1932, letter from William Kenney to Ralph W. Greenway, president of the Lethbridge Board of Trade. Glacier Park Co.: Roads and trails. Ibid.

17 January 1933, letter from E. T. Scoyen, superintendent of Glacier National Park. Great Northern president's subject files. Waterton Lakes Park: Prince of Wales Hotel construction and operation 1925-60. Ibid.

18 January 12, 1933, letter from William Kenney to H. H. Brown. Ibid.

19 *The Lethbridge Herald*, June 28, 1933.

  Although it would have been acceptable to hold the peace park dedication anywhere in Waterton, Canon Middleton knew too well the reasons for and power of tradition, and that meant the ceremony had to be held at the Prince of Wales Hotel. Middleton thought "much of ceremony. The symbolic pageant, usually with strong religious overtones, is part of the British tradition he represents. The ceremony to him is a way of pointing out achievement won, a necessary affirmation, a turning point for an individual or for mankind." The tradition has continued for five decades, except for four years during the Second World War, with the annual Rotary peace park meetings alternating between Glacier Park Lodge and the Prince of Wales Hotel.

20 July 2, 1929, letter from Fred Udell, head of security for the Prince of Wales Hotel, to Capt. R. Stanley Harrison, manager of the Prince of Wales Hotel. Louis Warren Hill Sr. papers, James Jerome Hill Library, St. Paul, Minn.

21 July 7, 1929, letter from Capt. R. S. Harrison to Louis Hill. Ibid.

22 Interview with Cam McKay on March 17, 1993, in Milk River, Alta.

23 Annual financial statements for the *Motor Vessel International*. Glacier Park Co.: Launches and Docks, *International* 1929-1960. Great Northern Railway company records, Minnesota Historical Society.

24 Mart Kenney, *Mart Kenney and His Western Gentlemen* (Saskatoon, Sask.: Western Producer Prairie Books, 1981), p. 25.

It took no small feat of ingenuity for Mart Kenney's band to land the job in Waterton. With limited funds, Kenney had no way to get to Waterton to audition and he "couldn't very well ask the owners to come to Vancouver," Kenney recalls in his memoirs. "My quandary was solved in a way that would never be possible today," Kenney says. "My good friend George Chandler, a (radio) broadcasting pioneer, came up with a brilliant and generous plan. He offered to stay on the air after midnight one night so that his station could reach Lethbridge. I then arranged for the McLeans [sic] to listen in on that night and we played live from CJOR (in Vancouver)." The audition went well and Kenney's group was hired.

25 Ibid., p. 26.

26 Ibid.

27 During the last summer Mart Kenney and his band played in Waterton, 1934, Kenney arranged for a radio program to be broadcast from the pavilion during the Saturday night dances. The program was broadcast across Canada on CBC via CJOC in Lethbridge, which picked up the feed from a telephone line/microphone at the hall. The exposure led to the band being hired by the Canadian Pacific Railway to perform at its hotel in Regina, the beginning of a long association with the CPR. Sadly, Kenney and his band would return to Waterton on only a few occasions over the next decades. The MacLean's pavilion was destroyed by fire in 1937 and rebuilt, continuing the tradition of weekend dances in Waterton for years to come. The dance hall has since been redesigned and expanded and now contains a saloon and convention centre.

28 January 19, 1933, statement of revenues and expenses for the *International*. Launches and Docks: *International*. Great Northern Railway company records, Minnesota Historical Society.

29 July 6, 1933, letter from Mrs. P. W. Primrose to George Anderegg, accountant for Glacier Park Hotel Company. Ibid.

30 *The Lethbridge Herald*, August 12, 1935.

31 Ibid.

See also Donald Robinson, *Through the Years in Glacier National Park*, p. 85.

32 *The Lethbridge Herald*, August 12, 1935.

33 Ibid., August 14, 1935.

34 August 10, 1935, radio-telephone message from the fire cache at St. Mary, Mont., to Arthur Harwood, postmaster at Waterton Park. Great Northern Railway company records, Minnesota Historical Society.

35 *The Lethbridge Herald*, August 14, 1935.

36 Ibid.

37 Ibid., August 15, 1935.

38 Ibid., August 12, 1935.

An inside sprinkler system would not be installed at the hotel until the late 1950s.

39 Ibid., August 15, 1935.

40 *St. Paul Dispatch*, April 21, 1939.

41 August 11, 1935, telegram from William Kenney, president of Great Northern Railway.

Also see April 1939 memo to Frank J. Gavin, Great Northern Railway president's subject files. Canadian Hotel Company 1926-40. Great Northern Railway company records, Minnesota Historical Society.

Ironically, Sleeger and Kenney played out the same "I saved the Hotel-Why?" exchange the following year when a fire raced down the Swiftcurrent Valley toward Many Glacier Hotel.

42 May 22, 1939, memo. Great Northern Railway company records, Minnesota Historical Society.

43 December 23, 1933, memo from A. J. Dickinson to William Kenney. Great Northern president's subject files. Waterton Lakes Park: Prince of Wales Hotel construction and operation 1925-60. Ibid.

44 January 4, 1934, memo from A. J. Dickinson to William Kenney. Ibid.

45 June 17, 1935, memo from Thomas McMahon to R. W. Davis. Ibid.

46 July 26, 1931, memo from Ray Sleeger to A. J. Binder. Ibid.

47 March 19, 1932, letter from A. J. Binder to William Kenney. Ibid.

48 July 26, 1931, letter from Ray Sleeger to A. J. Binder. Ibid.

49 August 15, 1931, letter from William Kenney to A. J. Binder. Ibid.

50 August 19, 1935, memo from Charles Jenks to William Kenney. Ibid.

51 August 13, 1935, memo from William Kenney to Charles Jenks. Ibid.

52 Heather Pringle, *A Guide to Waterton Lakes National Park* (Vancouver, B.C.: Douglas & McIntyre, 1986), p. 29.

53 February 15, 1936, Prince of Wales Hotel caretaker's report. Glacier Park Co.: Caretaker's Reports. Great Northern Railway company records, Minnesota Historical Society.

54 February 22, 1936, Prince of Wales Hotel caretaker's report. Ibid.

55 February 29, 1936, Prince of Wales Hotel caretaker's report. Ibid.

56 March 7, 1936, Prince of Wales Hotel caretaker's report. Ibid.

57 Parks Canada attendance figures for Waterton Lakes National Park.

58 Donald Robinson, *Through the Years in Glacier National Park*, p. 89.

59 *The Lethbridge Herald*, June 13, 1936.

60 Ibid.

61 November 3, 1937, memo from William Kenney. Great Northern president's subject files. Waterton Lakes Park: Prince of Wales Hotel construction and operation 1925-60. Great Northern Railway company records, Minnesota Historical Society.

While net revenue from operations was $13,000 in the red in 1936, the hotel managed to generate a profit of $2,600 in 1937, after which losses ($1,800 in 1938 and $778 in 1939) continued until 1940.

62 Despite the effort of Rotarians in having the two parks joined, Great Northern was reluctant to use "international peace park" in its advertising literature. The railway felt the name was too long, it didn't want to subordinate the name Glacier, which it had used as an advertising slogan for decades, and there was no support from its field representatives, who preferred "Glorious Glacier Park."

January 6, 1942, letter from O. J. McGillis to Canon Middleton.

Also see December 19, 1941, letter from Middleton to McGillis and January 10, 1942, letter from Middleton to McGillis. Personal and business papers of the Venerable Archdeacon Samuel H. Middleton in the possession of his daughter, Sophie Allison of Pincher Creek, Alta.

63 June 9, 1942, memo from A. S. Morgan, oil controller in Winnipeg, Manitoba. Great Northern president's subject files. Waterton Lakes Park: Prince of Wales Hotel construction and operation 1925-60. Great Northern Railway company records, Minnesota Historical Society.

64 June 12, 1942, memo from A. A. Aszmann to Charles Jenks. Ibid.

65 *The Lethbridge Herald*, June 9, 1942.

66 June 14, 1942, memo from A. A. Aszmann to Charles Jenks. Great Northern president's subject files. Waterton Lakes Park: Prince of Wales Hotel construction and operation 1925-60. Great Northern Railway company records, Minnesota Historical Society.

Resort hotels elsewhere in the Canadian Rockies, such as the Banff Springs Hotel, Chateau Lake Louise and Jasper Park Lodge, remained open during 1942 but were closed voluntarily by their respective railway owners, Canadian Pacific and Canadian National, in 1943 owing to curtailment of tourist traffic because of the war. The resulting closures freed hundreds of former staff members for other, more war-vital employment. *Calgary Herald*, March 24, 1943.

Chapter 10

1 Interview with Sophie Allison on August 10, 1975, in Waterton Park, Alta.

2 For an overview of the rise in auto tourism in the U.S., see Earl Pomeroy, *In Search of the Golden West: The Tourist in Western America* (New York: Alfred A. Knopf, 1957).

3 Donald Robinson, *Through the Years in Glacier National Park* (West Glacier, Mont.: Glacier Natural Historical Association, Inc., 1960), p. 127.

4 Ibid.

5 The superintendent of Glacier Park noticed the changing trend as early as 1933. "You will note that in 1926 twenty-six per cent of the people entering the park made horseback trips, while this had steadily decreased until 1932 only 3.5% of the trail visitors had indulged in this form of recreation. I think these figures prove very clearly that the Park Saddle Horse Company is neglecting the revenue which may be derived from the private motorists entering the park."

February 28, 1933, letter from E. T. Scoyen, superintendent of Glacier National Park, to the director of the National Park Service. Louis Warren Hill Sr. papers, James Jerome Hill Reference Library, St. Paul, Minn.

6 C. W. Buchholtz, *Man In Glacier* (West Glacier, Mont.: Glacier Natural History Association, 1993), p. 61.

7 A two-room cabin at Swiftcurrent rented for $2.50 US a day, compared with $6.50 to $14 a day for a room at nearby Many Glacier Hotel. The cabins were a bargain for travellers and for the railway, which paid $350 to $500 each to have them constructed versus over $500,000 to build Many Glacier Hotel, and required a much lower level of staffing and less maintenance.

April 10, 1936, letter from A. A. Aszmann to Ray Sleeger and George Anderegg, Glacier Park Hotel Company. Glacier Park Co. subject files: Contract, construction Swiftcurrent, 1936. Great Northern Railway company records, Minnesota Historical Society archive, St. Paul, Minn.

Also see U.S. Department of the Interior, *Glacier National Park (Montana)* (Washington, D.C., United States Government Printing Office, 1937), pp. 24-25.

8 Interview with Margaret Black on November 20, 1997, in St. Mary, Mont.

9 Ibid.

Hill was also paying his respects to Margaret Black, whom he would have known from her work as a full-time employee in the 1920s at Glacier Park Hotel Company's offices in St. Paul, Minn., and Glacier Park Hotel at East Glacier Park, Mont.

10 October 27, 1949, letter from Charles Curley, executive vice-president of First Trust Company of St. Paul, Minn, to Sarah Simon. Louis Hill papers, J. J. Hill Library.

11 Interview with Margaret Black.

12 Interview with Joan Tangren on September 9, 1990, in Waterton Park, Alta.

Initially, the day-to-day operation of Northland Lodge was left to Edna Leavitt, Earl Hacking's mother-in-law. Bessie, Earl's wife, took over in the 1950s and, with the help of her children—Don, George and particularly Joan—continued as manager until 1985.

13 Michael J. Ober, "Enmity and Alliance: Park service-concessioner relations in Glacier National Park 1892-1961" (Unpublished MA thesis, University of Montana, 1973), p. 156.

14 John Budd was born in 1907 and while growing up held summer jobs with Great Northern. He was educated at Yale, where he graduated as a civil engineer. The focus of his post-graduate studies was transportation. In 1947, at age 39, he became president of Chicago and Eastern Illinois Railway.

15 January 5, 1953, letter from John Budd to John Mauff of Chicago, Ill. Copy provided to the author by Mauff.

Budd wrote Mauff in reply to a letter appealing to Great Northern not to close or destroy its facilities at Two Medicine. In the letter, Budd recalls his time in the park and his divided loyalties. "I have spent a great deal of time in my life in Glacier Park. … As stated above, the decision to abandon Two Medicine was a difficult one for me because that site is one of the most delightful in the park in the eyes of both myself and my family."

16 Ibid.

17 Ralph W. Hidy, Muriel E. Hidy and Roy Scott with Don L. Hofsommer, *The Great Northern Railway—A History* (Boston, Mass.: Harvard Business School Press, 1988), p. 248.

The change in philosophy would eventually lead to a long-sought merger between Great Northern, Northern Pacific and Chicago Burlington & Quincy to create Burlington Northern, with an emphasis on freight rather than passengers. The passenger side of the business would be spun off to Amtrak.

18 Ober, "Enmity and Alliance," p. 157.

Also see May 15, 1951, letter from James V. Lloyd, acting regional director of the U.S. National Park Service, to the director of the National Park Service. Louis Hill papers, J. J. Hill Library.

19 Ibid., p. 162.

20 August 5, 1931, memo from William Kenney to A. J. Binder and June 17, 1935, letter from Thomas McMahon to R. W. Davis and August 5, 1950, letter from John Budd to F. J. Gavin. Great Northern Railway president's files. Waterton Lakes Park: Prince of Wales Hotel construction and operation 1925-60. Great Northern Railway company records, Minnesota Historical Society.

21 July 26, 1931, letter from Ray Sleeger to A. J. Binder. Ibid.

22 June 17, 1935, memo from Thomas McMahon to R. W. Davis. Ibid.

Also see August 5, 1950, memo from John Budd to F. J. Gavin. Ibid.

23 The original shingles have since been covered by a new roof surface in Parks Canada's preferred shade—green.

24 *Town and Country*, supplement to *The Lethbridge Herald*, May 1990.

25 *The Lethbridge Herald*, October 2, 1956.

Also see *Great Falls Tribune*, November 4, 1956, and February 8, 1957.

26 Ober, "Enmity and Alliance," p. 174.

27 *The Lethbridge Herald*, June 10, 1957.

28 Ibid., April 3, 1959 and April 30, 1959, memos. Great Northern Railway president's subject files. Waterton Lakes Park: Prince of Wales Hotel construction and operation 1925-60. Great Northern Railway company records, Minnesota Historical Society.

29 *Calgary Herald*, June 13, 1959, and November 25, 1959.

30 The Kainai chieftainship honours non-tribal members in such fields as science, the arts and community service. Candidates must also have integrity and the respect of Blood elders. In 1950, the Kainai Chieftanship Society limited membership to no more than 40 living persons. Charles, Prince of Wales, was inducted as Chief Red Crow in 1977.

31 Great Northern's reasons for phasing out native people in its promotional literature are unclear. It may have been in part to avoid conflicts with the cowboy and western heritage it was promoting in its "Ranch" coffee shop-lounge cars on the Empire Builder. The Indian art calendars managed to survive until 1958.

32 *Calgary Herald*, November 25, 1959.

The majority of pictographs, portraits and explanatory frames were turned over to Sophie Allison, the daughter of Canon Middleton, who, in turn, donated them to the Fort Macleod RCMP Museum, where some are now on display.

33 December 18, 1958, letter from John Budd to T. A. Jerraw.

Also see December 23, 1958, letter from Automatic Sprinkler Corp. of America to Robert Downing, vice-president of Great Northern, and February 3, 1959, letter from Robert Downing to J. B. Temple.

Great Northern Railway president's subject files. Waterton Lakes Park: Prince of Wales Hotel construction and operation 1925-60. Great Northern Railway company records, Minnesota Historical Society.

34 Some of the lanterns and lampshades were sold to private individuals and are prized possessions. A number were also salvaged and used in the lobby of Lake McDonald Lodge. They have since been replaced with copies.

35 September 15, 1957, letter from W. O. Derrough. Great Northern Railway company records, Minnesota Historical Society.

W. O. Derrough, a disgruntled and dismissed general manager of Glacier Park Company, charged Knutson was letting contracts to friends, making gifts to railway officials and charging them back to the company, employing drunken contractors and authorizing a public relations budget in excess of 10 per cent of the company's revenues.

36 *The Lethbridge Herald*, April 30, 1959.

37 Ober, "Enmity and Alliance," p. 179.

38 July 25, 1960, letter for file of Robert Downing. Great Northern Railway president's subject files. Glacier Park Transport Company 1935-37. Great Northern Railway company records, Minnesota Historical Society.

39 Ibid.

40 Don Hummel, *Wake Up, America! The Environmentalists are Stealing the National Parks—The Destruction of Concessions and Public Access* (Bellevue, Wash.: The Free Enterprise Press, 1987), p. 192.

41 Ober, "Enmity and Alliance," p. 175.

42 *The Calgary Herald*, June 8, 1964.

43 Ibid., June 9, 1964.

44 Ibid., June 10, 1964.

The elements came back to haunt Waterton in 1975 and 1995 when the townsite was again flooded, although not as extensively as in 1964. Town residents were again offered shelter at no cost in the Prince of Wales Hotel until the water abated.

45 Hummel, *Wake Up, America!*, p. 233.

46 *The Calgary Herald*, August 2, 1967.

47 Ibid.

48 December 7, 1976, letter to all members of the Conference of National Park Concessioners from Don Hummel. The Ray Djuff Fond at the Glenbow Museum archive in Calgary, Alta.

49 Hummel, *Wake Up, America!*, p. 353-354.

In 1977, Hummel entered into negotiations to sell the Glacier concessions to TWA Services, the concessioner at Zion, Bryce and North Rim Grand Canyon. They came to a tentative agreement, but couldn't hammer out final terms and the deal fell through.

50 *The Lethbridge Herald*, November 23, 1974.

51 *Toronto Globe and Mail*, August 10, 1974.

52 Ibid., August 16, 1974.

53 Ibid.

Daylight saving time was a war measure imposed by the federal government in Canada in 1918 and again in 1942 and was repealed after each war. When cities such as Calgary tried introducing daylight saving time on their own after the Second World War, it caused such havoc for railway, bus line, court and other employees, the Social Credit government banned the practice. Alberta remained on standard time until April 30, 1972, by which time it was the last province in Canada to introduce daylight saving time.

54 The author was present during the altercation between Don and Cliff Hummel.

55 Hummel, *Wake Up, America!*, p. 371.

Hummel claims he was forced to sell the assets of Glacier Park Inc. after the National Park Service refused to negotiate in good faith with him. He says he was the victim of a concerted effort to roust him from Glacier Park and only sold the company because there was no other option.

56 *The Lethbridge Herald*, October 7, 1988.

Chapter 11

1 *Service Regulations and Information for Employees*—1925 handbook for Glacier Park Hotel Company employees. Glacier Park Hotel Company—Instructions and Bulletins. Great Northern Railway company records, Minnesota Historical Society archive, St. Paul, Minn.

2 1973 Prince of Wales Hotel employee information circular from Glacier Park Inc. File 6 of the Ray Djuff Fond at the Glenbow Museum archive in Calgary, Alta.

3 March 22, 1975, letter from former Prince of Wales Hotel waitress Sally Pike to Anthony Flemming-Blake of Edmonton, Alta. Author's collection.

4 Ibid.

5 Ibid.

6 Ibid.

7 January 31, 1975, letter from hotel maid Helen Graham of Lethbridge, Alta., to author. Author's collection.

8 July 30, 1959, memo. Glacier Park Co.: Entertainment 1958-60. Great Northern Railway company records, Minnesota Historical Society.

9 Sheet of lyrics to *It's a Real Drag*. File 5, Ray Djuff Fond, Glenbow Museum.

10 Undated letter (circa 1975) from former Prince of Wales Hotel bellhop Ainslie Pankhurst of Lethbridge, Alta., to author. Author's collection.

11 February 14, 1975, letter from hotel bellhop Rob Armstrong to Anthony Flemming-Blake of Edmonton, Alta. Author's collection.

12 *Service Regulations and Information for Employees—1925 handbook for Glacier Park Hotel Company employees.* Glacier Park Co., Instructions and bulletins. Great Northern Railway company records, Minnesota Historical Society.

13 Interview with Sophie Allison on August 10, 1975, in Waterton Park, Alta.

14 June 29, 1927, letter from Howard Noble to all hotel managers. Glacier Park Co., Instructions and bulletins. Great Northern Railway company records, Minnesota Historical Society.

15 September 25, 1927, letter from Louis Hill to Charles Jenks. Louis Warren Hill Sr. papers at the James Jerome Hill Reference Library, St. Paul, Minn.

16 January 7, 1930, letter from R. Stanley Harrison to Louis Hill. Louis Hill papers, J. J. Hill Library.

17 December 21, 1991, letter from Frances Bellucci, niece of Harley and Anna Boswell, to author. Author's collection.

18 Ibid.

19 Ibid.

20 March 23, 1992, letter from Frances Bellucci to author.

21 Interview with Sophie Allison.

22 Letter from former Ainslie Pankhurst.

23 May 1, 1992, letter from Mary Weber Fuller, niece of Harley and Anna Boswell, to author. Author's collection.

24 March 23, 1992, letter from Frances Bellucci to author.

25 April 5, 1951, letter from Canon Samuel Middleton to J. S. Jeffries of Great Northern Railway. From a collection of letters, notes and clippings of Canon Middleton in the possession of his daughter, Sophie Allison of Pincher Creek, Alta.

26 August 27, 1951, letter from Canon Samuel Middleton to J. S. Jeffries of Glacier Park Hotel Company. Ibid.

27 Copy of photo supplied to author by William Kirwan, nephew of Harley and Anna Boswell.

28 Interview with Sophie Allison.

29 June 19, 1947, letter to L. Anderson from J. S. Jeffries. Great Northern Railway company records, Minnesota Historical Society.

30 March 11, 1952, letter from Harley Boswell to Andy Russell. Fond M153/21 Andy Russell papers, archive of the Whyte Museum of the Canadian Rockies, Banff, Alta.

In October 1951, Harley Boswell had surgery to remove 80 per cent of his stomach and a foot of intestines—"all of that area is subject to ulcers. So I will not be bothered with that trouble again." Doctors also found gallstones and removed his gall bladder. Boswell, then 63 years old, recovered without complications from the surgery, but was weaker as a result.

31 Interview with Cam McKay of Milk River, Alta., a customs officer at Chief Mountain border crossing, on March 17, 1993.

32 Letter from Sally Pike.

33 May 1, 1992, letter from Mary Weber Fuller to author.

34 Interview with Bea Armstrong on August 14, 1974, in Waterton, Alta.

35 Letter from Sally Pike.

36 Ibid.

37 Heather Pringle, *A Guide to Waterton Lakes National Park* (Vancouver, B.C.: Douglas & McIntyre, 1986), p. 28.

38 *Sunday Magazine* in the *Calgary Herald*, August 5, 1990.

39 The flagstones have since been removed and grass planted in their place.

40 Donald Robinson, *Through the Years in Glacier National Park* (West Glacier, Mont.: Glacier Natural History Association, 1960), pp. 79-82.

41 Ernie Pyle, *Home Country* (New York: William Sloane Associates, 1947), pp. 415-420.

42 Letter from Sally Pike.

Index

About the Author

Ray Djuff is a newspaper copy
editor with a passion for Waterton-Glacier International Peace
Park. His interest in the parks was
sparked during the four summers
he worked at the Prince of Wales
Hotel in the 1970s. He has written
two other books about Waterton.
Djuff lives with his wife, Gina, and
two children, Monika and Michael,
in Calgary, Alberta.